Matrix and Power Series Methods

John W. Lee • Stephen D. Scarborough • Forrest Parker • Dean C. Wills

Fifth Edition

Matrix and Power Series Methods / MTH 306

Wiley Custom Learning Solutions

To order books or for customer service, please call 1(800)-CALL-WILEY (225-5945).

Printed in the United States of America.

ISBN 978-1-118-81774-2
Printed and bound by Quad/Graphics.

V00324_061618

Brief Contents

MATRIX AND POWER SERIES METHODS
Mathematics 306

All You Ever Wanted to Know About

Matrix Algebra and Infinite Series

But Were Afraid To Ask

By

John W. Lee
Department of Mathematics
Oregon State University

Stephen D. Scarborough
Department of Mathematics
Oregon State University

July 2013

Special thanks and acknowledgment to
Forrest Parker
and
Dean C. Wills
for their hard work and expertise
in the preparation of this manuscript.

Contents

CONTENTS

3.5 Non-Square Systems 50
3.6 Efficient Evaluation of Determinants 51
3.7 Complex Linear Systems 52
3.8 Suggested Problems 53

4 Matrices and Linear Systems **55**
4.1 Goals 55
4.2 Overview 55
4.3 Basic Matrix Operations 55
4.4 Linear Systems in Matrix Form 59
4.5 The Inverse of a Square Matrix 61
4.6 Transpose of a Matrix 64
4.7 Suggested Problems 65

5 Linear Dependence and Independence **69**
5.1 Goals 69
5.2 Overview 69
5.3 Dependence and Independence 69
5.4 Suggested Problems 76

6 Matrices and Linear Transformations **79**
6.1 Goals 79
6.2 Overview 79
6.3 Matrices as Transformations 79
6.4 Matrix of a Linear Transformation 83
6.5 Projections 87
6.6 Suggested Problems 91

7 Eigenvalue Problems **97**
7.1 Goals 97
7.2 Overview 97
7.3 Basic Properties 98
7.4 Symmetric Matrices 104
7.5 Suggested Problems 110

8 Catch Up and Review **113**

III Series Methods **117**

9 Taylor Polynomial Approximation **119**
9.1 Goals 119
9.2 Overview and a Glance Ahead 119
9.3 Taylor Polynomials 120
9.4 Error in Approximation 123
9.5 Other Base Points 126

List of Figures

Introduction

WELCOME TO MTH 306!

READ THIS INTRODUCTION!!!
****

DON'T SKIP IT!
REALLY!

The material for MTH 306 is arranged in 19 lessons. Each lesson, except for the two catch up and review lessons, has the following format:

LESSON	Topic to be covered
GOALS	What you are supposed to learn
TEXT	Main ideas highlighted and discussed
SUGGESTED PROBLEMS	Homework

You should have the calculus text you used for MTH 251-254. That text also includes some topics covered in this course. You may find it helpful to use your calculus text as a complement to the required spiral-bound text for MTH 306.

More details follow.   READ ON!!!!

PREREQUISITES

The OSU General Catalog lists MTH 252, Integral Calculus, as the prerequisite for MTH 306 because this course adequately prepares you for the infinite series part of MTH 306; however, MTH 252 leaves a small gap in preparation for the matrix and linear algebra part of MTH 306 related to 3-dimensional Cartesian coordinates and elementary properties of 2- and 3-dimensional vectors. If you have taken MTH 254, Vector Calculus I, you are more than adequately prepared for the matrix and linear algebra part of MTH 306. If not, you can make up any gap in your background with a little self-study of 3-dimensional Cartesian coordinates and of the elementary properties of 2- and 3-dimensional vectors. Skim Lesson 2 to see the background in vectors you are expected to have. Then do some self-study before Lesson 3 is covered in class. Just go to the OSU Library, check out any calculus book or precalculus book that covers the elements of vectors in 2- and 3-dimensions, and study the material that is covered in Lesson 2.

THINGS TO WATCH FOR AND DO

Skim each upcoming lesson *before* you come to class. Read it *again*, carefully, afterwards. It will direct your attention to key points. Use the lesson first to help you learn the material and later to review for tests.

Suggested problems should be solved *shortly after* the class lecture - not two or three days after!

The problem sets are labeled as "suggested problems" because your instructor may choose to omit some problems, add other problems, or give entirely different problem assignments. Be on your toes!

IN THE END IT IS UP TO YOU

Mathematics is not a spectator sport! To learn mathematics you must get fully involved.

Take notes during the lectures. *Think hard* about difficult points. Don't let confusion stand. Get help as soon as difficulties arise. Don't wait. The Mathematics Learning Center is a valuable resource; use it. So is your instructor. Attend office hours regularly or make an appointment to get help.

Keep a notebook with your neatly written *reworked* lecture notes and solved homework problems. This will help you organize your study, prepare for tests, and provide a good personalized reference for the future.

GOOD LUCK

STUDY TIPS AND SUGGESTIONS FOR LEARNING

1. Attend class and sit close to the front.

2. Take an active role in class by answering and asking questions.

3. Take good notes, but do not expect to understand everything as it happens in class.

4. Recopy and expand your class notes in a permanent notebook before the next class meeting. Doing so will reinforce what you just learned. This also is the time to straighten out points that you didn't fully understand in class.

5. Study these lessons with pencil and paper at hand. Stop and workout missing steps or things that you don't understand. This is an effective way to study a math text.

6. Keep up with the assigned homework. Expect to spend *at least* 2 hours outside of class for each hour in lecture and in recitation.

7. Form a study group and work with them on a regular basis. You will be surprised at how much you can learn in this way.

EXAMINATIONS AND QUIZZES

Your instructor will tell you the dates of the midterm(s) for your section of MTH 306. Be sure to ask if there will be any quizzes and whether they will be regularly scheduled or of the pop-quiz variety. MTH 306 has a final examination time already scheduled in the Schedule of Classes. Check the day and time of the final and put them on your calendar now. Your instructor may or may not allow you to take a conflict exam. Ask you instructor about his or her policy. If allowed, conflict exams *will* only be scheduled under very special circumstances and must be arranged for well in advance with your instructor.

Expect to take the final at the regularly scheduled time. Do not make any travel arrangements that prevent you from taking the regularly scheduled final. Such arrangements are not an acceptable reason for scheduling a conflict final exam.

LAB/RECITATION

Labs may include some individual work, some group work, and either a short quiz or group project to turn in at the end of the lab period. There may be a group lab project that must be finished outside of class and a formal lab report turned in at the next lab meeting. Your (lab) instructor will give you explicit instructions about such reports. Homework assignments also may be due at certain recitation meetings. You will find Group Projects printed on tear-out sheets in Appendix A. Your instructor will decide which if any of these projects to use during the term.

INFORMATION FOR INSTRUCTORS (AND STUDENTS)

MTH 306 moves at a fast pace from day one. Certain topics need to be covered in the recitation sections in order to cover the full syllabus for the course. Two topics that are essential for MTH 306 and that are normally covered in two recitation meetings, as group work projects, are:

- Group Project: Special Limits

- Group Project: l'Hôpital's Rule and Taylor Polynomials

The complete list of group projects is tabulated here for easy reference and planning. The table is repeated at the start of Appendix A.

An * is appended to the name of a group project if the project covers material that is *essential* for MTH 306 and the topic of the project normally is covered in a recitation class meeting.

Group Project	Suitable for use with
Complex Numbers and the Complex Plane	Lesson 1
Solving Linear Systems I	Lesson 3
Solving Linear Systems II	Lesson 3
Finding the Inverse of a Matrix	Lesson 4
Linear Dependence and Independence	Lesson 5
Matrices and Linear Transformations	Lesson 6
Reflection Matrices	Lesson 6
Eigenvalue Problems I	Lesson 7
Eigenvalue Problems II	Lesson 7
Special Limits*	Lesson 9, 10
L'Hôpital's Rule and Taylor Polynomials*	Lessons 9
Taylor Polynomial Approximation	Lesson 9
Taylor Series Representations	Lesson 11
Series With Positive Terms and the Integral Test	Lesson 12
Comparison Tests	Lesson 13
Conditional and Absolute Convergence	Lesson 14
The Ratio and Root Tests	Lesson 15
Algebraic Manipulation of Power Series	Lesson 16
Enrichment Projects	
Population Dynamics	Lesson 7
Systems of Differential Equations	Lesson 7
Special Relativity 1	Lesson 9
Series in Action: Heat Conduction	Lesson 12 – 17
Effective Calculation of Logarithms	Lesson 17
The Binomial Series	Lesson 17
Special Relativity 2	Lesson 17

Enrichment projects indicate some areas in which the mathematical ideas of MTH 306 are applied and typically are a little more demanding.

ACKNOWLEDGEMENT

Since these materials for MTH 306 were first written, several of my colleagues have given me valuable suggestions for revisions and extensions of the text and have generously contributed copies of their exams and group projects for inclusion in the Supplemental Material. They also have been kind enough to read and critique various revisions. It is a pleasure to acknowledge their contributions and help here. Special thanks are extended to Chris Bryant, Larry Chen, Sam Cook, Christine Escher, David Finch, Mina Ossiander, Juha Pohjanpelto, Don Solmon, and Enrique Thomann.

PREFACE TO THE July 2013 EDITION

For the July 2013 edition, the text has been reset in standard LaTeX by Forrest Parker. All figures have been redone, with a few figures added, by Dean C. Wills. Other than a small bit of reworking here and there, there are no other substantial changes in this edition.

Please report errata to sscarbor@math.oregonstate.edu.

Stephen D. Scarborough

Department of Mathematics

Oregon State University

TEAR-OUT PAGES

This spiral bound text has perforated pages. In particular, the Lab/Recitation Group Projects that are included in Appendix A are designed to be torn out and handed in as homework assignments, as may be required by your instructor. The sample exams in Appendix B also can be torn out individually.

Part I

Background and Review

Lesson 1

Complex Numbers, Variables, and Functions

1.1 Goals

- Be able to add, subtract, multiply, and divide complex numbers

- Represent complex numbers as points or vectors in the complex plane and illustrate addition and subtraction with the parallelogram (or triangle) law

- Learn the algebraic properties of absolute values and complex conjugates given in the lesson

- Write equations or inequalities that define any circle, disk, or the interior or exterior of a disk in the complex plane

- Learn the terms real part, imaginary part, and complex conjugate of a complex number and be able to illustrate them geometrically

- Express complex numbers in polar form and use polar forms to calculate powers and roots of complex numbers

1.2 Overview

Most of Lesson 1 is designed for self-study and/or review. Your instructor will only cover a few highlights.

Complex numbers play an important role in engineering and scientific problems. Mathematical models of real-world problems that involve oscillatory behavior typically lead to calculations and graphical visualizations in which complex numbers and functions come up in very natural ways. In particular this is true for problems involving matrix methods and power series expansions, which are the principal areas of study in MTH 306. Thus, we begin our study with a review of some basic properties of complex numbers and with a brief introduction to complex functions.

1.3   The Complex Number System

The number systems you use today evolved over several thousand years. New types of numbers and their related rules of arithmetic were developed in order to solve increasingly sophisticated problems that were encountered as human societies became increasingly complex. You should be familiar will most of the kinds of numbers listed below (in the order of their historical development).

1. *natural numbers:*   1, 2, 3, 4, 5, ...

2. *integers:*   ..., $-5, -4, -3, -2, -1, 0, 1, 2, 3, 4, 5, ...$.

3. *rational numbers (fractions):*   numbers of the form p/q where p and q are integers and $q \neq 0$. For example, 2/3, and $-5/2$ are rational numbers.

4. *real numbers:*   numbers which can be represented in decimal form with a possibly infinite number of decimal digits following the decimal point.

5. *complex numbers:*   numbers of the form $a + ib$ where a and b are real numbers and i, called the *imaginary unit*, satisfies $i^2 = -1$.

Evidently each natural number is an integer. Each integer is a rational number. For example, the integer 5 can also be expressed as 5/1. Rational numbers are real numbers because each rational number has a finite or periodically repeating decimal expansion that can be found by long division. For instance,

$$3/8 = 0.375 \text{ and } 13/7 = 1.\underbrace{857142}\underbrace{857142} \cdots .$$

Finally, all real numbers are complex numbers. For example, $5 = 5 + i0$.

The primary reason for extending the natural number system to include the other numbers above was the need to solve increasingly complex equations that came up in agriculture, astronomy, economics, science, and engineering. Let's look at a few simple examples to motivate the need to introduce new number systems. The linear equation

$$x + 2 = 5$$

has solution $x = 3$ in the natural numbers. On the other hand,

$$x + 5 = 2$$

has no solution in the system of natural numbers. The same is true of the equation

$$x + 2 = 2.$$

The need to solve simple equations such as these led to the integers and their familiar arithmetic properties. More linear equations can be solved in the system of integers than in the system of natural numbers, but we still cannot solve all linear equations. For instance,

$$2x - 4 = 6$$

has solution $x = 5$ but we cannot solve

$$2x - 4 = 5$$

in the system of integers. You can see how the need to solve this last equation led naturally to the system of rational numbers, in which the equation has solution $x = 9/2$. Indeed, any linear equation with integer coefficients can be solved in the rational number system. The equation $ax + b = c$, with $a \neq 0$, has solution $x = (c - b)/a$. If a, b, and c are integers, the solution is a rational number.

Quadratic equations are more challenging. Not all quadratic equations can be solved in the rational number system. In fact, most quadratic equations do not have rational number solutions. This shortcoming of the rational numbers was known to the Greeks. In particular, the Pythagorean school knew that the quadratic equation $x^2 = 2$, in which x gives the length of a diagonal of a square with side 1, has no solution in the system of rational numbers. We simply cannot determine the diagonal of such a unit square within the rational number system. The real number system is needed in order to solve this equation and the solution is $x = \sqrt{2} = 1.414213562\cdots$, an unending nonperiodic decimal.

The introduction of the real number system enables us to solve more quadratic equations, but not all such equations. You probably encountered this short coming in connection with the quadratic formula which expresses the solutions to the quadratic equation

$$ax^2 + bx + c = 0, \qquad a \neq 0,$$

as

$$x = \frac{-b \pm \sqrt{b^2 - 4ac}}{2a}.$$

The resulting solution formula gives real number solutions only if $b^2 - 4ac \geq 0$. What are we to make of the formula when $b^2 - 4ac < 0$? For example, the quadratic formula applied to $x^2 + 2x + 3 = 0$ yields

$$x = \frac{-2 \pm \sqrt{4 - 12}}{2} = \frac{-2 \pm \sqrt{-8}}{2}.$$

Here is the dilemma: In the real number system, the product of a number by itself is always positive or zero. So if $\sqrt{-8}$ is real, then its product with itself must be positive or zero, but, on the other hand, its product with itself must be -8 if $\sqrt{-8}$ stands for a number whose square is -8. You can appreciate that mathematicians of the fifteenth century were puzzled. Indeed it was not until the nineteenth century that this dilemma was fully resolved and the complex number system was placed on a firm foundation. There is no real number whose square is -8 but there is a complex number with that property; one such number is $i\sqrt{8}$, where i is the imaginary unit.

Once complex numbers are available, all quadratic equations can be solved. In fact, the quadratic formula gives the solution not only for all quadratic equations with real coefficients, the same formula gives the solution to all quadratic equations with complex (number) coefficients. The complex number system is even more powerful when it comes to solving equations. It is a fact, called the *Fundamental Theorem of Algebra,* that every polynomial (regardless of its degree) with complex coefficients can be solved in the complex number system. That is, all the roots of any such polynomial equation are complex numbers.

The historical confusion that preceded a clear understanding of the complex number system has led to some unfortunate terminology that persists to this day. For example, given the complex number $-3 + 4i$, the real number -3 is called its real part, 4 is called its imaginary part, and i is called the imaginary unit. There is nothing "imaginary" about the imaginary part of a complex number nor is the imaginary unit somehow mathematically suspect. Complex numbers may be less familiar to you, but the system of complex numbers is just as valid and just as useful as the other number systems you have used. Nevertheless, the use of the word "imaginary" is firmly entrenched in mathematical usage.

Now for some good news. The complex numbers obey the familiar rules of arithmetic that you have been using for years.

> Complex numbers can be added, subtracted, multiplied, and divided according to the usual rules of arithmetic.

After the foregoing operations are performed, the resulting expressions can be simplified and put in the **standard form** (real) $+ i$(real) using the relations

$$
\begin{aligned}
i &= i, & i^5 &= i^4 \cdot i = 1 \cdot i = i, \\
i^2 &= -1, & i^6 &= i^4 \cdot i^2 = 1 \cdot i^2 = -1, \\
i^3 &= i \cdot i^2 = -i, & i^7 &= i^4 \cdot i^3 = 1 \cdot i^3 = -i, \\
i^4 &= i^2 \cdot i^2 = (-1)(-1) = 1, & i^8 &= i^4 \cdot i^4 = 1 \cdot i^4 = 1,
\end{aligned}
$$

and so on where the powers of i repeat in a cycle of length 4.

Example 1 *Evaluate the following.*
(a) $2 + 3i + (-6 + 7i)$
(b) $2 + 3i - (-6 + 7i)$
(c) $(2 + 3i)(-6 + 7i)$
(d) $\dfrac{2 + 3i}{-6 + 7i}$

Solution. The first three evaluations are straightforward:

(a) $2 + 3i + (-6 + 7i) = 2 + 3i - 6 + 7i = -4 + 10i$.

(b) $2 + 3i - (-6 + 7i) = 2 + 3i + 6 - 7i = 8 - 4i$.

(c) $(2 + 3i)(-6 + 7i) = -12 + 14i - 18i + 21i^2$

$$= -12 - 4i - 21 = -33 - 4i.$$

Part (d) requires more thought. The algebraic identity $(\alpha + \beta)(\alpha - \beta) = \alpha^2 - \beta^2$ is used to eliminate i from the denominator:

$$\frac{2 + 3i}{-6 + 7i} = \frac{2 + 3i}{-6 + 7i} \cdot \frac{-6 - 7i}{-6 - 7i}$$

$$= \frac{-12 - 14i - 18i - 21i^2}{36 + 42i - 42i - 49i^2}$$

$$= \frac{9 - 32i}{85} = \frac{9}{85} - \frac{32}{85}i. \quad \square$$

The process used to carry out division in (d) is called *rationalization*. It always works: Given a complex number $c = a + ib$ with a and b real the complex number $\bar{c} = a - ib$ is called the **complex conjugate** of c. To simplify the fraction

$$\frac{a' + ib'}{a + ib}$$

multiply numerator and denominator by $\bar{c} = a - ib$, the complex conjugate of the denominator. After a short calculation, as in (d), the quotient can be expressed in standard form.

If $c = a + ib$ is a complex number written in standard form so that a and b are real, then a is called the **real part** and b is called the **imaginary part** of the complex number c. Briefly

$$a = \text{Re}(c) \qquad \text{and} \qquad b = \text{Im}(c).$$

Two complex numbers are *equal* (by definition) when they have the same real and imaginary parts. For example,

$$\frac{1 + i}{2} = \frac{1}{2} + \frac{1}{2}i \text{ and } \frac{1}{1 - i} = \frac{1}{1 - i} \cdot \frac{1 + i}{1 + i} = \frac{1 + i}{2} = \frac{1}{2} + \frac{1}{2}i$$

therefore,

$$\frac{1 + i}{2} = \frac{1}{1 - i}.$$

You may have noticed that we have not mentioned anything about inequalities in the foregoing discussion of complex numbers. There is a very good reason why:

> There is no way to define a notion of inequality among complex numbers that preserves all the familiar rules of inequalities.

Thus, in general, it makes no sense to say one complex number is greater than or less than some other complex number and expressions like

$c < 2 - 3i$ have NO meaning (are NOT defined) in the complex numbers.

There is a useful notion of the **absolute value (modulus)**, denoted $|c|$, of a complex number c. If $c = a + ib$ is a complex number in standard form, then

$$|c| = \sqrt{a^2 + b^2}.$$

For example, the complex number $c = -3 + 4i$ has absolute value

$$|-3 + 4i| = \sqrt{(-3)^2 + 4^2} = \sqrt{25} = 5.$$

1.4   Properties of Absolute Values and Complex Conjugates

It is customary to use the symbols x and y to stand for real numbers and to reserve the letters z and w for complex numbers. We shall adhere to that custom throughout these lessons.

Here are a few useful properties of absolute values:

$$\begin{aligned} |z| &\geq 0, \\ |zw| &= |z|\,|w|, \\ \left|\frac{z}{w}\right| &= \frac{|z|}{|w|} \qquad w \neq 0. \end{aligned}$$

Since the complex conjugate of $z = x + iy$ is $\bar{z} = x - iy$,

$$z\bar{z} = (x + iy)(x - iy) = x^2 - ixy + iyx + y^2 = x^2 + y^2 = |z|^2.$$

This relation and a few additional useful properties of complex conjugation are summarized here for future reference:

$$\begin{aligned} \overline{z \pm w} &= \bar{z} \pm \bar{w}, \\ \overline{zw} &= \bar{z}\bar{w}, \\ \overline{\left(\frac{z}{w}\right)} &= \frac{\bar{z}}{\bar{w}} \qquad w \neq 0, \\ z &= \bar{z} \qquad \text{if and only if } z \text{ is real}, \\ |z|^2 &= z\bar{z}. \end{aligned}$$

1.5   The Complex Plane

Real numbers are represented geometrically as points on a number line. Complex numbers are represented as points (or vectors) in a number plane, called the complex plane. Let $z = x + iy$ be a complex number with real part x and imaginary part y. The complex number z is represented geometrically as follows:

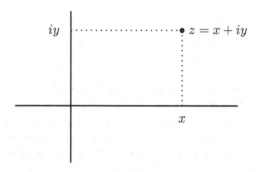

Figure 1.1: The Complex Plane

The plane in the figure is called the **complex plane**. The horizontal axis is called the **real axis**; it represents the real numbers $x = x + i0$ (thought of as complex numbers). The vertical axis is called the **imaginary axis**. Points on the imaginary axis represent special complex numbers of the form iy with y real. Such numbers are called **purely imaginary**. As you can see, the complex number $z = x + iy$ is represented by the point in the complex plane whose projection onto the real axis is x and whose projection onto the imaginary axis is iy.

Another fruitful way to represent a complex number is as a vector. Specifically the vector from the origin in the complex plane to the point used to represent the complex number. This representation is shown in the next figure.

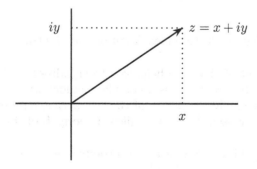

Figure 1.2: The Complex Plane

The vector representation fits together with the way addition and subtraction of complex numbers are defined and gives us a geometric visualization of these two algebraic operations. Indeed, if

$$z = x + iy \quad \text{and} \quad z' = x' + iy'$$

are in standard form, then

$$z + z' = (x + x') + i(y + y'),$$
$$z - z' = (x - x') + i(y - y').$$

These rules for addition and subtraction look just like the corresponding rules for addition and subtraction of two-dimensional vectors. In the case of complex numbers, real and imaginary parts are added or subtracted while in the case of two-dimensional vectors x-components and y-components are added or subtracted. Thus, addition and subtraction of complex numbers can be done geometrically using the familiar parallelogram (or triangle) law for vector addition:

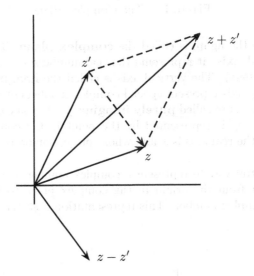

Figure 1.3: Complex Addition and Subtraction

The vector point of view also helps you to visualize the absolute value of a complex number. If $z = x + iy$ is a complex number with x and y real, then $|z| = \sqrt{x^2 + y^2}$ is simply the length of the vector that represents the complex number z. For this reason, $|z|$ is also called the **length** of the complex number z.

If $z = x + iy$ and $w = r + is$ are two complex numbers in standard form, then $z - w = (x - r) + i(y - s)$ and

$$|z - w| = \sqrt{(x - r)^2 + (y - s)^2}$$

which is the **distance** between z and w in the complex plane:

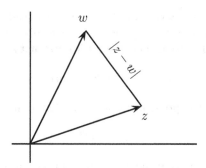

Figure 1.4: $|z - w|$ is the distance between z and w

Use of polar coordinates r and θ in the complex plane leads to the **polar form** for complex numbers as illustrated in the following figure.

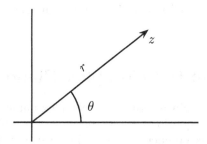

Figure 1.5: $z = r\cos\theta + ir\sin\theta$

Notice that

$$r = |z|$$

when a complex number z is expressed in polar form. Since the polar angle in a polar coordinate system is only determined up to multiples of 2π, z also has the polar forms

$$z = r\cos(\theta + 2\pi n) + ir\sin(\theta + 2\pi n)$$

for any integer n.

Multiplication and division of complex numbers have revealing geometric interpretations when the computations are expressed in polar form. Use of polar forms make it easy to calculate powers and roots of complex numbers. See the problems.

A Glimpse of Things to Come

In Lesson 18 you will learn that the real exponential function e^x with x real can be extended to a complex exponential function e^z with z complex. As you will see, if $z = i\theta$ with θ real, then the **Euler identity**

$$e^{i\theta} = \cos\theta + i\sin\theta$$

holds. Consequently, the polar form of a complex number can be expressed as

$$z = re^{i\theta}.$$

This is usually the most convenient way to express z in polar form. One reason for this is that the familiar rule of exponents

$$e^{i(\theta + \varphi)} = e^{i\theta}e^{i\varphi}$$

and

$$\left(e^{i\theta}\right)^n = e^{in\theta} \qquad n \text{ any integer}$$

hold.

1.6   Circles in the Complex Plane

Let z be a **complex variable**; that is, a complex number that can vary. Consider the graph of the equation $|z| = 1$. Since $|z| = |z - 0|$, the graph of $|z| = 1$ consists of all complex numbers z whose distance from the origin is 1. They comprise the points of the circle with center at the origin and radius 1 in the complex plane. This circle is called the **unit circle**.

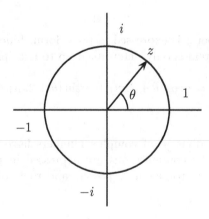

Figure 1.6: Unit Circle $|z| = 1$

Since $r = |z| = 1$ for each point on the unit circle, the polar form of z, which is $z = \cos\theta + i\sin\theta$, provides a parametric representation of points on the unit circle, with the central angle θ between z and the positive real axis as parameter. The circle is swept out once in the counterclockwise sense as θ increases from 0 to 2π.

Evidently the graph of $|z| < 1$ consists of all complex numbers inside the unit circle. The graph of $|z| < 1$ is called the **open unit disk**. (Open refers to the fact that the circular boundary of the disk is not part of the disk.)

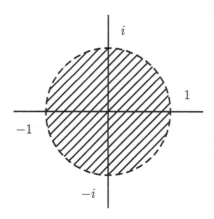

Figure 1.7: Open Unit Disk $|z| < 1$

Let c be a fixed complex number and $r > 0$ a fixed real number. Then the equation $|z - c| = r$ describes the points z in the complex plane whose distance from c is r. Thus, the graph of $|z - c| = r$ is the circle with center c and radius r in the complex plane. What is the graph of $|z - c| \leq r$?

Example 2 *Describe the graph of (a) the equation $|2z - 4i| = 6$ and (b) the inequality $|2z - 2 + 4i| \geq 6$ in the complex plane.*

Solution. The key to graphing such expressions is to express the left member in the form $|z - (\text{something})|$ and then make a distance interpretation of the resulting equality or inequality. Here are the details.
(a)

$$|2z - 4i| = 6,$$
$$|2(z - 2i)| = 6,$$
$$|2||z - 2i| = 6,$$
$$|z - 2i| = 3.$$

So the graph consists of all point z in the complex plane whose distance from $2i$ is 3, which is the circle with center $2i$ and radius 3 in the complex plane. Sketch this circle.

(b)

$$|2z - 2 + 4i| \geq 6,$$
$$|2(z - 1 + 2i)| \geq 6,$$
$$|z - 1 + 2i| \geq 3,$$
$$|z - (1 - 2i)| \geq 3.$$

So the graph consists of all point z in the complex plane whose distance from $1 - 2i$ is greater than or equal to 3, which consists of all points on or outside the circle with center $1 - 2i$ and radius 3 in the complex plane. $\square$

1.7   Complex Functions

Remember that complex variables are often denoted by z and w and, unless we say otherwise, x and y will always stand for real variables.

Functions involving complex numbers are defined in the same fashion as for the more familiar functions of algebra and calculus that involve only real numbers and variables. Thus,

$$f(z) = z^2,$$

with the understanding that z is a complex variable, defines a **complex-valued function of a complex variable**. For this function,

$$f(2 - i) = (2 - i)^2 = 4 - 4i + i^2 = 3 - 4i,$$
$$f\left(\frac{i}{1 + 2i}\right) = \frac{i^2}{(1 + 2i)^2} = \frac{-1}{-3 + 4i} = \frac{3}{25} + \frac{4}{25}i,$$
$$f(3) = 3^2 = 9,$$
$$f(i) = i^2 = -1.$$

The rule

$$g(x) = 2x - ix^2,$$

with x understood to be real, defines a **complex-valued function of a real variable**. For this function,

$$g(-3) = -6 - 9i,$$
$$g(0) = 0,$$
$$g\left(\sqrt{2}\right) = 2\sqrt{2} - 2i,$$

and so on. The rule

$$h(z) = \text{Re}(z) - \text{Im}(z)$$

defines a **real-valued function of a complex variable**. For this function,

$$h\left(2 - 3i\right) = 2 - \left(-3\right) = 5,$$
$$h\left(i\right) = 0 - 1 = -1,$$
$$h\left(\frac{2 - 3i}{1 + i}\right) = h\left(-\frac{1}{2} - \frac{5}{2}i\right) = -\frac{1}{2} - \left(-\frac{5}{2}\right) = 2.$$

All the common ways of expressing functions used earlier in calculus are used in the context of complex functions. For example, the function $f\left(z\right) = z^2$ also can be expressed by $w = z^2$.

Perhaps you are wondering what $f\left(z\right) = \sin z$ means when z is a complex variable. Your calculator knows. So should you. Stay tuned.

1.8   Suggested Problems

Evaluate and express in standard form:

1. $(3 - 2i) + (-7 + 5i)$

2. $(3 - 2i) - (-7 + 5i)$

3. $(3 - 2i)(-7 + 5i)$

4. $\dfrac{1}{1 - i}$

5. $\dfrac{3 - 2i}{-7 + 5i}$

6. $\overline{5 - 12i}$

7. $|5 - 12i|$

8. $|5 + 12i|$

9. i^{100}

10. i^{49}

Find all real or complex solutions:

11. $4x^2 + 9 = 0$

12. $z^2 + z = -2$

Illustrate on a graph the parallelogram or triangle law for the expressions:

13. $(2 + i) + (3 - 4i)$

14. $(2 + 2i) - (-3 + i)$

15. Let $z = 2 + i$ and $w = 3 - 4i$. Use a graph to illustrate z, w, $|z - w|$.

Express in polar form:

16. $-2 + 2i$

17. $1 + \sqrt{3}i$

Complex numbers z and w have polar forms

$$z = r\cos\theta + ir\sin\theta = re^{i\theta}$$
$$w = s\cos\varphi + is\sin\varphi = se^{i\varphi}$$

18. *(Geometric Interpretation of Multiplication of Complex Numbers)*

    (a) Use trigonometric identities to show that

    $$zw = rs \cos(\theta + \varphi) + irs \sin(\theta + \varphi)$$

    (b) Use Euler's identity and the rules of exponents to show that

    $$zw = rse^{i(\theta + \varphi)}$$

    (c) Explain briefly why (a) and (b) are consistent.

    (d) Explain why (a) or (b) establishes the identity $|zw| = |z|\,|w|$.

    (e) Based on (a) or (b) make a sketch and describe in geometric terms how to obtain the product zw from the polar forms of z and w.

19. *(Geometric Interpretation of Division of Complex Numbers)*

    (a) Use trigonometric identities to show that

    $$\frac{z}{w} = \frac{r}{s} \cos(\theta - \varphi) + i\frac{r}{s} \sin(\theta - \varphi)$$

    (b) Use Euler's identity and the rules of exponents to show that

    $$\frac{z}{w} = \frac{r}{s}e^{i(\theta - \varphi)}$$

    (c) Explain briefly why (a) and (b) are consistent.

    (d) Explain why (a) or (b) establishes the identity $|z/w| = |z|\,/\,|w|$.

    (e) Based on (a) or (b) make a sketch and describe in geometric terms how to obtain the quotient z/w from the polar forms of z and w.

20. *(Equality of Polar Forms)* Establish the following useful fact:

    $$re^{i\theta} \quad \text{and} \quad se^{i\varphi}$$

    are two polar forms of the same complex number z if and only if

    $$r = s \quad \text{and} \quad \varphi = \theta + 2\pi k \text{ for some integer } k.$$

    Make a sketch showing z, r, s, θ, φ that illustrates the geometric meaning of this result.

21. Let z be a complex number.

   (a) Express z in standard form and then express iz in standard form. Now find the angle between the vectors representing z and iz and plot them in the complex plane.

   (b) Express z and i in polar form using Euler's identity and then find iz in polar form. Now find the angle between the vectors representing z and iz and plot them in the complex plane.

22. *(DeMoivre's Formula)* In Problem 18 let $w = z = r\cos\theta + ir\sin\theta = re^{i\theta}$ and show, using the polar form you prefer, that

   (a) $z^2 = r^2\cos 2\theta + ir^2\sin 2\theta$ and $z^3 = r^3\cos 3\theta + ir^3\sin 3\theta$.

   (b) Express z^n in polar form using both polar representations. The result is called DeMoivre's formula. (If necessary first find z^4 in polar form.)

23. Find $(1+i)^{100}$ and express the result in standard form. *Hint.* First, write $1+i$ in polar form and apply DeMoivre's formula.

   Nth roots of complex numbers: A complex number z is an nth root of another complex number w if $z^n = w$. Each complex number except 0 has exactly n nth roots. (This statement applies to nonzero real numbers since they are particular complex numbers.) DeMoivre's formula can be used to find these roots as the following two examples illustrate.

24. Find the fourth roots z of $1+i$. Express your answer in standard from. *Hint.* Let $z = re^{i\theta}$ be a polar form of z, express $1+i$ in polar form, use DeMoivre's formula in the equation $z^4 = 1+i$, and finally determine r and θ. See Prob. 20. This gives the roots in polar form.

25. Find the cube roots of 1. *Hint.* See the hint for Problem 23.

   Graph the indicated equation or inequality.

26. $|z| = 4$

27. $|z - 1| = 3$

28. $|z + 1| = 3$

29. $|z| > 4$

30. $|z| \le 4$

31. $|z + i| \ge 1$

32. $|1 - z| < 1$

33. $|3z - 6| = 9$

34. $|2z + 3 + 4i| < 5$

Evaluate the given function at the given points. Express your answers in standard form.

35. $f(z) = z + 1/z \qquad z = i,\, z = 2 - i$

36. $g(z) = z^{-2} \qquad z = i,\, z = 1/(2 - i)$

37. $h(z) = \operatorname{Re}(z)/\operatorname{Im}(z) \qquad z = i,\, z = (5 - 2i)/(2 - i)$

38. $k(z) = (1 - z)/(z - i) \qquad z = 2i,\, z = 4$

Find the domain of each function. (That is, find the set of all z such that the function makes sense (is defined).)

39. $f(z) = z + 1/z$

40. $g(z) = z^2/(\operatorname{Re}(z) - \operatorname{Im}(z))$

If $z = x + iy$ with x and y real, express each function in the form (real) $+ i$(real).

41. $f(z) = z + 1/z$

42. $g(z) = z^2/(\operatorname{Re}(z) - \operatorname{Im}(z))$

Lesson 2

Vectors, Lines, and Planes

2.1 Goals

- Learn the algebraic and geometric descriptions of vectors

- Learn the basic rules of vector algebra and their geometric interpretations

- Learn the basic algebraic properties of dot products and use them to find angles between vectors and to test for orthogonality

- Be able to find the component and projection of one vector along another vector

- Learn the vector and scalar equations for lines and planes in 2-space and 3-space

2.2 Overview

Most of Lesson 2 is designed for self-study and/or review.
Your instructor will only cover a few highlights.

Reread the PREREQUISITES subsection in the Introduction to this book. Follow the advice there, as needed. The primary emphasis in this lesson will be on those properties of vectors, the dot product, and of lines and planes that will help you better understand the matrix and linear algebra topics that are the subject of the Part II of these lessons.

2.3   Vectors

Vectors in Ordinary 2-space and 3-space

Vectors have both algebraic and geometric descriptions. The algebraic description enables you to calculate easily with vectors. The geometric description helps with conceptual understanding and with applications, such as to problems involving motion or force. From the algebraic point of view, the bottom line is that vectors are added, subtracted, and multiplied by scalars (numbers) component-by-component. In this sense, vectors can be thought of as conceptual prototypes for modern parallel processors. From the geometric point of view, a **vector** has magnitude (or size) and direction. By contrast, a number, also called a **scalar**, has only magnitude. It has no direction. Mass, speed, and temperature are scalars while force and velocity are vectors.

Rectangular coordinates are introduced in 3-space by appending a third coordinate axis, the z-axis, to the two rectangular coordinates used in the xy-plane:

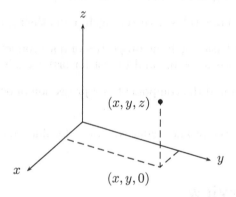

Figure 2.1: Regular Coordinates in 3-space

Vectors are represented geometrically by *arrows (directed line segments)* and algebraically by *components* relative to a Cartesian coordinate system:

$$\mathbf{a} = \langle a_1, a_2 \rangle \qquad \text{in 2-dimensions,}$$
$$\mathbf{a} = \langle a_1, a_2, a_3 \rangle \qquad \text{in 3-dimensions.}$$

The respective components of a vector give the displacements in the x-, y-, and z-directions of the tip of the arrow that represents the vector relative to its tail. One arrow that represents the vector $\mathbf{a} = \langle a_1, a_2, a_3 \rangle$ has its tail at the origin $(0, 0, 0)$ and its tip at the point (a_1, a_2, a_3). This arrow is called the **position vector** of the point (a_1, a_2, a_3) :

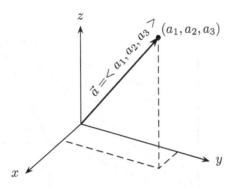

Figure 2.2: Regular Coordinates in 3-space

All other arrows that represent the vector **a** are parallel displacements of the position vector. What is the corresponding figure for a 2-dimensional vector?

The **magnitude (length)** of a vector **a**, denoted $|\mathbf{a}|$, is the (common) length of any arrow that represents it:

$$|\mathbf{a}| = \sqrt{a_1^2 + a_2^2} \qquad \text{in 2-dimensions,}$$
$$|\mathbf{a}| = \sqrt{a_1^2 + a_2^2 + a_3^2} \qquad \text{in 3-dimensions.}$$

These formulas follow easily from the Pythagorean theorem. See the problems. Vectors are added and subtract componentwise. For example, in 3-dimensions, if

$$\mathbf{a} = \langle a_1, a_2, a_3 \rangle \text{ and } \mathbf{b} = \langle b_1, b_2, b_3 \rangle,$$

then

$$\mathbf{a} \pm \mathbf{b} = \langle a_1 \pm b_1, a_2 \pm b_2, a_3 \pm b_3 \rangle.$$

Vector addition can be visualized geometrically through a **triangle law** and a **parallelogram law**, as in the following figures:

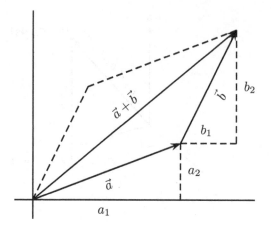

Figure 2.3: Triangle and Parallel Law of Vector Addition

Vector subtraction can be visualized as follows:

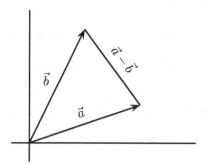

Figure 2.4: Triangle Law of Vector Subtraction

Notice the direction of the arrow representing $\mathbf{a} - \mathbf{b}$. To confirm the figure think of what vector must be added to $\mathbf{b}$ to get $\mathbf{a}$.

The **scalar multiple** of a vector $\mathbf{a}$ by a scalar c is the vector $c\mathbf{a}$ with magnitude $|c|$ times the magnitude of $\mathbf{a}$ and with direction the direction of $\mathbf{a}$ if $c \geq 0$ and the direction opposite to $\mathbf{a}$ if $c < 0$. Make a sketch that illustrates scalar multiplication. In terms of components

$$c\mathbf{a} = \langle ca_1, ca_2, ca_3 \rangle.$$

Use of the component description of vectors and familiar properties of numbers yields the following useful properties of vector addition and scalar multiplication:

A1.	$\mathbf{a} + \mathbf{b} = \mathbf{b} + \mathbf{a}$	A2.	$\mathbf{a} + (\mathbf{b} + \mathbf{c}) = (\mathbf{a} + \mathbf{b}) + \mathbf{c}$
A3.	$\mathbf{a} + \mathbf{0} = \mathbf{a}$	A4.	$\mathbf{a} + (-\mathbf{a}) = \mathbf{0}$
A5.	$c(\mathbf{a} + \mathbf{b}) = c\mathbf{a} + c\mathbf{b}$	A6.	$(c + d)\mathbf{a} = c\mathbf{a} + d\mathbf{a}$
A7.	$(cd)\mathbf{a} = c(d\mathbf{a})$	A8.	$1\mathbf{a} = \mathbf{a}$

In A3 and A4, $\mathbf{0}$ is a vector with all components equal to zero.

A **unit vector** is a vector that has length one. If $\mathbf{a} \neq \mathbf{0}$, then $\mathbf{u} = \mathbf{a}/\left|\mathbf{a}\right|$ is a unit vector with the same direction as $\mathbf{a}$. The unit vectors

$$\mathbf{i} = \langle 1, 0 \rangle, \quad \mathbf{j} = \langle 0, 1 \rangle \qquad \text{in 2-dimensions,}$$

$$\mathbf{i} = \langle 1, 0, 0 \rangle, \quad \mathbf{j} = \langle 0, 1, 0 \rangle, \quad \mathbf{k} = \langle 0, 0, 1 \rangle \qquad \text{in 3-dimensions.}$$

provide a convenient alternative to the angle-bracket notation for components:

$$\mathbf{a} = \langle a_1, a_2 \rangle = a_1\mathbf{i} + a_2\mathbf{j} \qquad \text{in 2-dimensions,}$$

$$\mathbf{a} = \langle a_1, a_2, a_3 \rangle = a_1\mathbf{i} + a_2\mathbf{j} + a_3\mathbf{k} \qquad \text{in 3-dimensions.}$$

The vectors $\mathbf{i}$ and $\mathbf{j}$ (or $\mathbf{i}$, $\mathbf{j}$, and $\mathbf{k}$) are called the **standard basis vectors** for 2-space (3-space).

n-Dimensional Vectors

Vectors in higher dimensions are just as useful and easy to use as the more familiar 2- and 3-dimensional vectors. An ***n*-dimensional vector** $\mathbf{a}$ has n components

$$\mathbf{a} = \langle a_1, a_2, a_3, ..., a_n \rangle$$

and such vectors are added, subtracted, and multiplied by scalars componen-twise. Consequently, the algebraic properties A1-A8 hold for vectors in n-dimensions.

The components of a vector can be either real or complex numbers. In either case the **magnitude** or **length** of $\mathbf{a}$ is

$$\left|\mathbf{a}\right| = \sqrt{\left|a_1\right|^2 + \left|a_2\right|^2 + \cdots + \left|a_n\right|^2}.$$

It is customary to denote by $\mathbb{R}^n$ the space of all n-vectors with real components and in which the scalars are real numbers. Likewise, $\mathbb{C}^n$ denotes the space of all n-vectors with complex components and in which the scalars are complex numbers.

The analogue in n-space of the standard basis $\mathbf{i}$, $\mathbf{j}$, $\mathbf{k}$ in 3-space is the set of unit vectors

$$
\begin{aligned}
\mathbf{e}_1 &= \langle 1, 0, 0, ..., 0, 0 \rangle, \\
\mathbf{e}_2 &= \langle 0, 1, 0, ..., 0, 0 \rangle, \\
\mathbf{e}_3 &= \langle 0, 0, 1, ..., 0, 0 \rangle, \\
&\ \ \vdots \\
\mathbf{e}_n &= \langle 0, 0, 0, ..., 0, 1 \rangle.
\end{aligned}
$$

These vectors are called the **standard basis in n-space**. Each vector $\mathbf{a}$ in n-space can be represented in terms of components as

$$\mathbf{a} = \langle a_1, a_2, a_3, ..., a_n \rangle = a_1\mathbf{e}_1 + a_2\mathbf{e}_2 + a_3\mathbf{e}_3 + \cdots + a_n\mathbf{e}_n.$$

2.4   Dot Products, Components, and Projections

For Vectors in 2-space and 3-space

The **dot product** of two vectors $\mathbf{a}$ and $\mathbf{b}$ in 2- or 3-space is

$$\boxed{\mathbf{a} \cdot \mathbf{b} = |\mathbf{a}|\,|\mathbf{b}|\cos\theta}$$

where θ is the smaller angle formed by $\mathbf{a}$ and $\mathbf{b}$, so that $0 \leq \theta \leq \pi$.

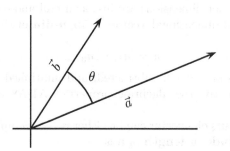

Figure 2.5: Angle θ between vectors $\vec{a}$ and $\vec{b}$

Notice that

$$\mathbf{a} \cdot \mathbf{a} = a_1^2 + a_2^2 + a_3^2 = |\mathbf{a}|^2$$

and likewise in 2 dimensions. The following algebraic properties of the dot product follow easily from its expression in terms of components.

DP1. $\mathbf{a} \cdot \mathbf{b} = \mathbf{b} \cdot \mathbf{a}$	DP2. $\mathbf{a} \cdot (\mathbf{b} + \mathbf{c}) = \mathbf{a} \cdot \mathbf{b} + \mathbf{a} \cdot \mathbf{c}$
DP3. $\mathbf{0} \cdot \mathbf{a} = 0$	DP4. $\mathbf{a} \cdot \mathbf{a} = |\mathbf{a}|^2$
DP5. $d\,(\mathbf{a} \cdot \mathbf{b}) = (d\mathbf{a}) \cdot \mathbf{b} = \mathbf{a} \cdot (d\mathbf{b})$	

Since $|\cos\theta| \leq 1$, an immediate consequence of $\mathbf{a} \cdot \mathbf{b} = |\mathbf{a}|\,|\mathbf{b}|\cos\theta$ is the **Schwarz Inequality**

$$|\mathbf{a} \cdot \mathbf{b}| \leq |\mathbf{a}|\,|\mathbf{b}|\,.$$

Dot products are very useful for finding the component or (vector) projection of one vector along another. The **component of b along a** is the scalar

$$\text{comp}_{\mathbf{a}}\,\mathbf{b} = |\mathbf{b}|\cos\theta,$$

where θ is the angle between $\mathbf{a}$ and $\mathbf{b}$. The geometric meaning is illustrated in the following figures.

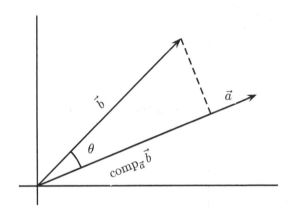

Figure 2.6: Component of $\vec{b}$ along $\vec{a}$

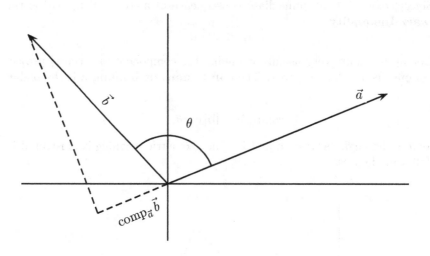

Figure 2.7: Component of $\vec{b}$ along $\vec{a}$

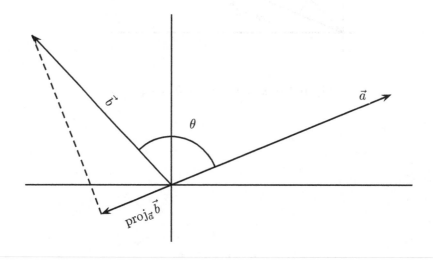

Figure 2.8: Projection of $\vec{b}$ onto $\vec{a}$

The $\mathrm{comp_a}\,\mathbf{b}$ is positive when the angle between $\mathbf{a}$ and $\mathbf{b}$ is acute and negative when it is obtuse. Also,

$$\mathrm{comp_a}\,\mathbf{b} = (|\mathbf{b}|\cos\theta)\frac{|\mathbf{a}|}{|\mathbf{a}|} = \frac{\mathbf{b}\cdot\mathbf{a}}{|\mathbf{a}|}.$$

The **(vector) projection of b along a** is the vector

$$\mathrm{proj_a}\,\mathbf{b} = (\mathrm{comp_a}\,\mathbf{b})\frac{\mathbf{a}}{|\mathbf{a}|} = \frac{\mathbf{b}\cdot\mathbf{a}}{|\mathbf{a}|^2}\mathbf{a}.$$

That is, $\mathrm{proj_a}\,\mathbf{b}$ is a vector whose length is $|\mathrm{comp_a}\,\mathbf{b}|$ and whose direction is the direction of $\mathbf{a}$ when $\mathrm{comp_a}\,\mathbf{b} \geq 0$ and whose direction is the direction of $-\mathbf{a}$ when $\mathrm{comp_a}\,\mathbf{b} < 0$. Draw a figure, analogous to the figure above, that illustrates $\mathrm{proj_a}\,\mathbf{b}$. A useful way to think about these formulas for components and projections is given in Problem 6.

For Vectors in $\mathbb{R}^n$

The **dot product** (also called **scalar product** or **inner product**) of two vectors

$$\mathbf{a} = \langle a_1, a_2, a_3, ..., a_n\rangle \ \text{ and } \ \mathbf{b} = \langle b_1, b_2, b_3, ..., b_n\rangle$$

in $\mathbb{R}^n$ is

$$\mathbf{a}\cdot\mathbf{b} = a_1 b_1 + a_2 b_2 + \cdots + a_n b_n.$$

The algebraic properties DP1-DP5 hold for vectors in $\mathbb{R}^n$. They follow by the same reasoning used to establish them in 2- or 3-dimensions. The Schwarz Inequality,

$$|\mathbf{a}\cdot\mathbf{b}| \leq |\mathbf{a}|\,|\mathbf{b}|$$

remains valid for any two n-vectors $\mathbf{a}$ and $\mathbf{b}$ and enables us to define angles between vectors in n-space. So the tables are turned. In 2- or 3-space properties of angles lead easily to the Schwarz inequality. In higher dimensions, the Schwarz inequality comes first and enables us to define angles, as follows. For nonzero vectors $\mathbf{a}$ and $\mathbf{b}$,

$$-1 \leq \frac{\mathbf{a}\cdot\mathbf{b}}{|\mathbf{a}|\,|\mathbf{b}|} \leq 1.$$

Consequently, there is a unique angle θ with $0 \leq \theta \leq \pi$ such that

$$\cos\theta = \frac{\mathbf{a}\cdot\mathbf{b}}{|\mathbf{a}|\,|\mathbf{b}|}.$$

By definition θ is the **angle between a and b**. Thus

$$\mathbf{a}\cdot\mathbf{b} = |\mathbf{a}|\,|\mathbf{b}|\cos\theta$$

just as for vectors in 2- and 3-space. We say two n-vectors $\mathbf{a}$ and $\mathbf{b}$ are **orthogonal (perpendicular)** if their dot product is zero:

$$\mathbf{a} \perp \mathbf{b} \Longleftrightarrow \mathbf{a} \cdot \mathbf{b} = 0.$$

The component and projection of one vector along another are defined just as in 2- or 3-space

$$\text{comp}_{\mathbf{a}} \mathbf{b} = \frac{\mathbf{b} \cdot \mathbf{a}}{|\mathbf{a}|},$$

$$\text{proj}_{\mathbf{a}} \mathbf{b} = \frac{\mathbf{b} \cdot \mathbf{a}}{|\mathbf{a}|^2} \mathbf{a}.$$

For Vectors in $\mathbb{C}^n$

The **(complex) dot product** (also called **scalar product** or **inner product**) of two vectors $\mathbf{a}$ and $\mathbf{b}$ in $\mathbb{C}^n$ is

$$\mathbf{a} \cdot \mathbf{b} = a_1 \overline{b_1} + a_2 \overline{b_2} + \cdots + a_n \overline{b_n}$$

where now the components are complex numbers and the overbar signifies complex conjugation. The algebraic properties DP2-DP4 hold for vectors in $\mathbb{C}^n$, but DP1 and DP5 change slightly:

DP1. $\overline{\mathbf{a} \cdot \mathbf{b}} = \mathbf{b} \cdot \mathbf{a}$

DP5. $d\left(\mathbf{a} \cdot \mathbf{b}\right) = (d\mathbf{a}) \cdot \mathbf{b} = \mathbf{a} \cdot \left(\overline{d}\mathbf{b}\right)$

The relation

$$\mathbf{a} \cdot \mathbf{a} = |\mathbf{a}|^2$$

and the **Schwarz Inequality**

$$|\mathbf{a} \cdot \mathbf{b}| \leq |\mathbf{a}| \, |\mathbf{b}|$$

hold for complex n-vectors $\mathbf{a}$ and $\mathbf{b}$. Since $\mathbf{a} \cdot \mathbf{b}$ is complex-valued we do not define the angle between any two complex vectors but it is useful to say that two complex n-vectors $\mathbf{a}$ and $\mathbf{b}$ are **orthogonal (perpendicular)** if their dot product is zero:

$$\mathbf{a} \perp \mathbf{b} \Longleftrightarrow \mathbf{a} \cdot \mathbf{b} = 0.$$

2.5 Row and Column Vectors

As you will see in subsequent lessons it is sometimes useful to think of a vector as a "row" vector and sometimes as a "column" vector. We express **row vectors** in component form as

$$\mathbf{a} = \langle a_1, a_2, a_3, ..., a_n \rangle \quad \text{or} \quad \mathbf{a} = [a_1 \ a_2 \ a_3 \ ... \ a_n]$$

using angle or square brackets. We express **column vectors** in component form as

$$\mathbf{a} = \begin{bmatrix} a_1 \\ a_2 \\ a_3 \\ \vdots \\ a_n \end{bmatrix}.$$

Vectors are most often thought of as column vectors in problems involving matrices.

2.6 Lines and Planes

Lines *in 3-space (and 2-space)*

A Line L in space is determined by a point P_0 on it and a vector $\mathbf{v}$ that orients the line in space; that is, L is parallel to $\mathbf{v}$. The following figure shows a position vector $\mathbf{r}_0$ to the point P_0, the vector $\mathbf{v}$ that gives the orientation of L in space, and a general (variable) point P on L with position vector $\mathbf{r}$.

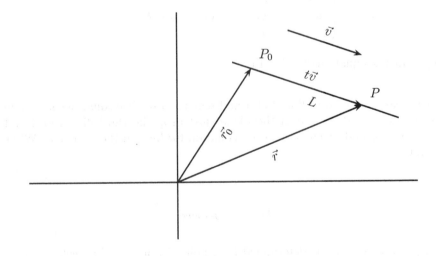

Figure 2.9: A Vector Equation for the line L

As indicated in the foregoing figure, the triangle law of vector addition leads to the following **vector (parametric) equation** for L

$$\mathbf{r} = \mathbf{r}_0 + t\mathbf{v}, \qquad \text{for } -\infty < t < \infty.$$

If $P = (x, y, z)$, $P_0 = (x_0, y_0, z_0)$, and $\mathbf{v} = \langle a, b, c \rangle$, equating corresponding components in this vector equation gives

$$\begin{cases} x = x_0 + at \\ y = y_0 + bt \\ z = z_0 + ct \end{cases} \qquad \text{for } -\infty < t < \infty.$$

These equations are called **(scalar) parametric equations** for the line L. Notice that the coefficients of t give the components of a vector parallel to the line L.

Example 1 *Find parametric equations for the line L determined by the two points $(2, -4, 3)$ and $(3, 2, 1)$.*

Solution. $P_0 = (2, -4, 3)$ is a point on L. The vector

$$\mathbf{v} = \langle 3 - 2, 2 - (-4), 1 - 3 \rangle = \langle 1, 6, -2 \rangle$$

that extends from $(2, -4, 3)$ to $(3, 2, 1)$ is parallel to L. So

$$\begin{cases} x = 2 + t \\ y = -4 + 6t \\ z = 3 - 2t \end{cases} \qquad \text{for } -\infty < t < \infty$$

are parametric equations for L. $\square$

The reasoning used to find vector and scalar parametric equations for a line in space works just as well in the plane (just drop the third dimension) and leads to vector and scalar parametric equation for lines in the xy-plane. What are they?

Planes *in 3-space*

A plane Π in space is determined by a point P_0 on it and a vector $\mathbf{N}$ perpendicular (normal) to it. The following figure shows a position vector $\mathbf{r}_0$ to the point P_0, the vector $\mathbf{N}$, and a general (variable) point P on Π with position vector $\mathbf{r}$.

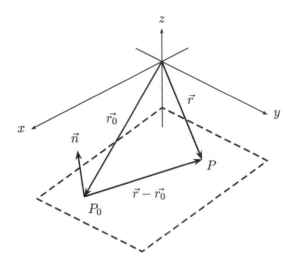

Figure 2.10: Vector Equation for a plane in space

Evidently P lies in the plane Π if and only if the vector $\mathbf{r} - \mathbf{r}_0$ lies in Π and this happens precisely when $\mathbf{r} - \mathbf{r}_0$ is perpendicular to $\mathbf{N}$. Hence, an equation for the plane Π is

$$\mathbf{N} \cdot (\mathbf{r} - \mathbf{r}_0) = 0.$$

If $P = (x, y, z)$, $P_0 = (x_0, y_0, z_0)$, and $\mathbf{N} = \langle a, b, c \rangle$, evaluating the dot product leads to the equivalent equation

$$a(x - x_0) + b(y - y_0) + c(z - z_0) = 0$$

for the plane Π. This equation may also be put in the form

$$ax + by + cz = d$$

by combining the constant terms. By reversing the steps, you can see that either of these equations has graph a plane with normal $\mathbf{N} = \langle a, b, c \rangle$ and, in the case of the first equation, that passes through the point (x_0, y_0, z_0).

Example 2 *A plane* Π *contains the point* $(1, -4, 7)$. *The line* L *with equation*

$$x = 4t, \ y = -2 + t, \ z = 3 - 5t \qquad \text{for } -\infty < t < \infty$$

is perpendicular to the plane. Find an equation for the plane Π.

Solution. The point $P_0 = (1, -4, 7)$ lies on Π and the vector $\mathbf{N} = \langle 4, 1, -5 \rangle$ is perpendicular to the plane. (Why?) So an equation for the plane is

$$4(x - 1) + 1(y - (-4)) - 5(z - 7) = 0$$

or

$$4x + y - 5z = -35. \quad \square$$

2.7   Suggested Problems

In Problems 1-6 use the algebraic properties DP1-DP5 whenever possible. Each problem has a short easy solution using these properties. No extensive calculation are needed nor is it helpful to express vectors in term of components.

1. Use dot product calculations to verify the identity

$$|\mathbf{a} + \mathbf{b}|^2 + |\mathbf{a} - \mathbf{b}|^2 = 2|\mathbf{a}|^2 + 2|\mathbf{b}|^2.$$

   Then give a geometric interpretation of this result for vectors in $\mathbb{R}^2$.

2. Let $\mathbf{u}_1$, $\mathbf{u}_2$, $\mathbf{u}_3$ be mutually orthogonal unit vectors. If $\mathbf{v} = c_1\mathbf{u}_1 + c_2\mathbf{u}_2 + c_3\mathbf{u}_3$ show that $c_1 = \mathbf{v} \cdot \mathbf{u}_1$, $c_2 = \mathbf{v} \cdot \mathbf{u}_2$, and $c_3 = \mathbf{v} \cdot \mathbf{u}_3$.

3. Let $\mathbf{a}$, $\mathbf{b}$, and $\mathbf{c}$ be vectors. Show, with the aid of the dot product, that:

   (a) $\mathbf{a} \perp \mathbf{b}$ and $\mathbf{a} \perp \mathbf{c}$ implies that $\mathbf{a} \perp \beta\mathbf{b}$ for any scalar β and $\mathbf{a} \perp (\mathbf{b} + \mathbf{c})$.

   (b) $\mathbf{a} \perp \mathbf{b}$ and $\mathbf{a} \perp \mathbf{c}$ implies that $\mathbf{a} \perp (\beta\mathbf{b}+\gamma\mathbf{c})$ for any scalars β and γ.

   (c) Interpret (b) geometrically for vectors in $\mathbb{R}^3$.

4. Let $\mathbf{a}$ and $\mathbf{b}$ be vectors.

   (a) Use the dot product to show that $\mathbf{a} \perp (\mathbf{b} - \mathrm{proj}_{\mathbf{a}}\,\mathbf{b})$.

   (b) $\mathrm{proj}_{\mathbf{a}}\,\mathbf{b}$ is a scalar multiple of which vector $\mathbf{a}$ or $\mathbf{b}$? Explain briefly.

5. A rhombus is a parallelogram with four equal sides. Use dot products to establish the following.

   (a) The diagonals of a rhombus are perpendicular to each other.

   (b) If the diagonals of a parallelogram are perpendicular, then the parallelogram is a rhombus.

6. Let $\mathbf{a}$ be a nonzero vector and let $\mathbf{u}$ be a unit vector in the direction of $\mathbf{a}$. For any vector $\mathbf{b}$ show:

   (a) $\mathrm{comp}_{\mathbf{a}}\,\mathbf{b} = \mathbf{b} \cdot \mathbf{u}$;

   (b) $\mathrm{proj}_{\mathbf{a}}\,\mathbf{b} = (\mathbf{b} \cdot \mathbf{u})\,\mathbf{u}$.

7. Use the Pythagorean theorem to verify the formulas for the length of a vector given in this lesson. *Hint.* In the 3-dimensional case use the figure for the position vector $\mathbf{a} = \langle a_1, a_2, a_3 \rangle$ and append to the rectangle in the figure its diagonal extending from the origin to the point $(a_1, a_2, 0)$.

8. Derive the vector and scalar parametric equations for a line in 2-space.

9. You may remember from geometry the statement: "Two points determine a line." Find scalar parametric equations for the line determined by the two points $(-2, 0, 3)$ and $(5, 4, -1)$.

10. A line in space passes through the point $(1, -2, 3)$ and is parallel to the line through the two points $(-2, 0, 3)$ and $(5, 4, -1)$. Find scalar parametric equations for the line.

11. You may remember from geometry the statement: "Three points determine a plane." Find an equation for the plane determined by the three points $(-2, 0, 3)$, $(6, -8, 10)$ and $(5, 4, -1)$. *Hint.* This is easy if you know about cross products. It is still not hard if you don't. In that case, start by finding two vectors in the plane. A normal vector $\mathbf{N} = \langle a, b, c \rangle$ to the plane must be perpendicular to both. Take dot products with $\mathbf{N}$ and you are on your way to finding the components of a normal to the plane.

12. A plane in space contains the point $(5, 4, 1)$ and has normal direction parallel to the line through the points $(0, -2, 0)$ and $(11, 7, -5)$. Find an equation for the plane.

Part II

Matrix Methods

Lesson 3

Linear Equations
and Determinants

3.1   Goals

- Be able to solve 2×2 and 3×3 linear systems by systematic elimination of unknowns without the aid of a calculator or computer

- Be able to evaluate 2×2 and 3×3 determinants without the aid of a calculator or computer

- Understand that systematic elimination of unknowns can be applied to any linear system of algebraic equations and is the basis for computer solutions of large systems

- Learn Theorems 1, 2, and 3. Be able to illustrate them geometrically for 2×2 and 3×3 linear systems

3.2   Overview

The lessons in Part II serve as an introduction to some important topics from matrix and linear algebra. We shall concentrate on general properties of solutions of linear systems of algebraic equations, systematic solution techniques, geometric aspects of matrices, and eigenvalue problems. We shall illustrate key concepts related to solving linear systems of equations in the computationally simple setting of 2×2 systems (two equations in two unknowns) and 3×3 systems. Many results that are easy to establish and interpret in the 2×2 or 3×3 case hold for $n \times n$ systems. When this is so, we will treat the 2×2 or 3×3 case and then state the results for general $n \times n$ linear systems. Many of you will have learned some of the computational techniques that follow in a previous algebra or precalculus course, but the point of view here will be different.

39

3.3   Three Basic Principles

You learned in algebra how to solve a system of two linear equations in two unknowns by elimination of unknowns. In this lesson, we will review that procedure, make it more systematic, and see that it can be applied to systems with any number of equations and unknowns.

Example 1 *Solve the system*

$$\begin{cases} x + y = 2 \\ 2x - 3y = 9 \end{cases}.$$

Solution. The graphs of the two equations are the straight lines in the figure:

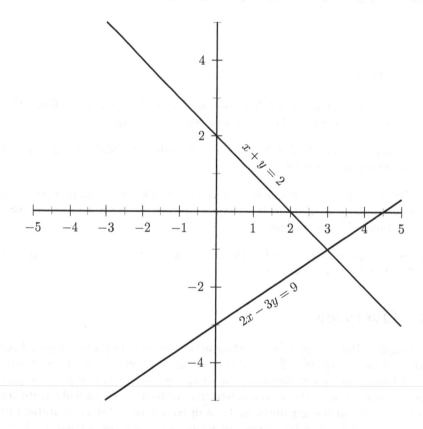

Figure 3.1: Graphical Solution of a System

The point (x, y) where the lines intersect satisfies both equations. It is the solution. The figure suggests that $x \approx 3$ and $y \approx -1$. To find the exact values of x and y, multiply the first equation by 3 and add the result to the second equation. This eliminates y and yields the equation $5x = 15$; so $x = 3$. Now the first equation gives $3 + y = 2$ or $y = -1$. (How can you eliminate x first and arrive at an equation for y? Do it.) $\square$

The set of solutions to the general system of two linear equations in two unknowns

$$\begin{cases} ax + by = e \\ cx + dy = f \end{cases} \tag{3.1}$$

where a, b, c, d, e, and f are given numbers, can be described geometrically much as in Example 1. Let L_1 be the straight line with equation $ax + by = e$ and L_2 be the straight line with equation $cx + dy = f$. Then one of three cases occurs:

Case I. L_1 and L_2 intersect in a *unique* point.

Case II. L_1 and L_2 are *distinct* parallel lines.

Case III. L_1 and L_2 *coincide.*

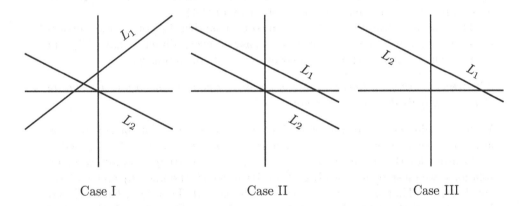

Case I   Case II   Case III

Figure 3.2: Cases of two lines in a plane

The points (x, y), if any, which lie on both lines L_1 and L_2 give the values of x and y which solve the system (3.1). Thus the linear system (3.1) either has exactly one solution (Case I), no solution (Case II), or infinitely many solutions (Case III). These conclusions for systems of two equations in two unknowns hold in general.

Theorem 1 *An $n \times n$ linear system of algebraic equations either has a unique solution, no solution, or infinitely many solutions.*

Later in the lesson when you learn systematic methods for solving linear systems, it will be advantageous to group the coefficients of the unknowns into a rectangular array called the **coefficient matrix** of the system. For the system (3.1) the coefficient matrix is

$$A = \begin{bmatrix} a & b \\ c & d \end{bmatrix}.$$

There are simple algebraic tests that distinguish which of the three possibilities in Theorem 1 actually occurs for a given system. The system (3.1) will have a unique solution precisely when L_1 and L_2 have different slopes,

$$-\frac{a}{b} \neq -\frac{c}{d},$$
$$ad - bc \neq 0. \tag{3.2}$$

The number $ad-bc$ is called a **determinant** of the system (3.1) or of the matrix A. The following notation is used for this determinant:

$$\begin{vmatrix} a & b \\ c & d \end{vmatrix} = ad - bc. \tag{3.3}$$

Notice that a matrix (which is a rectangular array of numbers) is indicated by square brackets and a determinant (which is a number) by vertical bars. We also express the determinant of A by $|A|$ or by $\det(A)$.

The reasoning leading to (3.2) assumed that neither L_1 nor L_2 was vertical because then b or d would be zero. It is easy to check directly that (3.2) still holds when either or both of the lines are vertical. In summary:

Theorem 2 *An $n \times n$ linear system of algebraic equations has a unique solution if and only if its determinant is not zero.*

We have confirmed this result for 2×2 systems but it is true for the general case as soon as we know what the determinant of an $n \times n$ system is. Stay tuned.

In order for the linear system (3.1) to have no solution or infinitely many solutions, we must be in Case II or Case III in which the lines L_1 and L_2 have equal slopes. That is, $-a/b = -c/d$ or $ad - bc = 0$. Therefore, Cases II and III occur when the determinant of the system is zero. Case III is distinguished from Case II by the fact that L_1 and L_2 have the same y-intercept,

$$\frac{e}{b} = \frac{f}{d},$$
$$\begin{vmatrix} b & e \\ d & f \end{vmatrix} = 0.$$

Similar determinant tests are available for $n \times n$ systems but they will not be given here.

The system (3.1) is **homogeneous** when $e = f = 0$. Thus, a homogeneous system of two equations in two unknowns has the form

$$\begin{cases} ax + by = 0 \\ cx + dy = 0 \end{cases}. \tag{3.4}$$

The lines L_1 and L_2 corresponding to a homogeneous system both pass through the origin. (Why?) These lines are either distinct (have different slopes) or coincide (have the same slopes).

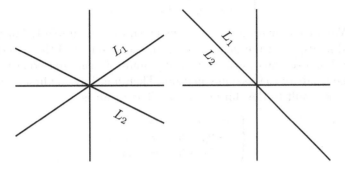

Only the trivial solution   Nontrivial solutions

Figure 3.3: Cases of two lines in a homogeneous system

The slopes of L_1 and L_2 are different precisely when the determinant

$$\begin{vmatrix} a & b \\ c & d \end{vmatrix} = ad - bc \neq 0.$$

In this case the homogeneous system (3.4) has the unique solution $x = 0$, $y = 0$. This (obvious) solution is called the **trivial solution** of the system. The homogeneous system (3.4) will have **nontrivial solutions** (solutions for which x and y are not both zero) when L_1 and L_2 have equal slopes, equivalently,

$$\begin{vmatrix} a & b \\ c & d \end{vmatrix} = ad - bc = 0.$$

Then any point $(x, y) \neq (0, 0)$ on the line $L_1 = L_2$ gives a nontrivial solution pair x, y of the homogeneous system. To recap:

Theorem 3 *An $n \times n$ homogeneous linear system of algebraic equations has nontrivial solutions if and only if its determinant is zero.*

Corollary 1 *An $n \times n$ homogeneous linear system of algebraic equations has only the trivial solution if and only if its determinant is not zero.*

Example 2 *Solve the system*

$$\begin{cases} x - 3y + z & = & 4 \\ 2x - 8y + 8z & = & -2 \\ -6x + 3y - 15z & = & 9 \end{cases}.$$

Solution. We use elimination of unknowns much as in Example 1. For instance, we can add multiples of the first equation to the second and third to eliminate x from the last two equations. Specifically, multiply the first equation by -2 and add the result to the second equation. Then multiply the first equation by 6 and add the result to the third equation. The result is

$$\begin{cases} x - 3y + z & = & 4 \\ -2y + 6z & = & -10 \\ -15y - 9z & = & 33 \end{cases}.$$

Simplify the last two equations by dividing by 2 and 3 respectively to obtain

$$\begin{cases} x - 3y + z & = & 4 \\ -y + 3z & = & -5 \\ -5y - 3z & = & 11 \end{cases}.$$

Add the second equation to the third to eliminate z from the last equation. This gives

$$\begin{cases} x - 3y + z & = & 4 \\ -y + 3z & = & -5 \\ -6y & = & 6 \end{cases}.$$

Therefore, $y = -1$. The second equation gives $-(-1) + 3z = -5$, $3z = -6$, $z = -2$. Now the first equation yields $x - 3(-1) + (-2) = 4$, $x = 3$. The system has solution $x = 3$, $y = -1$, $z = -2$. $\square$

The fact that the linear system in Example 2 has a unique solution $(x, y, z) = (3, -1, -2)$ can be interpreted geometrically. Each equation in the system graphs as a plane in space. Two planes intersect in a line or are parallel. Normally we expect the planes to intersect in a line. This is what happens for the first two planes in Example 2. The third plane cuts this line in a single point – the point $(3, -1, -2)$. In other examples, two or three of the planes may be parallel or coincide and the resulting system will have either no solutions or infinitely many solutions. Once again determinants can be used to distinguish the cases.

The determinant of the system of three linear equations

$$\begin{cases} ax + by + cz = j \\ dx + ey + fz = k \\ gx + hy + iz = l \end{cases}$$

in the three unknowns x, y, z and where a, b, c, ..., j, k, and l are given numbers is

$$\begin{vmatrix} a & b & c \\ d & e & f \\ g & h & i \end{vmatrix} = aei - ahf - bdi + bgf + cdh - cge.$$

This definition can be recast in the easily-remembered form

$$\begin{vmatrix} a & b & c \\ d & e & f \\ g & h & i \end{vmatrix} = a \begin{vmatrix} e & f \\ h & i \end{vmatrix} - b \begin{vmatrix} d & f \\ g & i \end{vmatrix} + c \begin{vmatrix} d & e \\ g & h \end{vmatrix}$$

which is called **the (Laplace) expansion of the determinant by its first row.** Do you see the pattern? Cross out the row and column containing a on the left to get the 2×2 determinant

$$\begin{vmatrix} e & f \\ h & i \end{vmatrix}$$

which multiplies a on the right. The second and third terms on the right are formed in the corresponding way. These terms are combined with the alternating sign pattern $+, -, +$.

Determinants for 4×4 systems and higher order systems can be defined in a similar way in terms of a Laplace expansion involving determinants of one lower order. For example, a 4×4 determinant is the sum formed as above from 4 products of first row entries of the 4×4 determinant multiplied by 3×3 determinants gotten by crossing out rows and columns and then combining the products with the alternating sign pattern $+, -, +, -$. You can find more details in any book on linear algebra or matrix theory.

3.4   Systematic Elimination of Unknowns

The system

$$\begin{cases} x + y = 2 \\ 2x - 3y = 9 \end{cases} \tag{3.5}$$

in Example 1 and the system

$$\begin{cases} u + v = 2 \\ 2u - 3v = 9 \end{cases} \tag{3.6}$$

are really the same. The symbols used for the unknowns is immaterial. What is essential is the coefficients that multiply the unknowns and the given right members. The unknowns simply serve as place holders. Thus, either system above is fully described by its **augmented matrix**

$$\begin{bmatrix} 1 & 1 & | & 2 \\ 2 & -3 & | & 9 \end{bmatrix} \tag{3.7}$$

which is composed of the coefficient matrix of the system augmented by the column vector of right-hand sides appended on the right. The vertical bar is just an aid to help you distinguish the coefficient matrix from the right members of the system. More precisely the augmented matrix is a 2×3 (read "2 by 3") matrix because it has 2 rows and 3 columns. We regard (3.7) as a compact version of (3.5) or (3.6). The first two columns in (3.7) keep track of the unknowns, either x and y in (3.5) or u and v in (3.6).

Let's recast our solution of (3.5) in Example 1 using the augmented matrix (3.7). We multiplied the first equation in (3.5) by 3 and added the result to the second equation. This amounts to multiplying each entry in the first row of (3.7) by 3 and adding these multiples to the corresponding entries of the second row. Now the system is described by the matrix

$$\begin{bmatrix} 1 & 1 & 2 \\ 5 & 0 & 15 \end{bmatrix}.$$

This means that (3.5) is reduced to

$$\begin{cases} x + y & = 2 \\ 5x & = 15 \end{cases}$$

or that (3.6) is reduced to

$$\begin{cases} u + v & = 2 \\ 5u & = 15 \end{cases}$$

As before we find that

$$x = 3, \ y = -1 \quad \text{or} \quad u = 3, \ v = -1$$

Example 3 *Solve the systems*

$$\begin{cases} 3x - 2y & = 12 \\ x + 4y & = 15 \end{cases} \quad and \quad \begin{cases} 3x - 2y & = -7 \\ x + 4y & = 7 \end{cases}.$$

Solution. The two augmented matrices are

$$\begin{bmatrix} 3 & -2 & 12 \\ 1 & 4 & -10 \end{bmatrix} \quad and \quad \begin{bmatrix} 3 & -2 & -7 \\ 1 & 4 & 7 \end{bmatrix}.$$

Since the coefficient matrices are the same, we can eliminate unknowns in both systems simultaneously using the matrix

$$\begin{bmatrix} 3 & -2 & 12 & -7 \\ 1 & 4 & -10 & 7 \end{bmatrix}.$$

The last two columns keep track of the right members of the two systems. Multiply the first row ("equations") by 2 and add the result to the second row ("equations") to obtain

$$\begin{bmatrix} 3 & -2 & 12 & -7 \\ 7 & 0 & 14 & -7 \end{bmatrix}.$$

Thus, the two systems have been reduced to

$$\begin{cases} 3x - 2y = 12 \\ 7x = 14 \end{cases} \quad and \quad \begin{cases} 3x - 2y = -7 \\ 7x = -7 \end{cases}.$$

Solve for x and substitute back into the first equation to obtain

$$x = 2, \ y = -3 \quad \text{and} \quad x = -1, \ y = 2$$

respectively. Since either systems has a unique solution its determinant must be nonzero. (Why?) Let's check this directly just for fun

$$\begin{vmatrix} 3 & -2 \\ 1 & 4 \end{vmatrix} = (3)(4) - (1)(-2) = 14 \neq 0. \quad \square$$

It should be apparent that augmented matrices can be used to solve systems with more equations and unknowns in much the same way.

Example 4 *Solve the system in Example 2 using an augmented matrix.*

Solution. The system is represented by the 3×4 matrix

$$\left[\begin{array}{ccc|c} 1 & -3 & 1 & 4 \\ 2 & -8 & 8 & -2 \\ -6 & 3 & -15 & 9 \end{array} \right].$$

For comparison purposes we lay out the solution carrying along the unknowns in the solution in the left column and using the augmented matrix approach in the right column:

With Unknowns Displayed	Via The Augmented Matrix
$\begin{cases} x - 3y + z = 4 \\ 2x - 8y + 8z = -2 \\ -6x + 3y - 15z = 9 \end{cases}$	$\left[\begin{array}{ccc|c} 1 & -3 & 1 & 4 \\ 2 & -8 & 8 & -2 \\ -6 & 3 & -15 & 9 \end{array} \right]$

Multiply Eqn 1 by -2 and add to Eqn 2

$\begin{cases} x - 3y + z = 4 \\ -2y + 6z = -10 \\ -6x + 3y - 15z = 9 \end{cases}$	$\left[\begin{array}{ccc|c} 1 & -3 & 1 & 4 \\ 0 & -2 & 6 & -10 \\ -6 & 3 & -15 & 9 \end{array} \right]$

Multiply Eqn 1 by 6 and add to Eqn 3

$\begin{cases} x - 3y + z = 4 \\ -2y + 6z = -10 \\ -15y - 9z = 33 \end{cases}$	$\left[\begin{array}{ccc|c} 1 & -3 & 1 & 4 \\ 0 & -2 & 6 & -10 \\ 0 & -15 & -9 & 33 \end{array} \right]$

Divide Eqn 2 by -2 and Eqn 3 by -3

$\begin{cases} x - 3y + z = 4 \\ y - 3z = 5 \\ 5y + 3z = -11 \end{cases}$	$\left[\begin{array}{ccc|c} 1 & -3 & 1 & 4 \\ 0 & 1 & -3 & 5 \\ 0 & 5 & 3 & -11 \end{array} \right]$

Multiply Eqn 2 by -5 and add to Eqn 3

$\begin{cases} x - 3y + z = 4 \\ y - 3z = 5 \\ 18z = -36 \end{cases}$	$\left[\begin{array}{ccc|c} 1 & -3 & 1 & 4 \\ 0 & 1 & -3 & 5 \\ 0 & 0 & 18 & -36 \end{array} \right]$

Divide Eqn 3 by 18

$\begin{cases} x - 3y + z = 4 \\ y - 3z = 5 \\ z = -2 \end{cases}$	$\left[\begin{array}{ccc|c} 1 & -3 & 1 & 4 \\ 0 & 1 & -3 & 5 \\ 0 & 0 & 1 & -2 \end{array} \right]$

So systematic elimination of unknowns has led us to the last system which is equivalent to the first (that is, both systems have the same solution(s)). The last step in the systematic solution process is call **back substitution**. We work from the last equation with only one unknown up through the previous equations finding one unknown from each equation. Here the last equation gives

$$z = -2.$$

The second to last equation $y - 3z = 5$ gives $y - 3(-2) = 5$ or

$$y = -1.$$

The third to last equation $x - 3y + z = 4$ gives $x - 3(-1) + (-2) = 4$ or

$$x = 3.$$

The original system has solution $x = 3$, $y = -1$, and $z = -2$. Once again the system has a unique solution so its determinant must be nonzero. Let's check this one more time

$$\begin{vmatrix} 1 & -3 & 1 \\ 2 & -8 & 8 \\ -6 & 3 & -15 \end{vmatrix} =$$

$$(1) \begin{vmatrix} -8 & 8 \\ 3 & -15 \end{vmatrix} - (-3) \begin{vmatrix} 2 & 8 \\ -6 & -15 \end{vmatrix} + (1) \begin{vmatrix} 2 & -8 \\ -6 & 3 \end{vmatrix} =$$

$$108 \neq 0. \quad \square$$

Example 5 *Solve*

$$\begin{cases} 2x - y + z = 1 \\ 3x + 2y - 4z = 4 \\ -6x + 3y - 3z = 2 \end{cases}.$$

Solution. Express the system as

$$\left[\begin{array}{ccc|c} 2 & -1 & 1 & 1 \\ 3 & 2 & -4 & 4 \\ -6 & 3 & -3 & 2 \end{array} \right].$$

Here it is more convenient to eliminate y rather than x from equations 2 and 3. (Why?) To eliminate y from the last two equations, multiply row 1 by 2 and add the result to row 2. Then multiply row 1 by 3 and add the result to row 3. The reduced system is

$$\left[\begin{array}{ccc|c} 2 & -1 & 1 & 1 \\ 7 & 0 & -2 & 6 \\ 0 & 0 & 0 & 5 \end{array} \right].$$

The last row represents the equation

$$0x + 0y + 0z = 5.$$

No values of x, y, z can satisfy this equation. (Why?) The system in this example has no solution. Since the system has no solution its determinant must be zero. Check directly that it is. $\quad \square$

Example 6 *Solve*

$$\begin{cases} 2x - y + z & = 1 \\ 3x + 2y - 4z & = 4 \\ 17x + 2y - 8z & = 16 \end{cases}.$$

Solution. Express the system as

$$\left[\begin{array}{ccc|c} 2 & -1 & 1 & 1 \\ 3 & 2 & -4 & 4 \\ 17 & 2 & -8 & 16 \end{array} \right].$$

For variety, we eliminate z from equations 2 and 3. To eliminate z from the last two equations, multiply row 1 by 4 and add the result to row 2. Then multiply row 1 by 8 and add the result to row 3. The reduced system is

$$\left[\begin{array}{ccc|c} 2 & -1 & 1 & 1 \\ 11 & -2 & 0 & 8 \\ 33 & -6 & 0 & 24 \end{array} \right].$$

Add -3 times row 2 to row 3 to reduce the system to

$$\left[\begin{array}{ccc|c} 2 & -1 & 1 & 1 \\ 11 & -2 & 0 & 8 \\ 0 & 0 & 0 & 0 \end{array} \right].$$

This means the system reduces to two equations in the three unknowns x, y, and z :

$$\begin{cases} 2x - y + z = 1 \\ 11x - 2y = 8 \end{cases}$$

or

$$\begin{cases} 2x - y & = 1 - z \\ 11x - 2y & = \quad 8 \end{cases}.$$

In this system z can be given any value and then we can solve for x and y in terms of z. Indeed, multiplying the first equation by -2 and adding it to the second gives

$$\begin{aligned} 7x & = 6 + 2z, \\ x & = \frac{6}{7} + \frac{2}{7}z, \end{aligned}$$

and then substituting this value for x into the first equation gives (check it)

$$y = \frac{5}{7} + \frac{11}{7}z$$

Thus, the system has infinitely many solutions given by

$$\begin{cases} x = \frac{6}{7} + \frac{2}{7}z \\ y = \frac{5}{7} + \frac{11}{7}z \qquad \text{for any choice of } z. \\ z = z \end{cases}$$

From the geometric point of view these equations are parametric equations (with parameter z) for the line in space through the point $(6/7, 5/7, 0)$ and parallel to the vector $\mathbf{v} = \langle 2/7, 11/7, 1 \rangle$. So in this example, the three planes that are the graphs of the three linear equations intersect in a common line. $\square$

Remember that when using systematic elimination of unknowns to solve linear systems that you can use the following steps, called *elementary row operations*, that always lead to an equivalent system:

- Interchange two rows

- Multiply (or divide) all the entries in a row by a nonzero constant

- Replace any row by the sum of itself and a multiple of *another* row

3.5   Non-Square Systems

In the foregoing sections we have concentrated on properties of square systems, those with as many equations as unknowns. Analogous properties hold for non-square systems in which there may be more equations than unknowns or more unknowns than equations. The treatment of non-square systems is mostly a story for another day and a course in linear algebra. We simply mention and illustrate with one example that systematic elimination of unknowns can be used to solve such systems.

Example 7 *Solve the system of three equations in four unknowns:*

$$\begin{cases} x - 2y - z + 3w & = & 0 \\ -2x + 4y + 5z - 5w & = & 3 \\ 3x - 6y - 6z + 8w & = & -3 \end{cases}$$

Solution. The augmented matrix for this system is

$$\left[\begin{array}{cccc|c} 1 & -2 & -1 & 3 & 0 \\ -2 & 4 & 5 & -5 & 3 \\ 3 & -6 & -6 & 8 & -3 \end{array} \right].$$

Multiply row 1 by 2 and add the result to row 2 and multiply row 1 by -3 and add the result to row 3 to obtain

$$\left[\begin{array}{cccc|c} 1 & -2 & -1 & 3 & 0 \\ 0 & 0 & 3 & 1 & 3 \\ 0 & 0 & -3 & -1 & -3 \end{array} \right].$$

Now add row 2 to row 3 to get

$$\left[\begin{array}{cccc|c} 1 & -2 & -1 & 3 & 0 \\ 0 & 0 & 3 & 1 & 3 \\ 0 & 0 & 0 & 0 & 0 \end{array} \right].$$

Systematic elimination of unknowns show us that the original system is equivalent to the system

$$\begin{cases} x - 2y - z + 3w & = 0 \\ 3z + w & = 3 \end{cases}.$$

The second equation reveals that z is determined by w (or vise versa). We choose to express w in terms of z to get $w = 3 - 3z$ for any choice of z. Substitute this value for w into the first equation to find

$$x - 2y = z - 3(3 - 3z) = 10z - 9.$$

This equation determines one of the variables in terms of the other two. We choose to express x in terms of y and z. Thus,

$$x = 2y + 10z - 9$$

for any y and z. Finally all solutions to the original system are given by

$$\begin{aligned} x &= 2y + 10z - 9, \\ y &= y, \\ z &= z, \\ w &= 3 - 3z, \end{aligned}$$

where y and z can be given any values. $\square$

3.6 Efficient Evaluation of Determinants

The direct evaluation of determinants using the Laplace expansion can be cumbersome. Procedures closely related to those used in the systematic elimination of unknowns can be used to evaluate determinants efficiently. Such methods are particularly useful for determinants of size 4×4 or higher. Since such higher order determinants are often evaluated by computers, we simply summarize here the procedures that underlie the efficient evaluation methods.

If A is an $n \times n$ matrix whose first, second, ..., n-th columns are respectively $\mathbf{a}_1, \mathbf{a}_2, ..., \mathbf{a}_n$, then we write

$$A = [\mathbf{a}_1, \mathbf{a}_2, ..., \mathbf{a}_n] \quad \text{and} \quad \det A = |\mathbf{a}_1, \mathbf{a}_2, ..., \mathbf{a}_n|.$$

The **main diagonal** of A is comprised of the entries that lie along the diagonal line segment extending from the upper left-hand corner of the matrix to its lower right-hand corner. The matrix A is **upper (lower) triangular** if all its entries below (above) its main diagonal are zero. The properties mentioned above for efficient evaluation of determinants are:

Prop. 1   *The determinant is a linear function of each of its columns.*

That is, if all but one column in a determinant is held fixed, then the determinant is linear in the remaining column. For example,

$$\begin{aligned} |\mathbf{a}_1 + \mathbf{a}_1', \mathbf{a}_2, ..., \mathbf{a}_n| &= |\mathbf{a}_1, \mathbf{a}_2, ..., \mathbf{a}_n| + |\mathbf{a}_1', \mathbf{a}_2, ..., \mathbf{a}_n|, \\ |r\mathbf{a}_1, \mathbf{a}_2, ..., \mathbf{a}_n| &= r|\mathbf{a}_1, \mathbf{a}_2, ..., \mathbf{a}_n| \quad \text{for any scalar } r. \end{aligned}$$

Prop. 2   *The determinant is zero whenever any two columns are equal.*

Prop. 3   *The value of a determinant is unchanged if a multiple of one column is added to another column.*

For example,

$$|\mathbf{a}_1, \mathbf{a}_2, \mathbf{a}_3, ..., \mathbf{a}_n| = |\mathbf{a}_1, \mathbf{a}_2 + r\mathbf{a}_j, \mathbf{a}_3, ..., \mathbf{a}_n|$$

for any column index $j \neq 2$ and any scalar r.

Prop. 4   *Interchanging two columns in a determinant changes its sign.*

For example,

$$|\mathbf{a}_1, \mathbf{a}_2, \mathbf{a}_3, \mathbf{a}_4, ..., \mathbf{a}_n| = -|\mathbf{a}_3, \mathbf{a}_2, \mathbf{a}_1, \mathbf{a}_4, ..., \mathbf{a}_n|.$$

Prop. 5   *Each of Properties 1-4 holds with column(s) replaced by row(s).*

Properties 1-5 can be used to put the matrix in upper (lower) triangular form. Then its determinant is easy to find.

Prop. 6   *The determinant of an upper (lower) triangular matrix is the product of its main diagonal entries.*

Another very useful property of determinants is:

Prop. 7   *The determinant of a product is the product of the determinants.*

That is,

$$\det AB = \det A \det B$$

for any two $n \times n$ matrices A and B.

See the next lesson for the meaning of the product of two matrices. You can find more information about these topics in virtually any book on matrix or linear algebra.

3.7   Complex Linear Systems

All of the foregoing examples involved only systems with real coefficients and right members. Nothing essential changes for systems with complex coefficients and right members. In this case, the solutions may be complex numbers, Theorems 1, 2, and 3 still hold, and the systematic solution techniques described earlier still apply. Determinants are defined and evaluated as previously described.

In Lesson 7 you will see that linear systems of equations involving complex numbers arise quite naturally in contexts where initially only real numbers are involved.

3.8 Suggested Problems

In problems 1-10 do the following

- Solve the given system by systematic elimination of unknowns using an augmented matrix.

- Check your answers.

- Give a geometric interpretation of your solution in terms of the graphs of the equations in the system.

1. $\begin{cases} 4x + 3y = 10 \\ 2x - 6y = -10 \end{cases}$ 2. $\begin{cases} 2x - y = 7 \\ -8x + 4y = 11 \end{cases}$

3. $\begin{cases} 2x + 3y = -6 \\ -x + \frac{3}{2}y = 3 \end{cases}$ 4. $\begin{cases} 3u - 2v = -1 \\ -5u + 3v = 2 \end{cases}$

5. $\begin{cases} x - z = 0 \\ 3x + y + z = 1 \\ -x + y + 2z = 2 \end{cases}$ 6. $\begin{cases} 3r - 2s + 4t = 6 \\ 2r + 3s - 5t = -8 \\ 5r - 4s + 3t = 7 \end{cases}$

7. $\begin{cases} x + 2y - z = 1 \\ 2x + y + z = 1 \\ x - y + 2z = 1 \end{cases}$ 8. $\begin{cases} x + 2y - z = 1 \\ 2x + y + z = 1 \\ 4x + 5y - z = 2 \end{cases}$

9. $\begin{cases} u + 2v - w = 2 \\ 2u + v + w = 1 \\ u - v + 2w = -1 \end{cases}$ 10. $\begin{cases} r + 2s - t = 2 \\ 6r + 9s - 3t = 9 \\ r - s + 2t = -1 \end{cases}$

In Problems 11-16 evaluate the determinant.

11. $\begin{vmatrix} 1 & -1 \\ 3 & 2 \end{vmatrix}$ 12. $\begin{vmatrix} 4 & 3 \\ 2 & 1 \end{vmatrix}$ 13. $\begin{vmatrix} 6 & 3 \\ 4 & 2 \end{vmatrix}$

14. $\begin{vmatrix} 0 & 1 & 0 \\ 1 & 0 & 0 \\ 0 & 0 & 1 \end{vmatrix}$ 15. $\begin{vmatrix} 1 & 2 & 3 \\ 4 & 5 & 6 \\ 7 & 8 & 9 \end{vmatrix}$ 16. $\begin{vmatrix} 4 & -6 & 3 \\ -1 & 4 & 1 \\ 5 & -6 & 3 \end{vmatrix}$

In Problems 17-20 use determinants to decide whether the system has (a) a unique solution or (b) either no solution or infinitely many solutions. Do *not* solve the system.

17. $\begin{cases} 3x - 4y = 7 \\ x + 2y = -4 \end{cases}$ 18. $\begin{cases} 2u - v = 5 \\ -8u + 4v = -11 \end{cases}$

19. $\begin{cases} 2x - 2y = 8 \\ -3x + y + 2z = -1 \\ x - 3y - z = 7 \end{cases}$ 20. $\begin{cases} 4u + 2v + 4w = 2 \\ 2u + v + 2w = 1 \\ 3u - 4v + w = -5 \end{cases}$

In Problems 21-24 determine the value(s) of λ for which the homogeneous system will have nontrivial solutions.

21. $\begin{cases} (1-\lambda)\,x + y = 0 \\ 4x + (1-\lambda)\,y = 0 \end{cases}$ 22. $\begin{cases} (1-\lambda)\,x + 2y = 0 \\ 3x + (2-\lambda)\,y = 0 \end{cases}$

23. $\begin{cases} (3-\lambda)\,x + 2y + 4z = 0 \\ 2x - \lambda y + 2z = 0 \\ 4x + 2y + (3-\lambda)\,z = 0 \end{cases}$ 24. $\begin{cases} -\lambda x - 2y - 3z = 0 \\ -x + (1-\lambda)\,y - z = 0 \\ 2x + 2y + (5-\lambda)\,z = 0 \end{cases}$

25. (a) Show, without explicitly solving, that the homogeneous system

$$\begin{cases} -x + 2y - z = 0 \\ 2x + y + z = 0 \\ x - y + 2z = 0 \end{cases}$$

has a unique solution. (b) Based on (a) what is the unique solution to the system?

Lesson 4

Matrices and Linear Systems

4.1 Goals

- Learn to add, subtract, multiply and scalar multiply matrices

- Be able to explain when addition, subtraction, and multiplication of particular matrices is defined

- Know when a matrix is invertible and be able to find its inverse using the systematic procedure described in this lesson

- Learn and apply the boxed results and Theorem 1

4.2 Overview

In this lesson you will study basic algebraic properties of matrices and matrix algebra. The algebra of matrices was developed as a consequence of and in conjunction with the systematic study of systems of linear equations. Even with the brief introduction given here you should begin to be able to appreciate the power and economy of the matrix notation and point of view.

4.3 Basic Matrix Operations

A **matrix** is just a rectangular array of numbers. For example

$$\begin{bmatrix} 2 & -1 \\ 3 & 7 \end{bmatrix}, \quad \begin{bmatrix} 1 & 2 & 3 \\ 4 & 5 & 6 \\ 7 & 8 & 9 \end{bmatrix}, \text{ and } \begin{bmatrix} 2 & 5 & -1 & 6 \\ 3 & 0 & 4 & -2 \\ 7 & -4 & 2 & 1 \end{bmatrix}$$

are matrices. An $n \times m$ matrix has n rows and m columns. [$n \times m$ is read "n by m".] The matrices above are 2×2, 3×3, and 3×4. Matrices came up naturally in Lesson 3 when linear systems were solved by elimination. They also come up in many other contexts.

It turns out to be useful to add, subtract, and scalar multiply matrices. This is done componentwise, just as for vectors. For example if

$$A = \begin{bmatrix} 1 & 2 \\ 3 & 4 \end{bmatrix} \quad \text{and} \quad B = \begin{bmatrix} -5 & 7 \\ 6 & -8 \end{bmatrix}$$

then

$$\begin{aligned} A + B &= \begin{bmatrix} 1+(-5) & 2+7 \\ 3+6 & 4+(-8) \end{bmatrix} = \begin{bmatrix} -4 & 9 \\ 9 & -4 \end{bmatrix}, \\ A - B &= \begin{bmatrix} 1-(-5) & 2-7 \\ 3-6 & 4-(-8) \end{bmatrix} = \begin{bmatrix} 6 & -5 \\ -3 & 12 \end{bmatrix}, \\ (-2)A &= \begin{bmatrix} (-2)1 & (-2)2 \\ (-2)3 & (-2)4 \end{bmatrix} = \begin{bmatrix} -2 & -4 \\ -6 & -8 \end{bmatrix}. \end{aligned}$$

Evidently, the componentwise operations of addition and subtraction can only be applied to matrices that have the **same size**; that is, matrices that have the same number of rows and the same number of columns. For example, we can add and subtract two 3×4 matrices, but we cannot add or subtract a 3×4 matrix and a 3×3 matrix. (Try it!)

Often it is useful to think of a matrix as composed of its rows and columns. For example, the matrix

$$\begin{bmatrix} 1 & 2 & 3 \\ 4 & 5 & 6 \\ 7 & 8 & 9 \end{bmatrix}$$

is composed of the three row vectors

$$[1\ 2\ 3], \quad [4\ 5\ 6], \text{ and} \quad [7\ 8\ 9]$$

and the three column vectors

$$\begin{bmatrix} 1 \\ 4 \\ 7 \end{bmatrix}, \quad \begin{bmatrix} 2 \\ 5 \\ 8 \end{bmatrix}, \text{ and} \quad \begin{bmatrix} 3 \\ 6 \\ 9 \end{bmatrix}.$$

In general an $n \times m$ matrix is composed of n row vectors and m column vectors.

In this section in order to describe matrix multiplication it will be convenient to define the sum of the products of the corresponding entries of two vectors (either row or column vectors) with the same number of components as the dot product of the vectors:

$$[1\ 2\ 3] \cdot [4\ 5\ 6] = (1)(4) + (2)(5) + (3)(6) = 32,$$

$$\begin{bmatrix} 1 \\ 4 \\ 7 \end{bmatrix} \cdot \begin{bmatrix} 2 \\ 5 \\ 8 \end{bmatrix} = (1)(2) + (4)(5) + (7)(8) = 78,$$

$$[1\ 2\ 3] \cdot \begin{bmatrix} 2 \\ 5 \\ 8 \end{bmatrix} = (1)(2) + (2)(5) + (3)(8) = 36.$$

The **product** $A\mathbf{x}$ of a matrix A and a column vector $\mathbf{x}$ turns out to be very useful. If

$$A = \begin{bmatrix} 1 & 2 \\ 3 & 4 \end{bmatrix} \quad \text{and} \quad \mathbf{x} = \begin{bmatrix} -2 \\ 5 \end{bmatrix}$$

then the product

$$A\mathbf{x} = \begin{bmatrix} 1 & 2 \\ 3 & 4 \end{bmatrix} \begin{bmatrix} -2 \\ 5 \end{bmatrix} = \begin{bmatrix} (1)(-2) + (2)(5) \\ (3)(-2) + (4)(5) \end{bmatrix} = \begin{bmatrix} 8 \\ 14 \end{bmatrix}.$$

Notice that the product $A\mathbf{x}$ is a vector. The first component of the vector $A\mathbf{x}$ is the dot product of the first row of A with $\mathbf{x}$. The second component of the vector $A\mathbf{x}$ is the dot product of the second row of A with $\mathbf{x}$. In general, we can define the product $A\mathbf{x}$ for any matrix A and column vector $\mathbf{x}$ for which the row vectors of A have the same number of components as the column vector $\mathbf{x}$. In this situation, we define the product $A\mathbf{x}$ to be the column vector whose successive components are the dot products of the rows of A with $\mathbf{x}$.

Example 1 *If*

$$A = \begin{bmatrix} 1 & 2 & 3 \\ 4 & 5 & 6 \end{bmatrix} \quad and \quad \mathbf{x} = \begin{bmatrix} -3 \\ 2 \\ -4 \end{bmatrix}$$

then

$$A\mathbf{x} = \begin{bmatrix} (1)(-3) + (2)(2) + (3)(-4) \\ (4)(-3) + (5)(2) + (6)(-4) \end{bmatrix} = \begin{bmatrix} -11 \\ -26 \end{bmatrix}. \quad \square$$

The linear properties of the a dot product carry over to the product $A\mathbf{x}$:

$$\boxed{\begin{aligned} A(\mathbf{x} + \mathbf{y}) &= A\mathbf{x} + A\mathbf{y}, \\ A(r\mathbf{x}) &= rA(\mathbf{x}) \quad \text{where } r \text{ is any scalar.} \end{aligned}}$$

It also is useful to define the product of certain matrices. Let A and B be matrices such that the row vectors of A and the column vectors of B have the same number of components. For example,

$$A = \begin{bmatrix} 1 & 2 & 3 \\ 4 & 5 & 6 \end{bmatrix} \quad \text{and} \quad B = \begin{bmatrix} -3 & 1 \\ 2 & 0 \\ -4 & 2 \end{bmatrix}$$

are such matrices and we can form the product of A with each column of B :

$$A\,(\text{first col. } B) \;=\; \begin{bmatrix} 1 & 2 & 3 \\ 4 & 5 & 6 \end{bmatrix} \begin{bmatrix} -3 \\ 2 \\ -4 \end{bmatrix} = \begin{bmatrix} -11 \\ -26 \end{bmatrix},$$

$$A\,(\text{second col. } B) \;=\; \begin{bmatrix} 1 & 2 & 3 \\ 4 & 5 & 6 \end{bmatrix} \begin{bmatrix} 1 \\ 0 \\ 2 \end{bmatrix} = \begin{bmatrix} 7 \\ 16 \end{bmatrix}.$$

By definition the product AB is the matrix with these columns

$$AB = \begin{bmatrix} -11 & 7 \\ -26 & 16 \end{bmatrix}.$$

In general, let A and B be matrices such that each row of A has the same number of entries as each column of B. If $B = [\mathbf{b}_1, \mathbf{b}_2, \cdots, \mathbf{b}_m]$, meaning that B has columns $\mathbf{b}_1$, $\mathbf{b}_2$,..., $\mathbf{b}_m$, then the **product** AB of the matrices A and B (in this order) is defined to be the matrix with columns $A\mathbf{b}_1$, $A\mathbf{b}_2$, ..., $A\mathbf{b}_m$:

$$\boxed{AB = A\,[\mathbf{b}_1, \mathbf{b}_2, \cdots, \mathbf{b}_m] = [A\mathbf{b}_1, A\mathbf{b}_2, \cdots, A\mathbf{b}_m]\,.}$$

If A is $n \times p$ and B is $p \times m$, then AB is an $n \times m$ matrix. The product AB has the same number of rows as A and the same number of columns as B.

Here is another way to describe the product AB. The first entry in the second column of AB is (see the box above) the first component of the column vector $A\mathbf{b}_2$. This component is the dot product of row 1 of A with column 2 of B. In the same way:

> The entry in row i and column j of AB is the dot product of row i of A with column j of B.

AB is called a (**matrix**) **product** because the following rules (which hold for multiplication of real and complex numbers) hold for matrix multiplication:

$$\begin{aligned} (AB)\,C &= A\,(BC), \\ A\,(B+C) &= AB + AC, \\ (B+C)\,A &= BA + CA, \\ c\,(AB) &= (cA)\,B = A\,(cB)\,. \end{aligned}$$

Since products of matrices are only defined for certain pairs of matrices, these rules hold in the following sense: If one side of each rule is defined, then so is the other and the stated equality is true.

It is important to realize that some familiar rules of algebra do *not* hold for matrices. For example, $ab = ba$ for any real or complex numbers a and b, but typically, even if AB and BA are both defined, $AB \neq BA$ for matrices.

Example 2 *If* $A = \begin{bmatrix} 1 & 2 \\ 3 & 4 \end{bmatrix}$ *and* $B = \begin{bmatrix} 0 & 2 \\ -5 & 1 \end{bmatrix}$, *then check that*

$$AB = \begin{bmatrix} -10 & 4 \\ -20 & 10 \end{bmatrix}, \quad BA = \begin{bmatrix} 6 & 8 \\ -2 & -6 \end{bmatrix}, \quad and \quad AB \neq BA. \quad \square$$

A matrix all of whose entries are zero is called a **zero matrix**. Thus,

$$O = \begin{bmatrix} 0 & 0 \\ 0 & 0 \\ 0 & 0 \end{bmatrix}$$

is the 3×2 zero matrix. Obviously,

$$\begin{bmatrix} 0 & 0 \\ 0 & 0 \\ 0 & 0 \end{bmatrix} + \begin{bmatrix} 1 & 4 \\ 2 & 5 \\ 3 & 6 \end{bmatrix} = \begin{bmatrix} 1 & 4 \\ 2 & 5 \\ 3 & 6 \end{bmatrix} = \begin{bmatrix} 1 & 4 \\ 2 & 5 \\ 3 & 6 \end{bmatrix} + \begin{bmatrix} 0 & 0 \\ 0 & 0 \\ 0 & 0 \end{bmatrix}.$$

In general,

$$O + A = A = A + O,$$

whenever A and O have the same size.

The special matrices

$$\begin{bmatrix} 1 & 0 \\ 0 & 1 \end{bmatrix} \quad and \quad \begin{bmatrix} 1 & 0 & 0 \\ 0 & 1 & 0 \\ 0 & 0 & 1 \end{bmatrix}$$

are called respectively the 2×2 and 3×3 identity matrix. The 1's are located on the **main diagonal** of these matrices. In general, an $n \times n$ matrix I whose main diagonal entries consist exclusively of 1's and whose other entries are all 0's is the $n \times n$ **identity matrix**. It is easy to check that

$$I\mathbf{x} = \mathbf{x}, \quad AI = A, \quad IB = B,$$

whenever the indicated products are defined.

4.4   Linear Systems in Matrix Form

The 2×2 system of linear equations

$$\begin{cases} x + y = 2 \\ 2x - 3y = 9 \end{cases} \tag{4.1}$$

can be expressed as a single matrix equation. Indeed, since

$$\begin{bmatrix} x+y \\ 2x-3y \end{bmatrix} = \begin{bmatrix} 1 & 1 \\ 2 & -3 \end{bmatrix} \begin{bmatrix} x \\ y \end{bmatrix}$$

the system (4.1) can be written as

$$\begin{bmatrix} 1 & 1 \\ 2 & -3 \end{bmatrix} \begin{bmatrix} x \\ y \end{bmatrix} = \begin{bmatrix} 2 \\ 9 \end{bmatrix}$$

or

$$A\mathbf{x} = \mathbf{b}$$

where

$$A = \begin{bmatrix} 1 & 1 \\ 2 & -3 \end{bmatrix}, \qquad \mathbf{x} = \begin{bmatrix} x \\ y \end{bmatrix}, \text{ and } \qquad \mathbf{b} = \begin{bmatrix} 2 \\ 9 \end{bmatrix}.$$

In the same way, the 3×3 system

$$\begin{cases} x - 3y + z & = & 4 \\ 2x - 8y + 8z & = & -2 \\ -6x + 3y - 15z & = & 9 \end{cases}$$

can be expressed as

$$\begin{bmatrix} 1 & -3 & 1 \\ 2 & -8 & 8 \\ -6 & 3 & -15 \end{bmatrix} \begin{bmatrix} x \\ y \\ z \end{bmatrix} = \begin{bmatrix} 4 \\ -2 \\ 9 \end{bmatrix}$$

or

$$A\mathbf{x} = \mathbf{b},$$

where

$$A = \begin{bmatrix} 1 & -3 & 1 \\ 2 & -8 & 8 \\ -6 & 3 & -15 \end{bmatrix}, \qquad \mathbf{x} = \begin{bmatrix} x \\ y \\ z \end{bmatrix}, \text{ and } \qquad \mathbf{b} = \begin{bmatrix} 4 \\ -2 \\ 9 \end{bmatrix}.$$

These examples make it plain that any 2×2, 3×3, or indeed any system of linear equations can be expressed as a single matrix equation of the form

$$A\mathbf{x} = \mathbf{b}$$

where

  A is the **coefficient matrix** of the system,
  $\mathbf{x}$ is the column vector of unknowns,
  $\mathbf{b}$ is the column vector of right members.

If the system is square (has as many equations as unknowns) then we express the determinant of the matrix A either by $|A|$ or $\det A$ or $\det(A)$ as seems most convenient. Then Theorems 2 and 3 of Lesson 3 can be expressed in matrix notation as follows:

> $A\mathbf{x} = \mathbf{b}$ has a *unique* solution $\Leftrightarrow \det A \neq 0$.
> $A\mathbf{x} = \mathbf{0}$ has *nontrivial solutions* $\Leftrightarrow \det A = 0$.

Another useful equivalent way to express the last result is

> $A\mathbf{x} = \mathbf{0}$ has *only the trivial solution* $\Leftrightarrow \det A \neq 0$.

4.5   The Inverse of a Square Matrix

The scalar equation $ax = b$ has solution

$$x = \frac{b}{a} \qquad \text{provided } a \neq 0.$$

When a linear system of equations is written in the matrix form $A\mathbf{x} = \mathbf{b}$, it is natural to inquire if a similar solution formula exists. The fraction b/a is a convenient way to write the product $a^{-1}b$, which defines division of numbers. It turns out that the inquiry just made has an affirmative answer. When you solve a linear system of equations by elimination of unknowns you perform a sequence steps such as multiplying one equation by a constant and adding the result to another equation, dividing an equation by a nonzero factor, and so forth. All these steps that ultimately lead to the solution $\mathbf{x}$ (when the system has a *unique* solution, that is, when $\det A \neq 0$) can be recorded in a matrix B. This matrix B has the property that $BA = I$, the identity matrix. Once you know B you can solve the system:

$$
\begin{aligned}
A\mathbf{x} &= \mathbf{b}, \\
BA\mathbf{x} &= B\mathbf{b}, \\
I\mathbf{x} &= B\mathbf{b}, \\
\mathbf{x} &= B\mathbf{b}.
\end{aligned}
$$

To summarize: If A is a square matrix with $\det A \neq 0$, then there is a *unique* matrix B, called the **inverse (matrix)** of A, such $BA = I$. A square matrix A is called **invertible** when there is square matrix B such that $BA = I$. The following result tells us when such a matrix exists.

Theorem 1 *A square matrix A is invertible if and only if $\det A \neq 0$.*

If A is invertible the inverse matrix B that satisfies $BA = I$ also satisfies $AB = I$. Furthermore, if either one of these equations holds for some matrix B, then A is invertible and B is its inverse. The inverse of an invertible matrix A is usually denoted by A^{-1}. So the inverse matrix satisfies

$$A^{-1}A = I = AA^{-1}.$$

When a linear system has a matrix that is invertible it can be solved simply by multiplying the matrix equation through by A^{-1},

$$\begin{aligned} A\mathbf{x} &= \mathbf{b}, \\ \mathbf{x} &= A^{-1}\mathbf{b}. \end{aligned}$$

It turns out that this solution formula is primarily of theoretical value as far as actually solving linear systems is concerned. The elimination process we have been using all along is more efficient from a computational point of view. There are however times when the inverse of a matrix A is needed for other purposes. Then the easiest way to find it is to use systematic elimination of unknowns. We illustrate how to do this in the case of a 3×3 matrix: Solve the following systems of equations

$$A\mathbf{x}_1 = \mathbf{e}_1, \quad A\mathbf{x}_2 = \mathbf{e}_2, \text{ and } \quad A\mathbf{x}_3 = \mathbf{e}_3$$

where $\mathbf{e}_1$, $\mathbf{e}_2$, and $\mathbf{e}_3$ are the columns of the 3×3 identity matrix. Then

$$A^{-1} = [\mathbf{x}_1, \mathbf{x}_2, \mathbf{x}_3].$$

To confirm this statement note that

$$A[\mathbf{x}_1, \mathbf{x}_2, \mathbf{x}_3] = [A\mathbf{x}_1, A\mathbf{x}_2, A\mathbf{x}_3] = [\mathbf{e}_1, \mathbf{e}_2, \mathbf{e}_3] = I$$

Example 3 *Show that the matrix*

$$A = \begin{bmatrix} 0 & 2 & 4 \\ 2 & 4 & 2 \\ 3 & 3 & 1 \end{bmatrix}$$

is invertible and find the inverse.

Solution. Since $\det A = -16$ (check this), the matrix is invertible. To find the inverse, we solve the three systems $A\mathbf{x}_1 = \mathbf{e}_1$, $A\mathbf{x}_2 = \mathbf{e}_2$, and $A\mathbf{x}_3 = \mathbf{e}_3$ all at once using the augmented matrix for the three systems

$$\left[\begin{array}{ccc|ccc} 0 & 2 & 4 & 1 & 0 & 0 \\ 2 & 4 & 2 & 0 & 1 & 0 \\ 3 & 3 & 1 & 0 & 0 & 1 \end{array}\right].$$

The plan is to use elimination of unknowns so that the final augmented matrix for the three systems has the form

$$\left[\begin{array}{ccc|ccc} 1 & 0 & 0 & * & * & * \\ 0 & 1 & 0 & * & * & * \\ 0 & 0 & 1 & * & * & * \end{array}\right].$$

Then the fourth column is $\mathbf{x}_1$, the solution to $A\mathbf{x}_1 = \mathbf{e}_1$, the fifth column is $\mathbf{x}_2$, and the sixth column is $\mathbf{x}_3$. (Why?) Since $A^{-1} = [\mathbf{x}_1, \mathbf{x}_2, \mathbf{x}_3]$, the inverse matrix of A is the matrix with the * entries. The overall strategy to reach the desired final form is to systematically put all 1's along the main diagonal of the matrix that composes the left half of the augmented matrix and use each newly created 1 to place zeros above and below it. Here are the arithmetical details for the example at hand. (Be sure to check each step!) To get a 1 in the 1,1 position of the augmented matrix interchange row 1 and row 2 and then divide the new row 1 by 2. This gives

$$\left[\begin{array}{ccc|ccc} 1 & 2 & 1 & 0 & \frac{1}{2} & 0 \\ 0 & 2 & 4 & 1 & 0 & 0 \\ 3 & 3 & 1 & 0 & 0 & 1 \end{array}\right].$$

Add -3 times row 1 to row 3 to get the first column of the identity matrix in column 1:

$$\left[\begin{array}{ccc|ccc} 1 & 2 & 1 & 0 & \frac{1}{2} & 0 \\ 0 & 2 & 4 & 1 & 0 & 0 \\ 0 & -3 & -2 & 0 & -\frac{3}{2} & 1 \end{array}\right].$$

Now we transform column 2 into the second column of the identity matrix. First, divide row 2 by 2 to get a 1 in the 2,2 position of the matrix:

$$\left[\begin{array}{ccc|ccc} 1 & 2 & 1 & 0 & \frac{1}{2} & 0 \\ 0 & 1 & 2 & \frac{1}{2} & 0 & 0 \\ 0 & -3 & -2 & 0 & -\frac{3}{2} & 1 \end{array}\right].$$

Second, multiply row 2 by -2 and add the result to row 1 and then multiply row 2 by 3 and add the result to row 3 to obtain

$$\left[\begin{array}{ccc|ccc} 1 & 0 & -3 & -1 & \frac{1}{2} & 0 \\ 0 & 1 & 2 & \frac{1}{2} & 0 & 0 \\ 0 & 0 & 4 & \frac{3}{2} & -\frac{3}{2} & 1 \end{array}\right].$$

Finally, we transform column 3 into the third column of the identity matrix. First divide row 3 by 4 to place a 1 in the 3,3 position:

$$\left[\begin{array}{ccc|ccc} 1 & 0 & -3 & -1 & \frac{1}{2} & 0 \\ 0 & 1 & 2 & \frac{1}{2} & 0 & 0 \\ 0 & 0 & 1 & \frac{3}{8} & -\frac{3}{8} & \frac{1}{4} \end{array}\right].$$

Now add multiples (what are they?) of row 3 to rows 1 and 2 to obtain

$$\left[\begin{array}{ccc|ccc} 1 & 0 & 0 & \frac{1}{8} & -\frac{5}{8} & \frac{3}{4} \\ 0 & 1 & 0 & -\frac{1}{4} & \frac{3}{4} & -\frac{1}{2} \\ 0 & 0 & 1 & \frac{3}{8} & -\frac{3}{8} & \frac{1}{4} \end{array}\right].$$

Consequently,

$$A^{-1} = \left[\begin{array}{ccc} \frac{1}{8} & -\frac{5}{8} & \frac{3}{4} \\ -\frac{1}{4} & \frac{3}{4} & -\frac{1}{2} \\ \frac{3}{8} & -\frac{3}{8} & \frac{1}{4} \end{array}\right]. \quad \square$$

Here is a useful fact about invertible matrices (see the problems) that is well worth remembering. If A and B are invertible matrices of the same size, then their product AB also is invertible and

$$(AB)^{-1} = B^{-1}A^{-1}.$$

Notice the reversal of order in the factors on the right.

4.6   Transpose of a Matrix

The **transpose** of a matrix A, denoted by A^T, is the matrix obtained from A by interchanging its rows with its columns. For example, if

$$A = \begin{bmatrix} -2 & 4 & 3 \\ 6 & 1 & -5 \end{bmatrix}$$

then

$$A^T = \begin{bmatrix} -2 & 6 \\ 4 & 1 \\ 3 & -5 \end{bmatrix}.$$

The transpose operation is used both in managing data in databases and in practical and theoretical matrix applications. Useful algebraic properties of the transpose operation include:

$$
\begin{aligned}
(A + B)^T &= A^T + B^T, \\
(cA)^T &= cA^T, \\
(AB)^T &= B^T A^T.
\end{aligned}
$$

These rules hold in the usual sense. If one side of the equality is defined so is the other and the stated equality is true.

Since vectors also are matrices, the transpose operation applies to vectors. What is the transpose of a column vector? If $\mathbf{v}$ and $\mathbf{w}$ are real column vectors with n components each, then their dot product can be expressed in terms of matrix multiplication as

$$\mathbf{v} \cdot \mathbf{w} = \mathbf{v}^T \mathbf{w}$$

where $\mathbf{v}^T \mathbf{w}$ is the product of the $1 \times n$ matrix $\mathbf{v}^T$ with the $n \times 1$ matrix $\mathbf{w}$. The corresponding result for vectors in $\mathbb{C}^n$ is

$$\mathbf{v} \cdot \mathbf{w} = \mathbf{v}^T \bar{\mathbf{w}}.$$

4.7 Suggested Problems

In Problems 1-4 find (a) $A + B$, (b) $A - 3B$, (c) AB, (d) BA, (e) $A\mathbf{x}$, and (f) $B\mathbf{x}$ whenever the indicated combination is defined. If the combination is *not* defined, briefly explain why.

1. $A = \begin{bmatrix} 1 & -2 \\ 0 & 3 \end{bmatrix}$, $B = \begin{bmatrix} 4 & 7 \\ -5 & -1 \end{bmatrix}$, $\mathbf{x} = \begin{bmatrix} 1 \\ -1 \end{bmatrix}$

2. $A = \begin{bmatrix} 1 & 2 \\ 3 & 4 \end{bmatrix}$, $B = \begin{bmatrix} -2 & 4 & 3 \\ 6 & 1 & -5 \end{bmatrix}$, $\mathbf{x} = \begin{bmatrix} 1 \\ -1 \end{bmatrix}$

3. $A = \begin{bmatrix} 1 & 4 & 0 \\ 2 & -4 & 3 \\ 1 & 5 & 2 \end{bmatrix}$, $B = \begin{bmatrix} 1 & -1 & 3 \\ 1 & 0 & 2 \\ 2 & 1 & 1 \end{bmatrix}$, $\mathbf{x} = \begin{bmatrix} 3 \\ -1 \\ 2 \end{bmatrix}$

4. $A = \begin{bmatrix} 1 & 2 & 3 \\ 4 & 5 & 6 \end{bmatrix}$, $B = \begin{bmatrix} -2 & 1 \\ 0 & 4 \\ 3 & -5 \end{bmatrix}$, $\mathbf{x} = \begin{bmatrix} 1 \\ 2 \end{bmatrix}$

5. Verify $(AB)^T = B^T A^T$ for the matrices in Problem 4.

6. Verify that $(AB)C = A(BC)$ when

$$A = \begin{bmatrix} 1 & 2 \\ 3 & -1 \end{bmatrix}, \quad B = \begin{bmatrix} 2 & 3 \\ -3 & 4 \end{bmatrix}, \quad C = \begin{bmatrix} 1 & 0 \\ 5 & 2 \end{bmatrix}$$

7. Verify that $A(B + C) = AB + AC$ when

$$A = \begin{bmatrix} 1 & 2 \\ 3 & -1 \end{bmatrix}, \quad B = \begin{bmatrix} 2 & 3 & 5 \\ -3 & 4 & 1 \end{bmatrix}, \quad C = \begin{bmatrix} 1 & 0 & -3 \\ 5 & 2 & 1 \end{bmatrix}$$

8. Are the following assertions true or false? Explain.

$$\begin{bmatrix} 1 & 2 \\ -1 & 5 \end{bmatrix} \begin{bmatrix} 4 \\ 3 \end{bmatrix} = \begin{bmatrix} 10 \\ 19 \end{bmatrix}$$

$$\begin{bmatrix} 1 & 3 & 7 \\ 2 & -1 & 6 \\ 1 & 0 & 1 \end{bmatrix} - 2 \begin{bmatrix} 1 & -2 & 0 \\ 3 & 2 & -1 \\ -2 & 1 & 3 \end{bmatrix} = \begin{bmatrix} -1 & 7 & 7 \\ -4 & -5 & 8 \\ 5 & -2 & -5 \end{bmatrix}$$

9. Solve for x, y, z, and w:

$$\begin{bmatrix} x & -7 \\ z & w \end{bmatrix} - 2 \begin{bmatrix} y & x \\ w & 4 - z \end{bmatrix} = \begin{bmatrix} -1 & -9 \\ -5 & 2 \end{bmatrix}$$

In Problems 10-13, express each system of linear equations in the matrix form $A\mathbf{x} = \mathbf{b}$.

10. $\begin{cases} 3x - 2y = 8 \\ 4x + 5y = -10 \end{cases}$

11. $\begin{cases} 4x - 2y + z = 6 \\ -5x + 7y + 4z = 0 \\ 3x - y = 5 \end{cases}$

12. $\begin{cases} 4x - 2y + z - 3w = -3 \\ x + y - 4z + 2w = 6 \\ 2x + 3y - 5z - w = 4 \end{cases}$

13. $\begin{cases} 4x - 2y + z = 6 \\ -5x + 7y + 4z = 0 \\ 3x - y = 5 \\ x - 2y + z = 3 \end{cases}$

In Problems 14-17 determine if the matrix has an inverse. If it does, find the inverse. If it doesn't explain briefly why not.

14. $\begin{bmatrix} 1 & 1 \\ 2 & 3 \end{bmatrix}$

15. $\begin{bmatrix} 1 & 0 & 1 \\ 1 & 1 & 0 \\ 0 & 1 & 1 \end{bmatrix}$

16. $\begin{bmatrix} 1 & 2 & 1 \\ -1 & 1 & 2 \\ 1 & 0 & 1 \end{bmatrix}$

17. $\begin{bmatrix} 1 & -2 & 3 \\ 3 & 0 & -3 \\ -1 & 2 & 3 \end{bmatrix}$

18. Let

$$A = \begin{bmatrix} a & b \\ c & d \end{bmatrix}$$

with $\det A \neq 0$. Use systematic elimination of unknowns to show that

$$A^{-1} = \frac{1}{\det A} \begin{bmatrix} d & -b \\ -c & a \end{bmatrix}$$

Hint. First assume $a \neq 0$. Then do the case $a = 0$.

19. The inverse of a 3×3 matrix can be expressed in terms of cross products and scalar triple products: Let A be a 3×3 matrix and think of A as composed of three row vectors

$$A = \begin{bmatrix} \mathbf{r}_1 \\ \mathbf{r}_2 \\ \mathbf{r}_3 \end{bmatrix}$$

Show that

$$A^{-1} = \frac{1}{\mathbf{r}_1 \cdot \mathbf{r}_2 \times \mathbf{r}_3} \begin{bmatrix} \mathbf{r}_2 \times \mathbf{r}_3 \\ \mathbf{r}_3 \times \mathbf{r}_1 \\ \mathbf{r}_1 \times \mathbf{r}_2 \end{bmatrix}^T$$

Hint. Let B be the matrix on the right. Calculate AB by expressing each entry of the matrix product as a scalar triple product. Then use what you know about the geometric interpretation of the scalar triple product.

20. Verify: If A and B are invertible matrices of the same size, then so is AB and $(AB)^{-1} = B^{-1}A^{-1}$. *Hint.* Don't make this hard! Let $C = AB$. By definition C is invertible if there is a matrix D so that $CD = I = DC$. Show by a simple one line calculation that $D = B^{-1}A^{-1}$ has the required property.

21. Find a matrix A such that AA^T and A^TA are defined and $AA^T \neq A^TA$.

Lesson 5

Linear Dependence and Independence

5.1 Goals

- Be able to define linear independence and linear dependence of a set of vectors

- Interpret independence and dependence in geometric terms for vectors in 2- and 3-space

- Use the determinant test for dependence or independence of n vectors in n-space

- Be able to find a nontrivial linear combination among linearly dependent vectors

5.2 Overview

Linear independence and linear dependence are fundamental concepts of matrix and linear algebra. They have both geometric and algebraic aspects and provide a precise way of distinguishing sets of vectors with redundant information from sets without redundant information.

5.3 Dependence and Independence

Vectors carry information. Often you will deal with sets of vectors and it is useful to determine whether there is redundancy (dependence) or no redundancy (independence) in the information carried by the vectors. The notions of linear dependence and independence make these ideas precise. These are fundamental ideas whose understanding is worth your best effort.

A finite sum of the form

$$c_1\mathbf{v}_1 + c_2\mathbf{v}_2 + c_3\mathbf{v}_3 + \cdots + c_k\mathbf{v}_k$$

is called a **linear combination** of the vectors $\mathbf{v}_1$, $\mathbf{v}_2$, $\mathbf{v}_3$, ..., $\mathbf{v}_k$. The set of all such linear combinations is called the **span** of the vectors $\mathbf{v}_1$, $\mathbf{v}_2$, $\mathbf{v}_3$, ..., $\mathbf{v}_k$.

Linear Dependence and Independence in $\mathbb{R}^n$

A set of vectors $\mathbf{v}_1$, $\mathbf{v}_2$, $\mathbf{v}_3$, ..., $\mathbf{v}_k$ is **linearly dependent (LD)** if (at least) one of the vectors is a linear combination of the others. Suppose, for example, that $\mathbf{v}_2$ is a linear combination of $\mathbf{v}_1$, $\mathbf{v}_3$, ..., $\mathbf{v}_k$. Then

$$\mathbf{v}_2 = c_1\mathbf{v}_1 + c_3\mathbf{v}_3 + \cdots + c_k\mathbf{v}_k$$

for certain real scalars $c_1, c_3, ..., c_k$. Equivalently,

$$c_1\mathbf{v}_1 + c_2\mathbf{v}_2 + c_3\mathbf{v}_3 + \cdots + c_k\mathbf{v}_k = \mathbf{0}$$

where $c_2 = -1$. Likewise, if $\mathbf{v}_j$ is a linear combination of the other vectors in the set, we would obtain the foregoing equation with $c_j = -1$. Thus, we can express linear dependence in the following convenient way:

> A set of vectors $\mathbf{v}_1$, $\mathbf{v}_2$, $\mathbf{v}_3$, ..., $\mathbf{v}_k$ is linearly dependent
> if there are (real) constants $c_1, c_2, ..., c_k$ *not all zero* such that
> $c_1\mathbf{v}_1 + c_2\mathbf{v}_2 + c_3\mathbf{v}_3 + \cdots + c_k\mathbf{v}_k = \mathbf{0}.$

A set of vectors $\mathbf{v}_1$, $\mathbf{v}_2$, $\mathbf{v}_3$, ..., $\mathbf{v}_k$ is **linearly independent (LI)** if it is not linearly dependent. Consequently:

> A set of vectors $\mathbf{v}_1$, $\mathbf{v}_2$, $\mathbf{v}_3$, ..., $\mathbf{v}_k$ is
> **linearly independent** if and only if the equation
> $c_1\mathbf{v}_1 + c_2\mathbf{v}_2 + c_3\mathbf{v}_3 + \cdots + c_k\mathbf{v}_k = \mathbf{0} \Rightarrow c_1 = 0,\ c_2 = 0,\ c_3 = 0, ...,\ c_k = 0.$

Linearly dependent sets of vectors contain redundant information and linearly independent sets do not. There is an important geometric way to think about LD and LI vectors. The next example points the way.

Example 1 *Let* $\mathbf{a}$ *and* $\mathbf{b}$ *be two vectors in* $\mathbb{R}^2$. *Show that*
    (a) $\mathbf{a}, \mathbf{b}$ *are LD* $\Longleftrightarrow$ $\mathbf{a}$ *is a (scalar) multiple of* $\mathbf{b}$ *or* $\mathbf{b}$ *is a multiple of* $\mathbf{a}$.
    (b) $\mathbf{a}, \mathbf{b}$ *are LI* $\Longleftrightarrow$ *the span of* $\mathbf{a}$ *and* $\mathbf{b}$ *is* $\mathbb{R}^2$.

Solution. (a) $\mathbf{a}, \mathbf{b}$ are LD if and only if there are constants r and s not both zero such that

$$r\mathbf{a} + s\mathbf{b} = \mathbf{0}.$$

Hence,

$$\mathbf{a} = -\frac{s}{r}\mathbf{b} \quad \text{if } r \neq 0,$$
$$\mathbf{b} = -\frac{r}{s}\mathbf{a} \quad \text{if } s \neq 0,$$

and (a) is verified.

(b) We give a geometric argument. By (a), the vectors $\mathbf{a}, \mathbf{b}$ are LI if neither is a scalar multiple of the other. Thus $\mathbf{a}$ and $\mathbf{b}$ point in different directions in $\mathbb{R}^2$. Then by the parallelogram law of vector addition it is clear (see the following figure) that any vector $\mathbf{v}$ in $\mathbb{R}^2$ is a linear combination of $\mathbf{a}$ and $\mathbf{b}$. $\square$

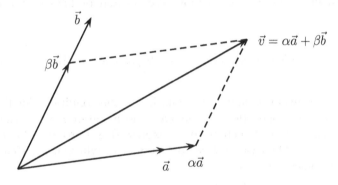

Figure 5.1: Linearly Independent Vectors span the Plane

Similarly in $\mathbb{R}^3$

(a) $\mathbf{a}, \mathbf{b}, \mathbf{c}$ are LD $\iff$ $\mathbf{a}, \mathbf{b}, \mathbf{c}$ all lie in a plane in $\mathbb{R}^3$.

(b) $\mathbf{a}, \mathbf{b}, \mathbf{c}$ are LI $\iff$ the span of $\mathbf{a}$, $\mathbf{b}$, and $\mathbf{c}$ is $\mathbb{R}^3$.

These results for $\mathbb{R}^2$ and $\mathbb{R}^3$ hint at similar results for higher dimensions, but that is a story for another day.

Example 2 *Determine whether the vectors* $\mathbf{a} = \langle 1, 2 \rangle$ *and* $\mathbf{b} = \langle -1, 4 \rangle$ *are LI or LD in* $\mathbb{R}^2$.

Solution 1. (Geometric) Neither vector is a scalar multiple of the other so they are LI. (Make a sketch.)

Solution 2. (Algebraic) Suppose

$$r\mathbf{a} + s\mathbf{b} = \mathbf{0}$$

for some scalars r and s. Then

$$
\begin{aligned}
r \langle 1, 2 \rangle + s \langle -1, 4 \rangle &= \langle 0, 0 \rangle, \\
\langle r - s, 2r + 4s \rangle &= \langle 0, 0 \rangle, \\
r - s &= 0 \quad \text{and} \quad 2r + 4s = 0, \\
r - s &= 0 \quad \text{and} \quad r + 2s = 0.
\end{aligned}
$$

Subtract the equation on the left from the equation of the right to obtain $3s = 0$ and $s = 0$. Then $r = 0$. So the equation

$$
r\mathbf{a} + s\mathbf{b} = \mathbf{0} \implies r = 0, \ s = 0
$$

and, hence, $\mathbf{a}$ and $\mathbf{b}$ are LI in $\mathbb{R}^2$. $\quad \square$

Evidently the geometric solution is easier in this example, but an algebraic solution usually is needed when more vectors and/or higher dimensions are involved.

Linear Independence and Linear Dependence in Matrix Form

There is a convenient matrix formulation of the conditions for linear independence and linear dependence. The matrix formulation rests on the fact that any linear combination of vectors can be expressed as a product of a matrix and a column vector. The case of 2 vectors in 3-space will make it clear how the matrix form comes about. If

$$
\mathbf{v} = \begin{bmatrix} a \\ c \\ e \end{bmatrix} \quad \text{and} \quad \mathbf{w} = \begin{bmatrix} b \\ d \\ f \end{bmatrix}
$$

the linear combination $c_1 \mathbf{v} + c_2 \mathbf{w}$ can be expressed as

$$
c_1 \mathbf{v} + c_2 \mathbf{w} = c_1 \begin{bmatrix} a \\ c \\ e \end{bmatrix} + c_2 \begin{bmatrix} b \\ d \\ f \end{bmatrix} = \begin{bmatrix} ac_1 + bc_2 \\ cc_1 + dc_2 \\ ec_1 + fc_2 \end{bmatrix} = \begin{bmatrix} a & b \\ c & d \\ e & f \end{bmatrix} \begin{bmatrix} c_1 \\ c_2 \end{bmatrix}.
$$

That is,

$$
c_1 \mathbf{v} + c_2 \mathbf{w} = A\mathbf{c}
$$

where

$$
A = \begin{bmatrix} a & b \\ c & d \\ e & f \end{bmatrix} \quad \text{and} \quad \mathbf{c} = \begin{bmatrix} c_1 \\ c_2 \end{bmatrix}.
$$

Notice that the matrix $A = [\mathbf{v}, \mathbf{w}]$ has for its columns the vectors $\mathbf{v}$ and $\mathbf{w}$ in the linear combination $c_1 \mathbf{v} + c_2 \mathbf{w}$ and that $\mathbf{c}$ is the column vector whose components are the corresponding scalar multiples of $\mathbf{v}$ and $\mathbf{w}$. The same reasoning establishes:

Any linear combination of vectors in n-space can be expressed as $A\mathbf{c}$ where A is the matrix whose columns are the vectors in the linear combination and $\mathbf{c}$ is the column vector whose components are the corresponding scalar multiples of the vectors in the linear combination.

Now it its easy to express the tests for linear independence and dependence of a set of vectors in matrix form. The vectors $\mathbf{v}_1, \mathbf{v}_2, ..., \mathbf{v}_k$ are linearly independent if and only if

$$c_1\mathbf{v}_1 + c_2\mathbf{v}_2 + c_3\mathbf{v}_3 + \cdots + c_k\mathbf{v}_k = \mathbf{0} \Rightarrow c_1 = 0,\ c_2 = 0,\ c_3 = 0, ...,\ c_k = 0$$

and this condition can be expressed as

$$A\mathbf{c} = \mathbf{0} \implies \mathbf{c} = \mathbf{0}$$

where $A = [\mathbf{v}_1, \mathbf{v}_2, ..., \mathbf{v}_k]$ is the matrix with the given vectors for its columns and $\mathbf{c}$ is the column vector with components $c_1,\ c_2, ...,\ c_k$. We have established the following general fact:

If $\mathbf{v}_1, \mathbf{v}_2, ..., \mathbf{v}_k$ are vectors of the same size and $A = [\mathbf{v}_1, \mathbf{v}_2, ..., \mathbf{v}_k]$ is the matrix with the given vectors for its columns, then $\mathbf{v}_1, \mathbf{v}_2, ..., \mathbf{v}_k$ are linearly independent if and only if the homogeneous system $A\mathbf{c} = \mathbf{0}$ has only the trivial solution $\mathbf{c} = \mathbf{0}$.

Of course, the vectors are linearly dependent if and only if the homogeneous system $A\mathbf{c} = \mathbf{0}$ has *nontrivial* solutions. In this case, each nontrivial solution $\mathbf{c}$ to $A\mathbf{c} = \mathbf{0}$ yields a nontrivial linear combination of the given vectors whose sum is $\mathbf{0}$.

The bottom line: Linear independence or linear dependence can be determined by solving an appropriate linear system.

A Determinant Test for Linear Independence or Dependence

In the case of n vectors each with n components, the system $A\mathbf{c} = \mathbf{0}$ is $n \times n$ and has *only* the trivial solution $\mathbf{c} = \mathbf{0}$ precisely when $\det(A) \neq 0$.

Theorem 1 *A set of n, n-vectors is linearly independent if and only if the determinant of the matrix whose columns are the given vectors is not zero.*

Example 3 *Determine whether the vectors*

$$\mathbf{u} = \begin{bmatrix} 1 \\ 2 \\ -1 \end{bmatrix}, \qquad \mathbf{v} = \begin{bmatrix} 2 \\ 1 \\ 3 \end{bmatrix}, \qquad \mathbf{w} = \begin{bmatrix} -4 \\ 1 \\ -11 \end{bmatrix}$$

are linearly independent or linearly dependent. If they are linearly dependent find a nontrivial linear combination of the vectors that has sum $\mathbf{0}$.

Solution. Since

$$\det\left[\mathbf{u}, \mathbf{v}, \mathbf{w}\right] = \begin{vmatrix} 1 & 2 & -4 \\ 2 & 1 & 1 \\ -1 & 3 & -11 \end{vmatrix}$$
$$= (1)(-11-3) - (2)(-22+1) + (-4)(6+1)$$
$$= -14 + 42 - 28 = 0,$$

the vectors $\mathbf{u}$, $\mathbf{v}$, and $\mathbf{w}$ are linearly dependent. So, there must be scalars x, y, and z not all zero such that

$$x\mathbf{u} + y\mathbf{v} + z\mathbf{w} = \mathbf{0}. \tag{5.1}$$

This vector equation can be expressed in matrix form as

$$\begin{bmatrix} 1 & 2 & -4 \\ 2 & 1 & 1 \\ -1 & 3 & -11 \end{bmatrix} \begin{bmatrix} x \\ y \\ z \end{bmatrix} = \begin{bmatrix} 0 \\ 0 \\ 0 \end{bmatrix}. \tag{5.2}$$

Note that the coefficient matrix is $[\mathbf{u}, \mathbf{v}, \mathbf{w}]$. We solve this system using the augmented matrix

$$\begin{bmatrix} 1 & 2 & -4 & | & 0 \\ 2 & 1 & 1 & | & 0 \\ -1 & 3 & -11 & | & 0 \end{bmatrix}.$$

Add -2 times row 1 to row 2 and then add row 1 to row 3 to eliminate x from the second and third equations of the system:

$$\begin{bmatrix} 1 & 2 & -4 & | & 0 \\ 0 & -3 & 9 & | & 0 \\ 0 & 5 & -15 & | & 0 \end{bmatrix}.$$

Divide the second row by -3 and the third row by 5 to reduce the system to

$$\begin{bmatrix} 1 & 2 & -4 & | & 0 \\ 0 & 1 & -3 & | & 0 \\ 0 & 1 & -3 & | & 0 \end{bmatrix}.$$

The last two equations impose the single requirement

$$y - 3z = 0 \qquad \text{or} \qquad y = 3z.$$

Then the first equation gives

$$x + 2(3z) - 4z = 0 \qquad \text{or} \qquad x = -2z.$$

Therefore equation (5.2), equivalently (5.1), holds for

$$x = -2z, \quad y = 3z, \quad \text{and any choice of } z.$$

Thus,

$$-2z\mathbf{u}+3z\mathbf{v}+z\mathbf{w} = \mathbf{0} \quad \text{for any choice of } z.$$

In particular, the choice $z = 1$ (or any choice of $z \neq 0$) yields

$$-2\mathbf{u}+3\mathbf{v} + \mathbf{w} = \mathbf{0}.$$

This is the required nontrivial linear relation satisfied by $\mathbf{u}, \mathbf{v}$, and $\mathbf{w}$. $\quad\square$

Did you notice in Example 3 that the column of zeros in the augmented matrix never changes during systematic elimination of unknowns? This always happens when you solve a homogeneous system. (Why?) Consequently, when systematic elimination of unknowns is used to solve a *homogeneous* system, the zero column of right members of the homogeneous system often is not written. That is, the augmented matrix is replaced by the coefficient matrix. This saves a little time and space.

Linear Dependence and Independence in $\mathbb{C}^n$

The formal definition of linear dependence and independence are the same in $\mathbb{R}^n$ and $\mathbb{C}^n$ except that the scalars are complex in the case of $\mathbb{C}^n$. A set of vectors $\mathbf{v}_1, \mathbf{v}_2, \mathbf{v}_3, ..., \mathbf{v}_k$ in $\mathbb{C}^n$ is **linearly dependent (LD)** if there are (complex) constants $c_1, c_2, ..., c_k$ *not all zero* such that

$$c_1\mathbf{v}_1 + c_2\mathbf{v}_2 + c_3\mathbf{v}_3 + \cdots + c_k\mathbf{v}_k = \mathbf{0}.$$

A set of vectors $\mathbf{v}_1, \mathbf{v}_2, \mathbf{v}_3, ..., \mathbf{v}_k$ is **linearly independent (LI)** if the equation

$$c_1\mathbf{v}_1 + c_2\mathbf{v}_2 + c_3\mathbf{v}_3 + \cdots + c_k\mathbf{v}_k = \mathbf{0} \Rightarrow c_1 = 0, \ c_2 = 0, \ c_3 = 0, ..., \ c_k = 0.$$

To distinguish between LI and LD in $\mathbb{R}^n$ and $\mathbb{C}^n$ we (sometimes) say the vectors are LI or LD *over* $\mathbb{R}$ or *over* $\mathbb{C}$ to emphasize which scalars are used.

5.4   Suggested Problems

In Problems 1-8 determine whether the given vectors are linearly dependent or linearly independent. If they are linearly dependent, find a nontrivial linear combination of the vectors that has sum **0**.

1. $\begin{bmatrix} 1 \\ 2 \end{bmatrix}, \begin{bmatrix} -1 \\ 3 \end{bmatrix}$

2. $\begin{bmatrix} 3 \\ 2 \end{bmatrix}, \begin{bmatrix} 6 \\ 4 \end{bmatrix}$

3. $\begin{bmatrix} 1 \\ 1 \\ 0 \end{bmatrix}, \begin{bmatrix} 0 \\ 1 \\ 1 \end{bmatrix}, \begin{bmatrix} 1 \\ 0 \\ 1 \end{bmatrix}$

4. $\begin{bmatrix} 2 \\ 1 \\ 0 \end{bmatrix}, \begin{bmatrix} 0 \\ 1 \\ 0 \end{bmatrix}, \begin{bmatrix} -1 \\ 2 \\ 0 \end{bmatrix}$

5. $\begin{bmatrix} -1 \\ 3 \\ -2 \end{bmatrix}, \begin{bmatrix} 3 \\ 1 \\ 0 \end{bmatrix}, \begin{bmatrix} 2 \\ -1 \\ 1 \end{bmatrix}$

6. $\begin{bmatrix} 1 \\ 2 \\ 3 \end{bmatrix}, \begin{bmatrix} 3 \\ 2 \\ 1 \end{bmatrix}, \begin{bmatrix} -7 \\ 2 \\ 11 \end{bmatrix}$

7. $\begin{bmatrix} 1 \\ 1 \\ 0 \\ 1 \end{bmatrix}, \begin{bmatrix} 0 \\ 1 \\ 1 \\ 0 \end{bmatrix}, \begin{bmatrix} 1 \\ 0 \\ 1 \\ 0 \end{bmatrix}$

8. $\begin{bmatrix} 1 \\ 1 \\ 0 \\ 1 \end{bmatrix}, \begin{bmatrix} 0 \\ 1 \\ 1 \\ 0 \end{bmatrix}, \begin{bmatrix} 4 \\ 2 \\ -2 \\ 4 \end{bmatrix}$

9. If **a**, **b**, **c** are three vectors in 3-space, their scalar triple product is $\mathbf{a} \cdot \mathbf{b} \times \mathbf{c}$. Use the standard volume interpretation of the scalar triple product to give a geometric justification of Theorem 1 when $n = 3$.

10. Let

$$\mathbf{a} = \begin{bmatrix} 1 \\ -1 \end{bmatrix}, \quad \mathbf{b} = \begin{bmatrix} 0 \\ 2 \end{bmatrix}, \quad \text{and} \quad \mathbf{c} = \begin{bmatrix} -3 \\ 5 \end{bmatrix}.$$

(a) Give a geometric argument that shows that the vectors are linearly dependent in $\mathbb{R}^2$.

(b) Give an algebraic argument that shows the vectors are linearly dependent in $\mathbb{R}^2$.

11. Let

$$\mathbf{v}_1 = \begin{bmatrix} a \\ c \end{bmatrix}, \quad \mathbf{v}_2 = \begin{bmatrix} b \\ d \end{bmatrix}, \quad \text{and} \quad \mathbf{v}_3 = \begin{bmatrix} e \\ f \end{bmatrix}$$

be vectors in in $\mathbb{R}^2$.

(a) Give a geometric argument that shows that the vectors are linearly dependent in $\mathbb{R}^2$.

(b) Give an algebraic argument that shows the vectors are linearly dependent in $\mathbb{R}^2$. *Hint.* First express

$$c_1 \mathbf{v}_1 + c_2 \mathbf{v}_2 + c_3 \mathbf{v}_3 = \mathbf{0}$$

in the form $A\mathbf{c} = \mathbf{b}$ where

$$A = \begin{bmatrix} a & b \\ c & d \end{bmatrix} \quad \text{and} \quad \mathbf{c} = \begin{bmatrix} c_1 \\ c_2 \end{bmatrix}.$$

What is $\mathbf{b}$? Now use what you know about solvability of linear systems.

be vectors in R^3.

Lesson 6

Matrices and Linear Transformations

6.1 Goals

- Understand how a matrix determines a linear transformation

- Describe in geometric terms the effect of particular linear transformations

- Find the matrix of a linear transformation relative to the standard basis

6.2 Overview

So far our treatment of matrices and their properties has been exclusively algebraic. However, there is an important and revealing geometric way to think about matrices which is the principal subject of this lesson; it is the *linear transformation (linear operator)* point of view. The basic idea is to think of the matrix as a function that takes input vectors and transforms them into output vectors obtained by multiplying by the given matrix.

6.3 Matrices as Transformations

We attach a geometric character to a matrix in a very natural way by observing the action of the matrix on input vectors. If A is an $n \times m$ matrix and $\mathbf{v}$ is any m-vector, then A transforms (maps, carries) $\mathbf{v}$ into the output n-vector $A\mathbf{v}$.

Example 1 *Give a geometric description of the transformation that is multiplication by the matrix*

$$A = \begin{bmatrix} 1 & 0 \\ 0 & -1 \end{bmatrix}.$$

Solution. A transforms the 2-vector

$$\mathbf{v} = \begin{bmatrix} x \\ y \end{bmatrix}$$

into the vector

$$A\mathbf{v} = \begin{bmatrix} 1 & 0 \\ 0 & -1 \end{bmatrix} \begin{bmatrix} x \\ y \end{bmatrix} = \begin{bmatrix} x \\ -y \end{bmatrix}.$$

The action of multiplication by A is shown in the following plot in the xy-plane:

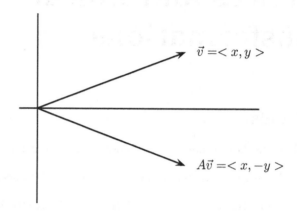

Figure 6.1: Multiplication by A in Example 1

Multiplication by A transforms each 2-vector $\mathbf{v}$ into its reflection (mirror image) $A\mathbf{v}$ across the x-axis. □

It is often convenient to represent transformations, such as in Example 1, with the same kind of notation used to represent functions in calculus. If A is an $n \times m$ matrix, we define a function T by

$$T(\mathbf{v}) = A\mathbf{v}.$$

For the right member to make sense $\mathbf{v}$ must be an m-vector. Then $T(\mathbf{v})$ is an n-vector. We express this relationship between input m-vectors and output n-vectors by writing

$$T : \mathbb{R}^m \to \mathbb{R}^n$$

which is read "T is a **transformation (operator, function) from $\mathbb{R}^m$ into $\mathbb{R}^n$**." This transformation T is referred to as **multiplication by A** and we sometimes write $T = T_A$ to indicate explicitly that the transformation is determined by the matrix A.

Example 2 *Give a geometric description of the transformation $T = T_A : \mathbb{R}^3 \rightarrow \mathbb{R}^3$ of multiplication by the matrix*

$$A = \begin{bmatrix} 2 & 0 & 0 \\ 0 & -3 & 0 \\ 0 & 0 & 4 \end{bmatrix}.$$

Solution. If

$$\mathbf{v} = \begin{bmatrix} x \\ y \\ z \end{bmatrix},$$

then

$$T(\mathbf{v}) = A\mathbf{v} = \begin{bmatrix} 2 & 0 & 0 \\ 0 & -3 & 0 \\ 0 & 0 & 4 \end{bmatrix} \begin{bmatrix} x \\ y \\ z \end{bmatrix} = \begin{bmatrix} 2x \\ -3y \\ 4z \end{bmatrix}.$$

The geometric effect of this transformation is most easily understood in terms of the superposition of three stretching actions. To see this more clearly, first let $\mathbf{v} = x\mathbf{i} = \langle x, 0, 0 \rangle$. Then

$$T(\mathbf{v}) = \langle 2x, 0, 0 \rangle = 2\mathbf{v}.$$

So, for any vector pointing along the x-axis, multiplication by the matrix A simply stretches the vector by the factor 2. Likewise, for any vector pointing along the z-axis, multiplication by the matrix A stretches the vector by the factor 4. If $\mathbf{v} = y\mathbf{j} = \langle 0, y, 0 \rangle$. Then

$$T(\mathbf{v}) = \langle 0, -3y, 0 \rangle = -3\mathbf{v}.$$

So, for any vector pointing along the y-axis, multiplication by the matrix A stretches the vector by the factor 3 and *reverses* its direction. Finally, returning to a general input vector $\mathbf{v} = \langle x, y, z \rangle$, multiplication by the matrix A stretches the projection of the input vector on the x-axis by 2 units, stretches the projection of the input vector on the y-axis by 3 units and reverses its direction, and stretches the projection of the input vector on the z-axis by 4 units. □

Example 3 *Give a geometric description of the transformation $T = T_A : \mathbb{R}^2 \rightarrow \mathbb{R}^3$ of multiplication by the matrix*

$$A = \begin{bmatrix} 1 & 0 \\ 0 & 1 \\ 1 & 1 \end{bmatrix}.$$

Solution. If

$$\mathbf{v} = \begin{bmatrix} x \\ y \end{bmatrix}$$

then

$$T(\mathbf{v}) = A\mathbf{v} = \begin{bmatrix} 1 & 0 \\ 0 & 1 \\ 1 & 1 \end{bmatrix} \begin{bmatrix} x \\ y \end{bmatrix} = \begin{bmatrix} x \\ y \\ x+y \end{bmatrix}.$$

Represent $\mathbf{v} = \langle x, y \rangle$ as the position vector of the point $(x, y, 0)$ in a 3-dimensional Cartesian xyz-coordinate system. Then $T(\mathbf{v}) = \langle x, y, x + y \rangle$ can be represented as the position vector of the point $(x, y, x + y)$ as show in the following figure:

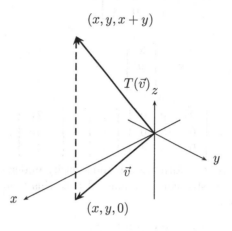

Figure 6.2: $T(\vec{v}) = A\vec{v}$ as in Example 3

$T(\mathbf{v})$ can be obtained from $\mathbf{v}$ by moving the tip of $\mathbf{v}$ vertically by the distance equal to the sum of the components of $\mathbf{v}$. $\square$

The transformation T_A of multiplication by a matrix A is linear, which means

$$
\begin{aligned}
T_A(\mathbf{v} + \mathbf{w}) &= T_A(\mathbf{v}) + T_A(\mathbf{w}), \\
T_A(r\mathbf{v}) &= rT_A(\mathbf{v}),
\end{aligned}
$$

for all vectors $\mathbf{v}$ and $\mathbf{w}$ (of the appropriate dimension) and all scalars r. These relations are immediate consequences of the corresponding properties of the product $A\mathbf{v}$:

$$
\begin{aligned}
A(\mathbf{v} + \mathbf{w}) &= A\mathbf{v} + A\mathbf{w}, \\
A(r\mathbf{v}) &= rA\mathbf{v}.
\end{aligned}
$$

In general, a transformation (operator, function) $T : \mathbb{R}^m \to \mathbb{R}^n$ is **linear** if

$$
\begin{aligned}
T(\mathbf{v} + \mathbf{w}) &= T(\mathbf{v}) + T(\mathbf{w}), \\
T(r\mathbf{v}) &= rT(\mathbf{v}),
\end{aligned}
$$

for all m-vectors $\mathbf{v}$ and $\mathbf{w}$ and all scalars r.

6.4 Matrix of a Linear Transformation

It is important to realize that any linear transformation between finite dimensional vector spaces is multiplication by an appropriate matrix. We begin with an example in which this conclusion is reasonably transparent.

Example 4 *Let $T : \mathbb{R}^3 \to \mathbb{R}^3$ be the operator that reflects a vector across the xy-plane in 3-space. Show that T is linear and find a matrix A such that $T = T_A$.*

Solution. The reflection of $\mathbf{v} = \langle x, y, z \rangle$ across the xy-plane is $\mathbf{w} = \langle x, y, -z \rangle$. So

$$T\left(\langle x, y, z \rangle\right) = \langle x, y, -z \rangle.$$

Now it is easy to check that T is linear:

$$
\begin{aligned}
T\left(\langle x, y, z \rangle + \langle x', y', z' \rangle\right) &= T\left(\langle x + x', y + y', z + z' \rangle\right) = \langle x + x', y + y', -(z + z') \rangle \\
&= \langle x, y, -z \rangle + \langle x', y', -z' \rangle \\
&= T\left(\langle x, y, z \rangle\right) + T\left(\langle x', y', z' \rangle\right)
\end{aligned}
$$

and, similarly,

$$T\left(r \langle x, y, z \rangle\right) = rT\left(\langle x, y, z \rangle\right).$$

In this example it is rather easy to guess a matrix A that will transform $\mathbf{v} = \langle x, y, z \rangle$ into $\mathbf{w} = \langle x, y, -z \rangle$:

$$
\begin{bmatrix} 1 & 0 & 0 \\ 0 & 1 & 0 \\ 0 & 0 & -1 \end{bmatrix} \begin{bmatrix} x \\ y \\ z \end{bmatrix} = \begin{bmatrix} x \\ y \\ -z \end{bmatrix}.
$$

So

$$T\left(\mathbf{v}\right) = A\mathbf{v} \quad \text{for} \quad A = \begin{bmatrix} 1 & 0 & 0 \\ 0 & 1 & 0 \\ 0 & 0 & -1 \end{bmatrix}. \quad \square$$

Here is a systematic way of finding a matrix that represents a given linear transformation. The matrix A in the following theorem is called the **matrix of T with respect to the standard basis in $\mathbb{R}^m$ and in $\mathbb{R}^n$**. Briefly, A is the **standard matrix of T**.

Theorem 1 *Let $T : \mathbb{R}^m \to \mathbb{R}^n$ be a linear transformation and $\mathbf{e}_1, \mathbf{e}_2, ..., \mathbf{e}_m$ be the standard basis for $\mathbb{R}^m$. Then $T = T_A$ where A is the $n \times m$ matrix*

$$A = [T\left(\mathbf{e}_1\right), T\left(\mathbf{e}_2\right), ..., T\left(\mathbf{e}_m\right)]$$

where $T\left(\mathbf{e}_i\right)$ is expressed as a column vector in $\mathbb{R}^n$.

We shall prove this theorem for the case $m = 2$ and $n = 3$. This special case will reveal clearly why the theorem is true in its full generality. In this case, $T : \mathbb{R}^2 \to \mathbb{R}^3$. In $\mathbb{R}^2$

$$\mathbf{e}_1 = \begin{bmatrix} 1 \\ 0 \end{bmatrix} \quad \text{and} \quad \mathbf{e}_2 = \begin{bmatrix} 0 \\ 1 \end{bmatrix}.$$

Since $T(\mathbf{e}_1)$ and $T(\mathbf{e}_2)$ are particular vectors in $\mathbb{R}^3$,

$$T(\mathbf{e}_1) = \begin{bmatrix} a \\ c \\ e \end{bmatrix} \quad \text{and} \quad T(\mathbf{e}_2) = \begin{bmatrix} b \\ d \\ f \end{bmatrix},$$

where a, c, e and b, d, f are the components of these vectors with respect to the standard basis in $\mathbb{R}^3$. Then for any

$$\mathbf{v} = \begin{bmatrix} x \\ y \end{bmatrix} = x\mathbf{e}_1 + y\mathbf{e}_2 \quad \text{in } \mathbb{R}^2,$$

$$
\begin{aligned}
T(\mathbf{v}) &= T(x\mathbf{e}_1 + y\mathbf{e}_2) = xT(\mathbf{e}_1) + yT(\mathbf{e}_2) \\
&= x\begin{bmatrix} a \\ c \\ e \end{bmatrix} + y\begin{bmatrix} b \\ d \\ f \end{bmatrix} = \begin{bmatrix} ax + by \\ cx + dy \\ ex + fy \end{bmatrix} \\
&= \begin{bmatrix} a & b \\ c & d \\ e & f \end{bmatrix} \begin{bmatrix} x \\ y \end{bmatrix} = [T(\mathbf{e}_1), T(\mathbf{e}_2)]\,\mathbf{v} = A\mathbf{v}. \quad \square
\end{aligned}
$$

From a practical point of view, Theorem 1 gives us an efficient way to evaluate a linear transformation. The evaluation reduces to a matrix multiplication. You find the appropriate matrix by determining the components of the images of the standard basis vectors under the transformation.

Example 5 *The transformation $T : \mathbb{R}^2 \to \mathbb{R}^2$ that rotates each vector counterclockwise by 60 degrees is a linear transformation. Find the matrix A such that $T = T_A$. Then find a convenient formula for $T(\mathbf{v})$ for any $\mathbf{v} = \langle x, y \rangle$ in $\mathbb{R}^2$.*

Solution. Let

$$\mathbf{e}_1 = \begin{bmatrix} 1 \\ 0 \end{bmatrix}, \quad \mathbf{e}_2 = \begin{bmatrix} 0 \\ 1 \end{bmatrix}.$$

Then, as the following figure reveals,

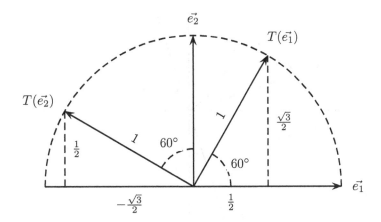

Figure 6.3: Counterclockwise rotation by 60 degrees

$$T\left(\mathbf{e}_1\right) = \left[\begin{array}{c} 1/2 \\ \sqrt{3}/2 \end{array}\right], \quad T\left(\mathbf{e}_2\right) = \left[\begin{array}{c} -\sqrt{3}/2 \\ 1/2 \end{array}\right].$$

So $T = T_A$ for

$$A = [T\left(\mathbf{e}_1\right), T\left(\mathbf{e}_2\right)] = \left[\begin{array}{cc} 1/2 & -\sqrt{3}/2 \\ \sqrt{3}/2 & 1/2 \end{array}\right].$$

Thus, for any $\mathbf{v} = \langle x, y \rangle$ in $\mathbb{R}^2$

$$T\left(\mathbf{v}\right) = A\mathbf{v} = \left[\begin{array}{cc} 1/2 & -\sqrt{3}/2 \\ \sqrt{3}/2 & 1/2 \end{array}\right] \left[\begin{array}{c} x \\ y \end{array}\right] = \left[\begin{array}{c} \frac{1}{2}x - \frac{1}{2}\sqrt{3}y \\ \frac{1}{2}\sqrt{3}x + \frac{1}{2}y \end{array}\right]. \quad \square$$

Example 6 *The transformation* $T : \mathbb{R}^2 \to \mathbb{R}^2$ *that reflects each vector across the line* $y = 3x$ *is a linear transformation. Find the matrix* A *such that* $T = T_A$. *Then find a convenient formula for* $T\left(\mathbf{v}\right)$ *for any* $\mathbf{v} = \langle x, y \rangle$ *in* $\mathbb{R}^2$.

Solution. The matrix we seek is

$$A = [T\left(\mathbf{e}_1\right), T\left(\mathbf{e}_2\right)]$$

where $\mathbf{e}_1$ and $\mathbf{e}_2$ are the standard basis vectors for $\mathbb{R}^2$. There are several reasonable ways to solve this problem. Some are suggested in the problems. Here is one way. It is motivated by the following figure:

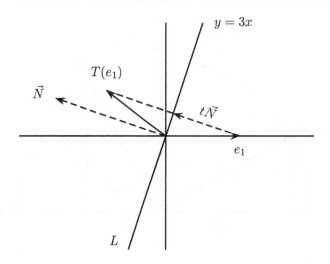

Figure 6.4: Reflection across $y = 3x$

Since the equation of the line L of reflection can be written as $-3x + y = 0$, the vector $\mathbf{N} = \langle -3, 1 \rangle$ is perpendicular to L. (Why?) If, see the figure, we can find the scalar t such that $\mathbf{e}_1 + t\mathbf{N}$ has its tip on L, then $T(\mathbf{e}_1) = \mathbf{e}_1 + 2t\mathbf{N}$ (note the factor 2). Why? Here is one way to find t. Since the tip of $\mathbf{e}_1 + t\mathbf{N}$ must lie on L which is given by the equation $y = 3x$, $\mathbf{e}_1 + t\mathbf{N}$ has components $\langle x, 3x \rangle$ for some x. Thus,

$$\langle x, 3x \rangle = \mathbf{e}_1 + t\mathbf{N} = \langle 1, 0 \rangle + t \langle -3, 1 \rangle$$

and equating components lead to a system of two equations in two unknowns

$$\begin{cases} x = 1 - 3t \\ 3x = t \end{cases}.$$

Since we only need t, multiply the first equation by -3 and add it to the second to find

$$0 = -3 + 10t,$$
$$t = \frac{3}{10}.$$

Thus,

$$T(\mathbf{e}_1) = \mathbf{e}_1 + 2t\mathbf{N} = \langle 1, 0 \rangle + \frac{3}{5} \langle -3, 1 \rangle = \left\langle -\frac{4}{5}, \frac{3}{5} \right\rangle.$$

Apply the same reasoning (do it) to find

$$T(\mathbf{e}_2) = \left\langle \frac{3}{5}, \frac{4}{5} \right\rangle.$$

Consequently, the matrix of T is

$$A = \begin{bmatrix} -4/5 & 3/5 \\ 3/5 & 4/5 \end{bmatrix}.$$

Finally, for any $\mathbf{v} = \langle x, y \rangle$ in $\mathbb{R}^2$

$$T(\mathbf{v}) = A\mathbf{v} = \begin{bmatrix} -4/5 & 3/5 \\ 3/5 & 4/5 \end{bmatrix} \begin{bmatrix} x \\ y \end{bmatrix} = \begin{bmatrix} -\frac{4}{5}x + \frac{3}{5}y \\ \frac{3}{5}x + \frac{4}{5}y \end{bmatrix}. \quad \square$$

Composition of Linear Transformations

The use of composite functions in calculus enables you to express some rather complicated functions as the successive effect of applying two or more simpler functions. Composition of functions plays a similar role when the functions are linear transformations. This is mostly a story for another day. For now we just make an important observation about composition of linear transformations and matrix multiplication: Suppose

$$S : \mathbb{R}^m \to \mathbb{R}^n \text{ and } T : \mathbb{R}^n \to \mathbb{R}^p$$

are linear transformations with standard matrices B and A respectively. (What are the dimensions of these matrices?) Just as in calculus, the composite function $T(S(\mathbf{v}))$ is denoted by $T \circ S$; that is,

$$T \circ S(\mathbf{v}) = T(S(\mathbf{v})).$$

Consequently,

$$T \circ S(\mathbf{v}) = T(S(\mathbf{v})) = T(B\mathbf{v}) = AB\mathbf{v}.$$

In other words, if S is multiplication by the matrix B and T is multiplication by the matrix A, then the composite transformation $T \circ S$ is multiplication by the matrix AB. Since multiplication by the matrix AB is a linear transformation, we have just confirmed that the composition of linear transformations is a linear transformation.

It is easy to confirm directly that the composition $T \circ S$ of the linear transformations S and T is a linear transformation. So this transformation has a standard matrix – say C. We have just shown that $C = AB$. That is, matrix multiplication was defined to correspond exactly to composition of linear transformations.

6.5 Projections

A square matrix P with the property that $P^2 = P$ is called a **projection matrix**. The next example will help explain the terminology.

Example 7 *Show that*

$$P = \begin{bmatrix} 1 & 0 \\ 0 & 0 \end{bmatrix}$$

is a projection matrix and describe the action of the corresponding linear transformation T_P that is multiplication by P.

Solution. It is easy to check that $P^2 = P$. (Do it.) So P is a projection matrix. Next, if $\mathbf{v} = [x \; y]^T$, then

$$T_P(\mathbf{v}) = \begin{bmatrix} 1 & 0 \\ 0 & 0 \end{bmatrix} \begin{bmatrix} x \\ y \end{bmatrix} = \begin{bmatrix} x \\ 0 \end{bmatrix} = \mathbf{w}.$$

The linear transformation $\mathbf{w} = T_P(\mathbf{v})$ takes any vector $\mathbf{v}$ and projects that vector onto the x-axis as in the following figure:

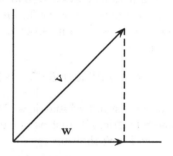

Figure 6.5: $\mathbf{w} = T_P(\mathbf{v})$

Notice that the range of T_P is the x-axis and that T_P projects any vector in the x-axis to itself. □

Any projection matrix P determines two important spaces:

$$R = \text{Range of } T_P = \{\mathbf{w} : \mathbf{w} = T_P(\mathbf{v}) \text{ for some } \mathbf{v}\},$$
$$N = \text{Null space of } T_P = \{\mathbf{v} : T_P(\mathbf{v}) = \mathbf{0}\}.$$

In Example 7

$$R = \left\{ \begin{bmatrix} x \\ 0 \end{bmatrix} : x \text{ is a real number} \right\},$$
$$N = \left\{ \begin{bmatrix} 0 \\ y \end{bmatrix} : y \text{ is a real number} \right\}.$$

Since

$$\mathbf{v} = \begin{bmatrix} x \\ y \end{bmatrix} = \begin{bmatrix} x \\ 0 \end{bmatrix} + \begin{bmatrix} 0 \\ y \end{bmatrix}$$

every vector in $\mathbb{R}^2$ is decomposed uniquely into a vector in R and a vector in N. This unique decomposition property is true for any projection matrix P and is given by

$$\mathbf{v} = P\mathbf{v} + (I - P)\,\mathbf{v}.$$

See the problems.

You probably noticed in Example 7 that every vector in R is orthogonal to every vector in N. In general, a projection matrix is called an **orthogonal projection** if $N \perp R$, meaning every vector in N is orthogonal to every vector in R. So P in Example 7 is an orthogonal projection. Orthogonal projection matrices are especially useful, but not all projection matrices are orthogonal. See the problems.

Example 8 (Projection onto a Line) *Show that for any unit vector $\mathbf{u}$ in $\mathbb{R}^3$, viewed as a column vector, that $P_u = \mathbf{u}\mathbf{u}^T$ is a 3×3 orthogonal projection matrix.*

Solution. It is easy to verify that $P_u^2 = P_u$ so P_u is a projection matrix:

$$P_u^2 = \left(\mathbf{u}\mathbf{u}^T\right)\left(\mathbf{u}\mathbf{u}^T\right) = \mathbf{u}\left(\mathbf{u}^T\mathbf{u}\right)\mathbf{u}^T = \mathbf{u}\mathbf{u}^T = P_u$$

because $\mathbf{u}^T\mathbf{u} = \mathbf{u} \cdot \mathbf{u} = 1$. Notice also that

$$P_u\mathbf{v} = \left(\mathbf{u}\mathbf{u}^T\right)\mathbf{v} = \mathbf{u}\left(\mathbf{u}^T\mathbf{v}\right) = \mathbf{u}\left(\mathbf{u} \cdot \mathbf{v}\right)$$

or, equivalently,

$$P_u\mathbf{v} = (\mathbf{v} \cdot \mathbf{u})\,\mathbf{u} = \mathrm{proj}_{\mathbf{u}}\,\mathbf{v}.$$

Make a sketch as follows: The line L that is parallel to $\mathbf{u}$ and passes through the origin and an arbitrary vector $\mathbf{v}$ determine a plane in space. Sketch $\mathbf{v}$ and L in this plane. Now add $P_u\mathbf{v}$ to your sketch. Now you can see that P_u projects each vector $\mathbf{v}$ onto the line L. Also the only vectors $\mathbf{v}$ whose projections are the zero vector are perpendicular to the line L. (Algebraically, $P_u\mathbf{v} = (\mathbf{v} \cdot \mathbf{u})\,\mathbf{u} = \mathbf{0}$ if and only $\mathbf{v} \cdot \mathbf{u} = 0$; that is, if and only if $\mathbf{v} \perp \mathbf{u}$.) Consequently,

$$R = \text{Range of } P_u = L,$$
$$N = \text{Null space of } P_u = \{\mathbf{v} : \mathbf{v} \cdot \mathbf{u} = 0\} = L^{\perp},$$

the line through the origin perpendicular to L. Since $R \perp N$, P_u is an orthogonal projection matrix. P_u projects each vector in 3-space (orthogonally) onto the line L. $\square$

Example 9 (Projection onto a Plane) *The plane Π with equation $x - y + 2z = 0$ has $\mathbf{n} = \langle 1, -1, 2 \rangle$ as a normal vector. Two orthogonal unit vectors that span the plane are*

$$\mathbf{a} = \left\langle \frac{-1}{\sqrt{3}}, \frac{1}{\sqrt{3}}, \frac{1}{\sqrt{3}} \right\rangle \quad and \quad \mathbf{b} = \left\langle \frac{1}{\sqrt{2}}, \frac{1}{\sqrt{2}}, 0 \right\rangle.$$

(Check that $\mathbf{a}$ and $\mathbf{b}$ lie in Π and $\mathbf{a} \cdot \mathbf{b} = 0$.) Let $P_{\mathbf{a}}$ and $P_{\mathbf{b}}$ be projection matrices as in Example 8. Show that the matrix $P = P_{\mathbf{a}} + P_{\mathbf{b}}$ is a 3×3 orthogonal projection matrix.

Solution. You are asked to check in Problem 22 that P is a projection matrix; that is, that $P^2 = P$. To see that it is an orthogonal projection matrix, draw a figure that shows the plane Π in a horizontal position with orthogonal unit vectors $\mathbf{a}$ and $\mathbf{b}$ in Π and the vector $\mathbf{n}$ perpendicular to Π. Sketch a general position vector $\mathbf{v}$ and consult your sketch as you read what follows. From Example 8, for each vector $\mathbf{v}$ in $\mathbb{R}^3$

$$P\mathbf{v} = \text{proj}_\mathbf{a}\,\mathbf{v} + \text{proj}_\mathbf{b}\,\mathbf{v} = (\mathbf{v}\cdot\mathbf{a})\,\mathbf{a} + (\mathbf{v}\cdot\mathbf{b})\,\mathbf{b}.$$

Since $\mathbf{a}$ and $\mathbf{b}$ lie in Π, $P\mathbf{v}$ lies in Π. So the projection matrix P projects any vector $\mathbf{v}$ in $\mathbb{R}^3$ into the plane Π. Since $\mathbf{a}$ and $\mathbf{b}$ are orthonormal vectors in Π, if $\mathbf{w}$ lies in Π to begin with, then

$$\text{proj}_\mathbf{a}\,\mathbf{w} + \text{proj}_\mathbf{b}\,\mathbf{w} = \mathbf{w}.$$

(Make a sketch that confirms this.) That is, $P\mathbf{w} = \mathbf{w}$ for each $\mathbf{w}$ in Π. Combining these observations gives

$$R = \text{Range of } P = \Pi.$$

Furthermore, $P\mathbf{v} = \mathbf{0}$ if and only if $(\mathbf{v}\cdot\mathbf{a})\,\mathbf{a} = -(\mathbf{v}\cdot\mathbf{b})\,\mathbf{b}$. Dot this equation with $\mathbf{a}$ and then with $\mathbf{b}$ to conclude that $\mathbf{v}\cdot\mathbf{a} = 0$ and $\mathbf{v}\cdot\mathbf{b} = 0$. It follows that $\mathbf{v}$ is orthogonal to the plane Π and hence parallel to $\mathbf{n}$. That is, $P\mathbf{v} = \mathbf{0}$ if and only if $\mathbf{v} = t\mathbf{n}$ for some t. Thus,

$$N = \text{Null space of } P = \{\mathbf{v} : \mathbf{v} = t\mathbf{n} \text{ for some } t \text{ in } \mathbb{R}\}\,.$$

Once again $R \perp N$, and P is an orthogonal projection matrix. P projects each vector in 3-space (orthogonally) onto the plane Π. $\square$

The language used above for matrices has its natural counterpart for linear transformations. A linear transformation T is called a projection (or projection operator) if $T^2 = T$ and is an orthogonal projection if its range and null space are orthogonal to each other. With this agreement, if P is a projection (orthogonal projection) matrix then the corresponding linear transformation of multiplication by P is a projection (orthogonal projection) operator.

6.6 Suggested Problems

1. Give a geometric description of the linear transformation that is multiplication by the given matrix.

   (a) $A = \begin{bmatrix} -1 & 0 \\ 0 & 1 \end{bmatrix}$ (b) $A = \begin{bmatrix} -1 & 0 \\ 0 & -1 \end{bmatrix}$

   (c) $A = \begin{bmatrix} 1 & 0 & 0 \\ 0 & -1 & 0 \\ 0 & 0 & 1 \end{bmatrix}$ (d) $A = \begin{bmatrix} 0 & 1 \\ 1 & 0 \end{bmatrix}$.

   (e) $A = \begin{bmatrix} 0 & 1 & 0 \\ 1 & 0 & 0 \\ 0 & 0 & 1 \end{bmatrix}$ (f) $A = \begin{bmatrix} 0 & -1 \\ 1 & 0 \end{bmatrix}$

   (g) $A = \begin{bmatrix} 1 & 0 & 0 \\ 0 & 2 & 0 \\ 0 & 0 & 3 \end{bmatrix}$ (h) $A = \begin{bmatrix} 2 & 0 & 0 \\ 0 & 1/2 & 0 \\ 0 & 0 & -1 \end{bmatrix}$

2. Each transformation T below is linear. For each transformation
   (i) make a sketch that illustrates how $\mathbf{v}$ is mapped to $T(\mathbf{v})$, and
   (ii) find the matrix of T with respect to the standard basis.

   (a) For each $\mathbf{v}$ in $\mathbb{R}^2$, $T(\mathbf{v})$ is the reflection of $\mathbf{v}$ across the line $y = x$.

   (b) For each $\mathbf{v}$ in $\mathbb{R}^2$, $T(\mathbf{v})$ is the reflection of $\mathbf{v}$ across the line $y = -x$.

   (c) For each $\mathbf{v}$ in $\mathbb{R}^2$, $T(\mathbf{v})$ is the reflection of $\mathbf{v}$ across the y-axis.

   (d) For each $\mathbf{v}$ in $\mathbb{R}^2$, $T(\mathbf{v})$ is the reflection of $\mathbf{v}$ across the line $y = 2x$.

   (e) For each $\mathbf{v}$ in $\mathbb{R}^2$, $T(\mathbf{v})$ is the reflection of $\mathbf{v}$ in the origin.

   (f) For each $\mathbf{v}$ in $\mathbb{R}^3$, $T(\mathbf{v})$ obtained by projecting $\mathbf{v}$ onto the xy-plane and then reflecting the projected vector across the plane $y = x$.

   (g) For each $\mathbf{v}$ in $\mathbb{R}^2$, $T(\mathbf{v})$ is the vector obtained by a counterclockwise rotation of $\mathbf{v}$ by $\pi/4$ radians.

   (h) For each $\mathbf{v}$ in $\mathbb{R}^2$, $T(\mathbf{v})$ is the vector obtained by a counterclockwise rotation of $\mathbf{v}$ by θ radians.

   (i) For each $\mathbf{v}$ in $\mathbb{R}^2$, $T(\mathbf{v})$ is the vector obtained by a clockwise rotation of $\mathbf{v}$ by θ radians.

   (j) For each $\mathbf{v}$ in $\mathbb{R}^3$, $T(\mathbf{v})$ is the vector with the same length as $\mathbf{v}$ and whose projection onto the xy-plane is obtained by rotating the projection of $\mathbf{v}$ onto the xy-plane counterclockwise by $\pi/6$ radians. There are two distinct linear transformations with these properties. Find the matrix of each one.

   (k) For each $\mathbf{v}$ in $\mathbb{R}^3$, $T(\mathbf{v})$ is the projection of $\mathbf{v}$ onto the xy-plane in $\mathbb{R}^3$.

   (l) For each $\mathbf{v}$ in $\mathbb{R}^3$, $T(\mathbf{v})$ is the projection of $\mathbf{v}$ onto the xy-plane in $\mathbb{R}^2$.

3. Solve Example 6 by making use of the dot product to find the projection of one vector along another. *Hint.* What is the vector $\mathbf{e}_1$ minus its projection on the line L of reflection?

4. Solve Example 6 by first finding a formula for $T(\mathbf{v})$ in terms of $\mathbf{v} = \langle v_1, v_2 \rangle$. *Hint.* Reason along the lines of Example 6 or the foregoing problem but with $\mathbf{e}_1$ replaced by $\mathbf{v}$.

5. It was assumed in Example 5 that a counterclockwise rotation by 60 degrees in the xy-plane is a linear transformation. Confirm this with a geometric argument. *Hint.* Use the parallelogram (triangle) law of vector addition.

6. A linear transformation $T : \mathbb{R}^3 \to \mathbb{R}^3$ has matrix

$$A = \begin{bmatrix} 1 & -3 & 1 \\ 2 & -8 & 8 \\ -6 & 3 & -15 \end{bmatrix}.$$

Find a vector $\mathbf{v}$ in $\mathbb{R}^3$ that satisfies $T(\mathbf{v}) = [4 \ -2 \ 9]^T$.

7. A linear transformation $T : \mathbb{R}^3 \to \mathbb{R}^3$ has matrix

$$A = \begin{bmatrix} 2 & -1 & 1 \\ 3 & 2 & -4 \\ -6 & 3 & -3 \end{bmatrix}.$$

Find a vector $\mathbf{v}$ in $\mathbb{R}^3$ that satisfies $T(\mathbf{v}) = [1 \ 4 \ 2]^T$.

8. A linear transformation $T : \mathbb{R}^3 \to \mathbb{R}^2$ has matrix

$$A = \begin{bmatrix} 1 & -3 & 1 \\ 2 & -8 & 8 \end{bmatrix}.$$

Find all vectors $\mathbf{v}$ in $\mathbb{R}^3$ that satisfies $T(\mathbf{v}) = [-2 \ 12]^T$ or show that no such vector $\mathbf{v}$ exists.

9. A linear transformation $T : \mathbb{R}^2 \to \mathbb{R}^3$ has matrix

$$A = \begin{bmatrix} 1 & -3 & 1 \\ 2 & -8 & 8 \end{bmatrix}^T.$$

Find all vectors $\mathbf{v}$ in $\mathbb{R}^2$ that satisfies $T(\mathbf{v}) = [-2 \ 12 \ -20]^T$ or show that no such vector $\mathbf{v}$ exists.

10. A linear transformation $T : \mathbb{R}^2 \to \mathbb{R}^3$ has matrix

$$A = \begin{bmatrix} 1 & -3 & 1 \\ 2 & -8 & 8 \end{bmatrix}^T.$$

Find all vectors $\mathbf{v}$ in $\mathbb{R}^2$ that satisfies $T(\mathbf{v}) = [9 \ 0 \ 2]^T$ or show that no such vector $\mathbf{v}$ exists.

11. A linear transformation $T : \mathbb{R}^2 \to \mathbb{R}^3$ has matrix

$$A = \begin{bmatrix} 1 & -3 & 1 \\ 2 & -8 & 8 \end{bmatrix}^T.$$

Find all vectors $\mathbf{v}$ in $\mathbb{R}^2$ that satisfies $T(\mathbf{v}) = [-6 \ -11 \ 7]^T$ or show that no such vector $\mathbf{v}$ exists.

12. A linear transformation $T : \mathbb{R}^5 \to \mathbb{R}^6$. What is the size of the standard matrix of T?

13. A linear transformation $T : \mathbb{R}^7 \to \mathbb{R}^4$. What is the size of the standard matrix of T?

14. Let $T : \mathbb{R}^2 \to \mathbb{R}^2$ be the linear transformation that reflects each vector across the line $y = x$. Let $S : \mathbb{R}^2 \to \mathbb{R}^2$ be the linear transformation that projects each vector orthogonally onto the y-axis.

    (a) Find the standard matrices for T and S.

    (b) Use geometric reasoning to find $T \circ S(\mathbf{e}_1)$ and $T \circ S(\mathbf{e}_2)$ and, in this way, find the standard matrix of the linear transformation $T \circ S$.

    (c) Check that the matrix of $T \circ S$ is the product of the matrix of T and the matrix of S (in this order).

    (d) Repeat (b) and (c) but for the transformation $S \circ T$.

    (e) Does $T \circ S = S \circ T$? Give a geometric explanation for your answer.

15. Let $R_\alpha : \mathbb{R}^2 \to \mathbb{R}^2$ be the linear transformation that rotates each vector counterclockwise by the angle α. Let $R_\beta : \mathbb{R}^2 \to \mathbb{R}^2$ be the linear transformation that rotates each vector counterclockwise by the angle β.

    (a) Use matrix multiplication to find the matrix for $R_\alpha \circ R_\beta$.

    (b) Then use trigonometric identities to show that the matrix for $R_\alpha \circ R_\beta$ is the same as the matrix for $R_{\alpha+\beta}$.

    (c) Finally give a simple geometric argument to explain the equality $R_{\alpha+\beta} = R_\alpha \circ R_\beta$.

16. Find the matrix of the transformation $T : \mathbb{R}^2 \to \mathbb{R}^2$ that is reflection across the line $y = -x$, followed by rotation counterclockwise by $45°$, followed by orthogonal projection onto the line $y = 2x$. Finally, find $T\left([3 \ 3]^T\right)$.

17. Find the matrix of the transformation $T : \mathbb{R}^2 \to \mathbb{R}^2$ that is reflection across the line $y = x$, followed by rotation counterclockwise by $45°$, followed by orthogonal projection onto the line $y = -2x$. Finally, find $T\left([3 \ -3]^T\right)$.

18. The transformation $T : \mathbb{R}^3 \to \mathbb{R}^3$ that reflects each vector across the plane $x + y + z = 0$ is a linear transformation. Find the matrix A such that $T = T_A$. Then find a convenient formula for $T(\mathbf{v})$ for any $\mathbf{v} = \langle x, y, z \rangle$ in $\mathbb{R}^3$. *Hint.* Review the reasoning needed for reflection across a line in Example 6 or in Problems 3 and 4.

19. Solve Problem 18 for reflection across the plane $2x - 3y + 4z = 0$. *Hint.* See the hint for Problem 18.

20. A linear transformation $T : \mathbb{R}^2 \to \mathbb{R}^2$ is defined as follows. For any vector $\mathbf{v}$ in $\mathbb{R}^2$ define $\mathbf{w} = T(\mathbf{v})$ to be the vector whose tip is obtained from the tip of $\mathbf{v}$ by displacing the tip of $\mathbf{v}$ parallel to the vector $\langle -1, 1 \rangle$ until the displaced tip lies on the y-axis.

    (a) Find the matrix P of T.

    (b) Show that P is a projection matrix.

    (c) What does P project onto? Is P an orthogonal projection?

21. A linear transformation $T : \mathbb{R}^2 \to \mathbb{R}^2$ is defined as follows. For any vector $\mathbf{v}$ in $\mathbb{R}^2$ define $\mathbf{w} = T(\mathbf{v})$ to be the vector whose tip is obtained from the tip of $\mathbf{v}$ by displacing the tip of $\mathbf{v}$ parallel to the vector $\langle -1, 1 \rangle$ until the displaced tip lies on the line L with equation $y = 2x$.

    (a) Find the matrix P of T. *Hint.* Reason along the lines of Example 6 or Problems 3 or 4.

    (b) Show that P is a projection matrix.

    (c) What does P project onto? Is P an orthogonal projection?

22. *(Reflection via Projection)* Find the matrix of the linear transformation in Example 6 using projections by means for the following steps. Let L be the line with equation $y = 3x$ shown in the figure accompanying the example. Let $\mathbf{a}$ be the unit vector in L whose tail is at the origin and whose tip is in the first quadrant.

    (a) Find the components of $\mathbf{a}$.

    (b) Explain why $T(\mathbf{v}) = \mathbf{v} + 2(\text{proj}_{\mathbf{a}} \mathbf{v} - \mathbf{v}) = 2\,\text{proj}_{\mathbf{a}} \mathbf{v} - \mathbf{v}$.

    (c) Use (b) to conclude that T is multiplication by the matrix $Q = 2P_a - I$, where P_a is the projection matrix on the line L as in Example 8.

    (d) Show that $Q^2 = I$, equivalently, $T^2 = I$.

    (e) Now explain in geometric language, without any calculation, why the result in (d) is obvious.

23. Show that the matrix $P = P_a + P_b$ in Example 9 is a projection matrix as follows: (Recall that P_a and P_b are projection matrices as in Example 8.)

    (a) Show that $P^2 = P_a^2 + P_a P_b + P_b P_a + P_b^2$.

    (b) Show $P_a P_b = 0$ and $P_b P_a = 0$. *Hint.* For a unit column vector $\mathbf{u}$ recall that $P_u = \mathbf{u}\mathbf{u}^T$.

24. Let P be any projection matrix. Let T_P be the corresponding linear transformation of multiplication by P and let R and N be, respectively, the range and null space of T.

    (a) Show that $\mathbf{0}$ is the only vector in $R \cap N$.

    (b) Show that $\mathbf{v} = \mathbf{r} + \mathbf{n}$ with $\mathbf{r}$ in R and $\mathbf{n}$ in N is true if and only if $\mathbf{r} = P\mathbf{v}$ and $\mathbf{n} = (I - P)\mathbf{v}$.

Lesson 7

Eigenvalue Problems

7.1 Goals

- Know the definitions of eigenvalue, eigenvector, characteristic equation

- Be able to find eigenvalues and eigenvectors for particular matrices, usually 2×2 or 3×3

- Learn the general properties of eigenvalues and eigenvectors given in Theorems $1 - 4$

- Learn the properties of eigenvalues and eigenvectors of a symmetric matrix given in Theorem 5

7.2 Overview

Let A be an $n \times n$ matrix of constants (which may be real or complex numbers). A problem of central importance in several areas of mathematics and its applications is to find all *nonzero* vectors $\mathbf{v}$ such that

$$A\mathbf{v} = \lambda\mathbf{v} \tag{7.1}$$

where λ is a scalar. This equation always has the trivial solution $\mathbf{v} = \mathbf{0}$, whatever λ may be. We call λ an **eigenvalue** of the matrix A if there is a *nonzero* vector $\mathbf{v}$, called an **eigenvector** corresponding to λ, which satisfies (7.1). The problem of finding all the eigenvalues and eigenvectors of a given matrix A is called an **eigenvalue problem**. Depending on the context, eigenvectors may determine steady-state population proportions among several competing species, or may determine the principal axes of rotation of a rigid body, or may determine the normal (natural) modes of oscillation of a mechanical or electrical network, just to list a few areas where eigenvalue problems arise. Corresponding eigenvalues give related information. For example, in oscillation problems, eigenvalues determine natural frequencies of oscillation.

7.3   Basic Properties

Evidently, the eigenvalues and eigenvectors of a matrix A satisfy a rather specialized equation. Here is a geometric interpretation of the eigenvalue problem. Think of A as a linear transformation on 2- or 3-dimensional space that takes input vectors $\mathbf{x}$ and transforms them into output vectors $A\mathbf{x}$. Typically, a *nonzero* input vector $\mathbf{x}$ and its corresponding output $A\mathbf{x}$ will point in different directions in space. Is it possible that for some special nonzero input vector $\mathbf{v}$ the output vector $A\mathbf{v}$ will point in the same or opposite direction in space as $\mathbf{v}$? If this happens, $A\mathbf{v}$ must be a scalar multiple of $\mathbf{v}$. That is, there must be a scalar λ such that $A\mathbf{v} = \lambda\mathbf{v}$, which is just the eigenvalue-eigenvector equation above. In other words, the eigenvectors of a matrix A are either the nonzero vectors (directions in space) that the matrix leave invariant (input and output have the same direction) or the vectors (directions in space) that the matrix reverses. This same interpretation is made in higher dimensional spaces.

To better understand the eigenvalue problem for matrices, we shall work primarily with 2×2 and 3×3 matrices. The principal properties of the general eigenvalue problem can be illustrated in this setting and the calculations involved are much easier. In the 2×2 and 3×3 cases, we shall write

$$\mathbf{v} = \begin{bmatrix} v_1 \\ v_2 \end{bmatrix} \quad \text{or} \quad \mathbf{v} = \begin{bmatrix} v_1 \\ v_2 \\ v_3 \end{bmatrix}$$

respectively. It is important to recognize that (7.1) can be expressed as a *homogeneous* system of linear equations.

Example 1 *If* $A = \begin{bmatrix} 1 & 2 \\ 3 & 4 \end{bmatrix}$, *express the eigenvalue problem* $A\mathbf{v} = \lambda\mathbf{v}$ *as a homogeneous system of linear equations.*

Solution. With the notation just introduced, $A\mathbf{v} = \lambda\mathbf{v}$ can be expressed as

$$\begin{bmatrix} 1 & 2 \\ 3 & 4 \end{bmatrix} \begin{bmatrix} v_1 \\ v_2 \end{bmatrix} = \lambda \begin{bmatrix} v_1 \\ v_2 \end{bmatrix},$$

$$\begin{bmatrix} v_1 + 2v_2 \\ 3v_1 + 4v_2 \end{bmatrix} = \begin{bmatrix} \lambda v_1 \\ \lambda v_2 \end{bmatrix}.$$

Equate components in this vector equation to obtain

$$\begin{cases} v_1 + 2v_2 = \lambda v_1 \\ 3v_1 + 4v_2 = \lambda v_2 \end{cases} \quad \text{or} \quad \begin{cases} (1 - \lambda)v_1 + 2v_2 = 0 \\ 3v_1 + (4 - \lambda)v_2 = 0 \end{cases},$$

a homogeneous linear system for the components of $\mathbf{v}$. You also can express the homogeneous system in matrix form:

$$\begin{bmatrix} 1 - \lambda & 2 \\ 3 & 4 - \lambda \end{bmatrix} \begin{bmatrix} v_1 \\ v_2 \end{bmatrix} = \begin{bmatrix} 0 \\ 0 \end{bmatrix}. \quad \square$$

In general, the equation $A\mathbf{v} = \lambda\mathbf{v}$ can be expressed as

$$
\begin{aligned}
A\mathbf{v} - \lambda\mathbf{v} &= \mathbf{0}, \\
A\mathbf{v} - \lambda I\mathbf{v} &= 0 \qquad \text{since } I\mathbf{v} = \mathbf{v}, \\
(A - \lambda I)\,\mathbf{v} &= \mathbf{0}, \tag{7.2}
\end{aligned}
$$

which is a linear homogeneous equation for $\mathbf{v}$. Notice that the matrix $A - \lambda I$ can be obtained from A by subtracting λ from each of its main diagonal elements. As illustrated in the foregoing example, the vector equation (7.2) represents a system of linear homogeneous equations for the components of the vector $\mathbf{v}$. By Theorem 3 in Lesson 3, (7.2) has a nontrivial solution $\mathbf{v}$ if and only if $\det(A - \lambda I) = 0$. The equation

$$
\det(A - \lambda I) = 0 \tag{7.3}
$$

is called the **characteristic equation** of the matrix A, and we have established the following result.

Theorem 1 *The eigenvalues λ of a square matrix A are the roots of its characteristic equation, $\det(A - \lambda I) = 0$.*

In most cases an eigenvalue problem is solved by first solving (7.3) to find its eigenvalues, λ; then we solve the homogeneous linear system (7.2) to find the corresponding eigenvectors. The following examples show what can happen when A is a 2×2 matrix.

Example 2 *Find the eigenvalues and eigenvectors for the matrix*

$$
A = \begin{bmatrix} 1 & 1 \\ 4 & 1 \end{bmatrix}.
$$

Solution. The characteristic equation of A is

$$
\begin{aligned}
\det(A - \lambda I) &= \begin{vmatrix} 1 - \lambda & 1 \\ 4 & 1 - \lambda \end{vmatrix} = (1 - \lambda)^2 - 4 = 0, \\
(1 - \lambda)^2 &= 4, \\
\lambda &= -1, 3.
\end{aligned}
$$

Thus, A has eigenvalues $\lambda = -1$ and $\lambda = 3$. For these two values of λ (and only for these two values) the homogeneous system $(A - \lambda I)\mathbf{v} = \mathbf{0}$ has nontrivial solutions

$$
\mathbf{v} = \begin{bmatrix} v_1 \\ v_2 \end{bmatrix}. \tag{7.4}
$$

Written out in detail the system (7.2) for $\mathbf{v}$ is

$$
\begin{cases} (1 - \lambda)v_1 + v_2 = 0 \\ 4v_1 + (1 - \lambda)v_2 = 0 \end{cases}. \tag{7.5}
$$

The next step is to find the nontrivial solutions to this homogeneous system when $\lambda = -1$ and when $\lambda = 3$.

When $\lambda = -1$ the system (7.5) is

$$\begin{cases} 2v_1 + v_2 = 0 \\ 4v_1 + 2v_2 = 0 \end{cases}.$$

This pair of equations imposes the single requirement $2v_1 + v_2 = 0$. Thus, (7.4) will satisfy the system $(A - (-1)I)\mathbf{v} = \mathbf{0}$ provided $v_2 = -2v_1$:

$$\mathbf{v} = \begin{bmatrix} v_1 \\ v_2 \end{bmatrix} = \begin{bmatrix} v_1 \\ -2v_1 \end{bmatrix} = v_1 \begin{bmatrix} 1 \\ -2 \end{bmatrix}.$$

Consequently, the eigenvectors of A belonging to the eigenvalue $\lambda = -1$ are the nonzero multiples of the vector

$$\mathbf{v}_1 = \begin{bmatrix} 1 \\ -2 \end{bmatrix}.$$

When $\lambda = 3$ the system (7.5) becomes

$$\begin{cases} -2v_1 + v_2 = 0 \\ 4v_1 - 2v_2 = 0 \end{cases}$$

and this pair of equations imposes the single requirement $-2v_1 + v_2 = 0$. Thus, (7.4) will satisfy $(A - 3I)\mathbf{v} = \mathbf{0}$ when $v_2 = 2v_1$:

$$\mathbf{v} = \begin{bmatrix} v_1 \\ v_2 \end{bmatrix} = \begin{bmatrix} v_1 \\ 2v_1 \end{bmatrix} = v_1 \begin{bmatrix} 1 \\ 2 \end{bmatrix}.$$

So, the eigenvectors of A belonging to the eigenvalue $\lambda = 3$ are the nonzero multiples of the vector

$$\mathbf{v}_2 = \begin{bmatrix} 1 \\ 2 \end{bmatrix}.$$

In summary, the matrix A has eigenvalues $\lambda_1 = -1$ and $\lambda_2 = 3$ and corresponding eigenvectors

$$\mathbf{v}_1 = \begin{bmatrix} 1 \\ -2 \end{bmatrix} \quad \text{and} \quad \mathbf{v}_2 = \begin{bmatrix} 1 \\ 2 \end{bmatrix}. \quad \square$$

You may have noticed in the summary that we did not mention that all nonzero multiples of $\mathbf{v}_1$ and $\mathbf{v}_2$ are also eigenvectors corresponding to $\lambda_1 = -1$ and $\lambda_2 = 3$, respectively. The fact that nonzero multiples of a given eigenvector are again eigenvectors is automatic (Problem 15) and therefore often suppressed because no really new information is gained. Another important feature of Example 2 is that the eigenvectors $\mathbf{v}_1$ and $\mathbf{v}_2$ are linearly independent. This follows at once from the meaning of linear independence, or it can also be checked using Theorem 1 in Lesson 5 because

$$\begin{vmatrix} 1 & 1 \\ -2 & 2 \end{vmatrix} = 4 \neq 0.$$

This special case reflects the following general fact.

Theorem 2 *Eigenvectors of a matrix belonging to distinct eigenvalues are linearly independent.*

We prove this result in the case of two eigenvectors. The general case is argued along similar lines. Assume that

$$A\mathbf{v} = \lambda\mathbf{v} \quad \text{and} \quad A\mathbf{w} = \mu\mathbf{w}$$

where $\mathbf{v} \neq \mathbf{0}$ and $\mathbf{w} \neq \mathbf{0}$ are eigenvectors of the matrix A. Consider the relation

$$\alpha\mathbf{v} + \beta\mathbf{w} = \mathbf{0}$$

where α and β are constants. Apply A to both sides of this equality and use the linearity of A to get

$$\alpha\lambda\mathbf{v} + \beta\mu\mathbf{w} = \mathbf{0}.$$

Now, multiply the first equation by λ and subtract the second equation from the result to find

$$\beta(\lambda - \mu)\mathbf{w} = \mathbf{0}.$$

Since $\lambda - \mu \neq 0$ and $\mathbf{w} \neq \mathbf{0}$, we conclude that $\beta = 0$. Then $\alpha\mathbf{v} = \mathbf{0}$ and we find that $\alpha = 0$. Thus, $\mathbf{v}$ and $\mathbf{w}$ are linearly independent.

Example 3 *Solve the eigenvalue problem for the matrix*

$$A = \begin{bmatrix} 1 & -1 \\ 5 & -3 \end{bmatrix}.$$

Solution. First,

$$\det(A - \lambda I) = \begin{vmatrix} 1 - \lambda & -1 \\ 5 & -3 - \lambda \end{vmatrix} = -3 + 2\lambda + \lambda^2 + 5$$

and the characteristic equation of A, $\lambda^2 + 2\lambda + 2 = 0$, has roots

$$\lambda = -1 + i, -1 - i,$$

which are the eigenvalues of the matrix A. Here $i = \sqrt{-1}$. To find the eigenvectors (7.4) we must solve $(A - \lambda I)\mathbf{v} = \mathbf{0}$ or

$$\begin{cases} (1 - \lambda)v_1 - v_2 = 0 \\ 5v_1 + (-3 - \lambda)v_2 = 0 \end{cases}. \tag{7.6}$$

When $\lambda = -1 + i$ the system (7.6) is

$$\begin{cases} (2-i)v_1 - v_2 = 0 \\ 5v_1 + (-2-i)v_2 = 0 \end{cases}.$$

Multiplication (check it) of the second equation by $(2-i)/5$ reduces it to the first equation, so the pair of equations above reduces to the single requirement

$$\begin{aligned} (2-i)v_1 - v_2 &= 0, \\ v_2 &= (2-i)v_1, \end{aligned}$$

and we deduce that the eigenvectors corresponding to $\lambda = -1 + i$ have the form

$$\mathbf{v} = \begin{bmatrix} v_1 \\ v_2 \end{bmatrix} = \begin{bmatrix} v_1 \\ (2-i)\,v_1 \end{bmatrix} = v_1 \begin{bmatrix} 1 \\ 2-i \end{bmatrix}.$$

Thus, the eigenvectors of A corresponding to $\lambda_1 = -1 + i$ are the nonzero multiples of

$$\mathbf{v}_1 = \begin{bmatrix} 1 \\ 2-i \end{bmatrix}.$$

An entirely similar calculation shows that $\lambda_2 = -1 - i$ has for its eigenvectors the nonzero multiples of

$$\mathbf{v}_2 = \begin{bmatrix} 1 \\ 2+i \end{bmatrix}.$$

Of course, the eigenvectors $\mathbf{v}_1$ and $\mathbf{v}_2$ are linearly independent by Theorem 2. This independence also can be deduced from the determinant test

$$\begin{vmatrix} 1 & 1 \\ 2-i & 2+i \end{vmatrix} = 2i \neq 0. \quad \square$$

Observe that the eigenvectors $\mathbf{v}_1$ and $\mathbf{v}_2$ are complex conjugate vectors; that is

$$\overline{\mathbf{v}_1} = \overline{\begin{bmatrix} 1 \\ 2-i \end{bmatrix}} = \begin{bmatrix} \bar{1} \\ \overline{2-i} \end{bmatrix} = \begin{bmatrix} 1 \\ 2+i \end{bmatrix} = \mathbf{v}_2.$$

It is an elementary property of complex numbers that $\bar{c} = c$ when c is real and that $\overline{c_1 c_2} = \bar{c}_1 \bar{c}_2$; moreover, it is routine to check that these properties carry over to the product $A\mathbf{v}$ of a matrix and a vector. Then for any *real* matrix A the calculation

$$A\mathbf{v} = \lambda\mathbf{v}, \quad \overline{A\mathbf{v}} = \overline{\lambda\mathbf{v}}, \quad \bar{A}\bar{\mathbf{v}} = \bar{\lambda}\bar{\mathbf{v}}, \quad A\bar{\mathbf{v}} = \bar{\lambda}\bar{\mathbf{v}}$$

establishes the following useful fact.

Theorem 3 *Let A be a real matrix. If λ is an eigenvalue of A with eigenvector $\mathbf{v}$, then $\bar{\lambda}$ is an eigenvalue of A with corresponding eigenvector $\bar{\mathbf{v}}$.*

Given this theorem, once we have found

$$\lambda_1 = -1 + i \quad \text{and} \quad \mathbf{v}_1 = \begin{bmatrix} 1 \\ 2 - i \end{bmatrix}$$

in Example 3, we get the eigenvalue-eigenvector pair

$$\lambda_2 = -1 - i \quad \text{and} \quad \mathbf{v}_2 = \begin{bmatrix} 1 \\ 2 + i \end{bmatrix}$$

free of charge by taking complex conjugates!

In both Examples 2 and 3, the 2×2 matrix A had two, linearly independent eigenvectors. In general, an $n \times n$ matrix A has **simple structure** (is **diagonalizable**) if it has n linearly independent eigenvectors. A notable consequence of Theorem 2 follows.

Theorem 4 *An $n \times n$ matrix A has simple structure (is diagonalizable) if it has n distinct eigenvalues.*

Most applications in which eigenvalue problems play a role are easiest to deal with in the case that A has simple structure. Unfortunately, not every matrix has simple structure. Here is an example.

Example 4 *Solve the eigenvalue problem for the matrix*

$$A = \begin{bmatrix} 1 & -1 \\ 1 & 3 \end{bmatrix}.$$

Solution. The characteristic equation of A is

$$\det(A - \lambda I) = \begin{vmatrix} 1 - \lambda & -1 \\ 1 & 3 - \lambda \end{vmatrix} = \lambda^2 - 4\lambda + 4 = (\lambda - 2)^2 = 0.$$

So A has an eigenvalue of algebraic multiplicity two and we write $\lambda_1 = \lambda_2 = 2$. To find corresponding eigenvectors (7.4), we must solve $(A - 2I)\mathbf{v} = \mathbf{0}$ or

$$\begin{cases} -v_1 - v_2 = 0 \\ v_1 + v_2 = 0 \end{cases}.$$

Evidently, this pair of equations reduces to the single requirement that $v_2 = -v_1$, and we conclude that the eigenvectors of A corresponding to $\lambda_1 = \lambda_2 = 2$ are

$$\mathbf{v} = \begin{bmatrix} 1 \\ -1 \end{bmatrix}$$

and all its nonzero multiples. □

Based on Examples 2 and 3, the matrix A in Example 4 seems to be "short" one eigenvector. The plain fact is (as Example 4 shows) that there is no second eigenvector that is independent of $\mathbf{v}$. This deficiency (shortage) of eigenvectors presents practical difficulties in applications, but that is a story for another day and a course in linear algebra.

Multiplicity of an Eigenvalue

Each eigenvalue λ of a matrix A has two multiplicities associated with it – an *algebraic multiplicity* and a *geometric multiplicity*. The algebraic multiplicity of λ is its multiplicity as a root of the characteristic equation of A. Recall that every polynomial with real or complex coefficients factors into linear factors. If a particular linear factor is repeated k times in the factorization the corresponding root is said to have multiplicity k. It is customary to call a root of a polynomial *simple* if it has multiplicity 1. The geometric multiplicity of an eigenvalue is the number of linearly independent eigenvectors that correspond to the eigenvalue. With this language, the eigenvalue $\lambda = 2$ in Example 4 has algebraic multiplicity 2 and geometric multiplicity 1. It is true in general that the geometric multiplicity is less than or equal to the algebraic multiplicity.

7.4   Symmetric Matrices

There is an important class of matrices, symmetric matrices, that come up often in applications and which are never "short" any eigenvectors. A *real*, square matrix is **symmetric** if $A = A^T$; equivalently, a matrix is symmetric if its entries in mirror-image positions across the main diagonal are equal. For example,

$$\begin{bmatrix} 3 & 2 \\ 2 & 5 \end{bmatrix} \quad \text{and} \quad \begin{bmatrix} 1 & 2 & 3 \\ 2 & 4 & 5 \\ 3 & 5 & 6 \end{bmatrix}$$

are 2×2 and 3×3 symmetric matrices.

Here is a deceptively important property of a symmetric matrix:

$$\boxed{A\mathbf{x} \cdot \mathbf{y} = \mathbf{x} \cdot A\mathbf{y} \qquad \text{for } A \text{ a symmetric matrix}}$$

and any compatible column vectors $\mathbf{x}$ and $\mathbf{y}$. To establish this property for the case of vectors in $\mathbb{R}^n$, recall that $\mathbf{v} \cdot \mathbf{w} = \mathbf{v}^T \mathbf{w}$ and, hence,

$$A\mathbf{x} \cdot \mathbf{y} = (A\mathbf{x})^T \mathbf{y} = \left(\mathbf{x}^T A^T\right)\mathbf{y} = \left(\mathbf{x}^T A\right)\mathbf{y} = \mathbf{x}^T (A\mathbf{y}) = \mathbf{x} \cdot A\mathbf{y}.$$

Virtually the same reasoning applies with the complex dot product.

Example 5 *Solve the eigenvalue problem for the symmetric matrix*

$$A = \begin{bmatrix} 3 & 2 & 4 \\ 2 & 0 & 2 \\ 4 & 2 & 3 \end{bmatrix}.$$

Solution. Here

$$A - \lambda I = \begin{bmatrix} 3-\lambda & 2 & 4 \\ 2 & -\lambda & 2 \\ 4 & 2 & 3-\lambda \end{bmatrix}$$

and

$$
\begin{aligned}
\det\left(A-\lambda I\right) &= \left(3-\lambda\right)\left\{-\lambda\left(3-\lambda\right)-4\right\}-2\left\{2\left(3-\lambda\right)-8\right\}+4\left\{4+4\lambda\right\} \\
&= \left(3-\lambda\right)\left(\lambda^2-3\lambda-4\right)+4\left(\lambda+1\right)+16\left(\lambda+1\right) \\
&= \left(3-\lambda\right)\left(\lambda+1\right)\left(\lambda-4\right)+4\left(\lambda+1\right)+16\left(\lambda+1\right) \\
&= \left(\lambda+1\right)\left(\left(3-\lambda\right)\left(\lambda-4\right)+20\right) \\
&= \left(\lambda+1\right)\left(-\lambda^2+7\lambda+8\right)=-\left(\lambda+1\right)^2\left(\lambda-8\right).
\end{aligned}
$$

The characteristic equation for A,

$$
\left(\lambda+1\right)^2\left(\lambda-8\right)=0,
$$

has roots

$$
\lambda_1=\lambda_2=-1 \quad \text{and} \quad \lambda_3=8,
$$

where the double root is listed to its algebraic multiplicity. The eigenvectors

$$
\mathbf{v}=\left[\begin{array}{c} v_1 \\ v_2 \\ v_3 \end{array}\right]
$$

satisfy the equation $\left(A-\lambda I\right)\mathbf{v}=\mathbf{0}$, which can be expressed as

$$
\left[\begin{array}{ccc} 3-\lambda & 2 & 4 \\ 2 & -\lambda & 2 \\ 4 & 2 & 3-\lambda \end{array}\right]\left[\begin{array}{c} v_1 \\ v_2 \\ v_3 \end{array}\right]=\left[\begin{array}{c} 0 \\ 0 \\ 0 \end{array}\right]. \tag{7.7}
$$

Case 1. $\lambda_1=\lambda_2=-1$. Then (7.7) is

$$
\left[\begin{array}{ccc} 4 & 2 & 4 \\ 2 & 1 & 2 \\ 4 & 2 & 4 \end{array}\right]\left[\begin{array}{c} v_1 \\ v_2 \\ v_3 \end{array}\right]=\left[\begin{array}{c} 0 \\ 0 \\ 0 \end{array}\right].
$$

Since the first and third equation are just twice the second equation, the 3×3 system imposes the single requirement

$$
2v_1+v_2+2v_3=0 \tag{7.8}
$$

among the components of $\mathbf{v}$. One way to get all solutions to (7.8) is to assign *any values* to v_1 and v_3 and then solve for $v_2=-2v_1-2v_3$. Thus,

$$
\mathbf{v} = \left[\begin{array}{c} v_1 \\ v_2 \\ v_3 \end{array}\right]=\left[\begin{array}{c} v_1 \\ -2v_1-2v_3 \\ v_3 \end{array}\right]=\left[\begin{array}{c} v_1 \\ -2v_1 \\ 0 \end{array}\right]+\left[\begin{array}{c} 0 \\ -2v_3 \\ v_3 \end{array}\right]
$$

$$
\mathbf{v} = v_1\left[\begin{array}{c} 1 \\ -2 \\ 0 \end{array}\right]+v_3\left[\begin{array}{c} 0 \\ -2 \\ 1 \end{array}\right] \qquad \text{for any } v_1,v_3.
$$

Geometrically speaking, the eigenvectors corresponding to the double eigenvalue $\lambda_1 = \lambda_2 = -1$ are the nonzero vectors in the plane Π spanned by the two vectors

$$\begin{bmatrix} 1 \\ -2 \\ 0 \end{bmatrix} \quad \text{and} \quad \begin{bmatrix} 0 \\ -2 \\ 1 \end{bmatrix}$$

which are themselves eigenvectors. (Why?) For most applications, it is convenient to single out two eigenvectors in the plane Π that are orthogonal. This is easy to do. For example, pick

$$\mathbf{v}_1 = \begin{bmatrix} 1 \\ -2 \\ 0 \end{bmatrix} \quad \text{and} \quad \mathbf{v}_2 = \begin{bmatrix} v_1 \\ -2v_1 - 2v_3 \\ v_3 \end{bmatrix}$$

where v_1 and v_3 are chosen to make

$$\mathbf{v}_1 \cdot \mathbf{v}_2 = v_1 + 4v_1 + 4v_3 = 5v_1 + 4v_3 = 0.$$

Convenient choices for v_1 and v_3 are $v_1 = 4$, $v_3 = -5$. Then

$$\mathbf{v}_1 = \begin{bmatrix} 1 \\ -2 \\ 0 \end{bmatrix} \quad \text{and} \quad \mathbf{v}_2 = \begin{bmatrix} 4 \\ 2 \\ -5 \end{bmatrix}$$

are orthogonal eigenvectors belonging to the double eigenvalue $\lambda_1 = \lambda_2 = -1$. Notice that the eigenvalue -1 has geometric multiplicity 2 because $\mathbf{v}_1$ and $\mathbf{v}_2$ are linearly independent eigenvectors and every other eigenvector is a linear combination of these two eigenvectors.

Case 2. $\lambda_3 = 8$. Then (7.7) is

$$\begin{bmatrix} -5 & 2 & 4 \\ 2 & -8 & 2 \\ 4 & 2 & -5 \end{bmatrix} \begin{bmatrix} v_1 \\ v_2 \\ v_3 \end{bmatrix} = \begin{bmatrix} 0 \\ 0 \\ 0 \end{bmatrix}.$$

We solve by elimination. Divide the second equation by 2 and write it first to obtain the augmented matrix

$$\begin{bmatrix} 1 & -4 & 1 & 0 \\ -5 & 2 & 4 & 0 \\ 4 & 2 & -5 & 0 \end{bmatrix}.$$

Now, eliminate v_1 from the second and third equations to obtain

$$\begin{bmatrix} 1 & -4 & 1 & 0 \\ 0 & -18 & 9 & 0 \\ 0 & 18 & -9 & 0 \end{bmatrix}.$$

The system reduces to

$$\begin{cases} v_1 - 4v_2 + v_3 = 0 \\ \phantom{v_1 - {}} 2v_2 - v_3 = 0 \end{cases}.$$

Thus,

$$v_3 = 2v_2, \quad v_1 = 4v_2 - v_3 = 2v_2$$

for any choice of v_2 and, hence,

$$\mathbf{v} = \begin{bmatrix} v_1 \\ v_2 \\ v_3 \end{bmatrix} = \begin{bmatrix} 2v_2 \\ v_2 \\ 2v_2 \end{bmatrix} = v_2 \begin{bmatrix} 2 \\ 1 \\ 2 \end{bmatrix}.$$

The eigenvectors corresponding to $\lambda_3 = 8$ are

$$\mathbf{v}_3 = \begin{bmatrix} 2 \\ 1 \\ 2 \end{bmatrix}$$

and its nonzero multiples. $\square$

The solution to Example 5 illustrates some important properties shared by all 3×3 symmetric matrices: First, notice that all the eigenvalues are real. Also, despite the fact that the characteristic equation has a multiple root (compare with the deficient situation in Example 4), the 3×3 symmetric matrix still has 3 linearly independent eigenvectors, namely,

$$\mathbf{v}_1 = \begin{bmatrix} 1 \\ -2 \\ 0 \end{bmatrix}, \quad \mathbf{v}_2 = \begin{bmatrix} 4 \\ 2 \\ -5 \end{bmatrix}, \quad \text{and} \quad \mathbf{v}_3 = \begin{bmatrix} 2 \\ 1 \\ 2 \end{bmatrix}.$$

(Check the linearly independence using the determinant test.) Even more is true. Observe that

$$\mathbf{v}_1 \cdot \mathbf{v}_2 = 0, \quad \mathbf{v}_1 \cdot \mathbf{v}_3 = 0, \quad \text{and} \quad \mathbf{v}_2 \cdot \mathbf{v}_3 = 0.$$

That is, $\mathbf{v}_1$, $\mathbf{v}_2$, and $\mathbf{v}_3$ are pairwise orthogonal vectors. We arranged the orthogonality of $\mathbf{v}_1$ and $\mathbf{v}_2$ but the orthogonality of $\mathbf{v}_3$ to both of $\mathbf{v}_1$ and $\mathbf{v}_2$ appears to have come free of charge. The general properties just highlighted hold for symmetric matrices of any size:

Theorem 5 *If A is an $n \times n$ symmetric matrix, then*
(a) all its eigenvalues are real;
(b) eigenvectors corresponding to distinct eigenvalues are mutually orthogonal; and
(c) there are always n linearly independent eigenvectors which can be chosen to be real and pairwise orthogonal.

By Theorem 5 any symmetric matrix has simple structure (is diagonalizable).

One final comment is in order about Example 5 and its eigenvectors $\mathbf{v}_1$ and $\mathbf{v}_2$ that belong to the same eigenvalue ($\lambda_1 = \lambda_2 = -1$). You already know that a nonzero multiple of any eigenvector is again an eigenvector. Since $\mathbf{v}_1$ and $\mathbf{v}_2$ are linearly independent eigenvectors belonging to the *same* eigenvalue, even more is true: Any *nontrivial* linear combination of the eigenvectors $\mathbf{v}_1$ and $\mathbf{v}_2$ is again an eigenvector belonging to that eigenvalue. In fact, it is always true that a *nontrivial* linear combination of linearly independent eigenvectors that belong to the same eigenvalue is again an eigenvector belonging that eigenvalue. (See Problem 17.) When results about eigenvalue problems are recorded it is assume that you know this fact.

Symmetric Matrices and Orthogonal Projections

There is a more geometric way of thinking about the content of Theorem 5 which can be illustrated in the context of Example 5. The orthogonal eigenvectors $\mathbf{v}_1 = \langle 1, -2, 0 \rangle$ and $\mathbf{v}_2 = \langle 4, 2, -5 \rangle$ span a plane Π that contains all the eigenvectors corresponding to the eigenvalues $\lambda_1 = \lambda_2 = -1$. The eigenvector $\mathbf{v}_3 = \langle 2, 1, 2 \rangle$ spans a line L that is orthogonal to the plane Π and contains all the eigenvectors corresponding to the eigenvalue $\lambda_3 = 8$. Since the vectors $\mathbf{v}_1$, $\mathbf{v}_2$ and $\mathbf{v}_3$ are mutually orthogonal, they are linearly independent and span 3-space (just like $\mathbf{i}$, $\mathbf{j}$ and $\mathbf{k}$). Consequently, any vector $\mathbf{v}$ in $\mathbb{R}^3$ can be uniquely expressed as $\mathbf{v} = c_1 \mathbf{v}_1 + c_2 \mathbf{v}_2 + c_3 \mathbf{v}_3$. Now $T(\mathbf{v}) = c_1 \mathbf{v}_1 + c_2 \mathbf{v}_2$ defines a linear transformation that projects each vector in $\mathbb{R}^3$ orthogonally onto Π and $U(\mathbf{v}) = c_3 \mathbf{v}_3$ defines a linear transformation that projects each vector in $\mathbb{R}^3$ orthogonally onto L, as illustrated in the following figure.

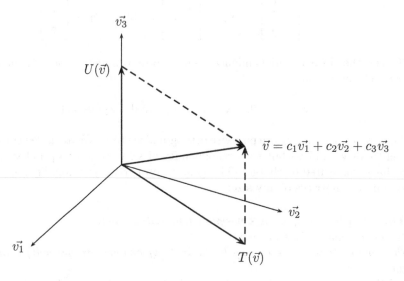

Figure 7.1: The transformations T and U

The matrix P_1 of T and P_3 of U are both orthogonal projection matrices with the properties

$$\mathbf{v} = c_1\mathbf{v}_1 + c_2\mathbf{v}_2 + c_3\mathbf{v}_3 \implies P_1\mathbf{v} = c_1\mathbf{v}_1 + c_2\mathbf{v}_2, \quad P_3\mathbf{v} = c_3\mathbf{v}_3$$

$$\mathbf{v} = P_1\mathbf{v} + P_3\mathbf{v}, \quad P_1\mathbf{v} \text{ lies in } \Pi, \quad P_3\mathbf{v} \text{ lies in } L$$

for each vector $\mathbf{v}$ in $\mathbb{R}^3$. Moreover,

$$\begin{aligned}
A\mathbf{v} &= A\left(c_1\mathbf{v}_1 + c_2\mathbf{v}_2 + c_3\mathbf{v}_3\right) \\
&= -c_1\mathbf{v}_1 - c_2\mathbf{v}_2 + 8c_3\mathbf{v}_3 = -P_1\mathbf{v} + 8P_3\mathbf{v} \\
&= \lambda_1 P_1\mathbf{v} + \lambda_3 P_3\mathbf{v} = \left(\lambda_1 P_1 + \lambda_3 P_3\right)\mathbf{v}.
\end{aligned}$$

Hence,

$$A = \lambda_1 P_1 + \lambda_3 P_3.$$

That is, A can be decomposed into a linear combination of orthogonal projection matrices (weighted the distinct eigenvalues of the matrix). Moreover the fact that $P_1\mathbf{v}$ lies in Π, and $P_3\mathbf{v}$ lies in L implies that $P_1 P_3 = P_3 P_1 = 0$.

The same type decomposition is true for a general symmetric matrix A. If A has *distinct* eigenvalues $\lambda_1, \lambda_2, ..., \lambda_m$ and if

$$\mathcal{E}_k = \{\mathbf{v} : A\mathbf{v} = \lambda_k\mathbf{v}\}$$

is the so-called **eigenspace** of the eigenvalue λ_k, then there are orthogonal projection matrices $P_1, P_2, ..., P_m$ such that

$$I = P_1 + P_2 + \cdots + P_m,$$
$$P_j P_k = 0 \text{ for } j \neq k,$$
$$A = \lambda_1 P_1 + \lambda_2 P_2 + \cdots + \lambda_m P_m.$$

Thus every symmetric matrix is a linear combination of orthogonal projection matrices.

A Note on Factoring Polynomials

Factoring cubic or higher order polynomials in normally challenging. Here is a hint for factoring characteristic polynomials. Try the following special case of the *rational roots theorem:* The only *possibilities* for integer roots of the polynomial

$$\lambda^n + a_{n-1}\lambda^{n-1} + \cdots + a_1\lambda + a_0$$

all of whose coefficients are integers are among the divisors of a_0. To take advantage of the rational roots theorem you must know the *factor theorem:* r is a root (also called a zero) of a polynomial $p(\lambda)$ if and only if $\lambda - r$ is a factor of the polynomial $p(\lambda)$.

7.5   Suggested Problems

In Problems 1-14 solve the eigenvalue problem for the given matrix. If the matrix is symmetric find a set of pairwise orthogonal eigenvectors. Check your answers.

1. $\begin{bmatrix} 5 & -1 \\ 3 & 1 \end{bmatrix}$ 2. $\begin{bmatrix} 1 & 1 \\ 1 & 3 \end{bmatrix}$

3. $\begin{bmatrix} 1 & -4 \\ 4 & -7 \end{bmatrix}$ 4. $\begin{bmatrix} 3 & -4 \\ 1 & -1 \end{bmatrix}$

5. $\begin{bmatrix} 3 & -2 \\ 4 & -1 \end{bmatrix}$ 6. $\begin{bmatrix} 2 & 5 \\ -1 & -2 \end{bmatrix}$

7. $\begin{bmatrix} 1 & -1 & 4 \\ 3 & 2 & -1 \\ 2 & 1 & -1 \end{bmatrix}$ 8. $\begin{bmatrix} 0 & -1 & 4 \\ 3 & 1 & -1 \\ 2 & 1 & -2 \end{bmatrix}$

9. $\begin{bmatrix} 1 & 0 & 0 \\ 2 & 1 & -2 \\ 3 & 2 & 1 \end{bmatrix}$ 10. $\begin{bmatrix} 1 & 0 & 0 \\ -4 & 1 & 0 \\ 3 & 6 & 2 \end{bmatrix}$

11. $\begin{bmatrix} 4 & 2 & 4 \\ 2 & 1 & 2 \\ 4 & 2 & 4 \end{bmatrix}$ 12. $\begin{bmatrix} 2 & 2 & 4 \\ 2 & -1 & 2 \\ 4 & 2 & 2 \end{bmatrix}$

13. $\begin{bmatrix} 0 & 2 & -1 \\ 2 & 5 & -6 \\ -1 & -6 & 8 \end{bmatrix}$ 14. $\begin{bmatrix} -3 & 2 & -1 \\ 2 & 2 & -6 \\ -1 & -6 & 5 \end{bmatrix}$

15. Show that any nonzero multiple of an eigenvector is again an eigenvector. That is, if $A\mathbf{v} = \lambda\mathbf{v}$ and $\mathbf{v} \neq \mathbf{0}$, then $\mathbf{w} = c\mathbf{v}$ for $c \neq 0$ also is an eigenvector of A.

16. Consider the equation $A\mathbf{v} = \lambda\mathbf{v}$.

    (a) For *any* value of λ, explain briefly why the equation $A\mathbf{v} = \lambda\mathbf{v}$ always has the trivial solution $\mathbf{v} = \mathbf{0}$.

    (b) Part of the definition of an eigenvalue is that there is a *nonzero* vector $\mathbf{v}$ such that $A\mathbf{v} = \lambda\mathbf{v}$. Students usually remember the equation $A\mathbf{v} = \lambda\mathbf{v}$ but often forget that $\mathbf{v} \neq \mathbf{0}$ is important. Use (a) to explain why the condition $\mathbf{v} \neq \mathbf{0}$ is important in the definition of an eigenvalue.

17. Let $\mathbf{v}$ and $\mathbf{w}$ be linearly independent eigenvectors that correspond to the same eigenvalue λ. Show that $c\mathbf{v} + d\mathbf{w}$ is also an eigenvector corresponding to the eigenvalue λ, provided that the constants c and d are not both zero. Interpret this result geometrically.

18. In Problem 17 take $\mathbf{v}_1 = \mathbf{v}$ and $\mathbf{v}_2 = c\mathbf{v} + \mathbf{w}$. Show how to choose c so that $\mathbf{v}_1$ and $\mathbf{v}_2$ are orthogonal. Consequently, any pair of linearly independent eigenvectors belonging to the same eigenvalue can be replaced by a pair of orthogonal eigenvectors belonging to the given eigenvalue.

19. Find a simple expression for $A^4\mathbf{v}$ in terms of $\mathbf{v}$ and λ if $\mathbf{v}$ and λ are an eigenvector-eigenvalue pair for the matrix A.

20. Let A be a matrix with eigenvector-eigenvalue pair $\mathbf{v}$ and λ. Find a simple expression for $\left(A^3 + 2A^2 - A + 3I\right)\mathbf{v}$ in terms $\mathbf{v}$ and λ.

21. Prove: If P is a projection matrix and λ is an eigenvalue of P, then $\lambda = 0$ or $\lambda = 1$. *Hint.* Let $\mathbf{v}$ be a corresponding eigenvector. Compare $P\mathbf{v}$ and $P^2\mathbf{v}$.

22. Prove: If R is a matrix, $R^2 = I$, and λ is an eigenvalue of R, then $\lambda = 1$ or $\lambda = -1$. *Hint.* See the hint of the previous problem.

23. Let A be the standard matrix of the linear transformation $T : \mathbb{R}^2 \to \mathbb{R}^2$ that rotates each vector counterclockwise by the angle θ with $0 \le \theta < 2\pi$.

    (a) If $\theta = 0$ use geometric arguments to find the eigenvalues and eigenvectors of A.

    (b) If $\theta = \pi$ use geometric arguments to find the eigenvalues and eigenvectors of A.

    (c) If $\theta \ne 0$ or π use geometric arguments to explain, without any calculations, why the eigenvalues and corresponding eigenvectors must be non-real.

24. Let A be the standard matrix in Problem 23. Find A and solve the eigenvalue problem for this matrix to confirm by algebraic means the results of Problem 23.

25. Let A be a symmetric matrix so that $A\mathbf{x} \cdot \mathbf{y} = \mathbf{x} \cdot A\mathbf{y}$ where $\cdot$ is the *complex* dot product.

    (a) Show that any eigenvalue λ of A must be *real*. *Hint.* If $A\mathbf{v} = \lambda\mathbf{v}$ with $\mathbf{v} \ne \mathbf{0}$ apply the dot product relation with $\mathbf{x} = \mathbf{y} = \mathbf{v}$.

    (b) Show that eigenvectors belonging to *distinct* eigenvalues are orthogonal. *Hint.* If $A\mathbf{v} = \lambda\mathbf{v}$ with $\mathbf{v} \ne \mathbf{0}$, $A\mathbf{w} = \mu\mathbf{w}$ with $\mathbf{w} \ne \mathbf{0}$, and $\lambda \ne \mu$ apply the dot product relation with $\mathbf{x} = \mathbf{v}$ and with $\mathbf{y} = \mathbf{w}$.

Problems 17, 18, and 25 show that the hard part of Theorem 5 is proving that there always is a full set of n linearly independent eigenvectors for an $n \times n$ symmetric matrix.

26.   *(On Diagonalizability)* The 2×2 matrix A in Example 2 has simple structure. To get a hint about why the terminology *diagonalizable* is used in
this context let

$$P = [\mathbf{v}_1, \mathbf{v}_2] = \begin{bmatrix} 1 & 1 \\ -2 & 2 \end{bmatrix} \qquad D = \begin{bmatrix} \lambda_1 & 0 \\ 0 & \lambda_2 \end{bmatrix} = \begin{bmatrix} -1 & 0 \\ 0 & 3 \end{bmatrix}$$

Verify that

$$AP = PD \qquad \text{equivalently} \qquad P^{-1}AP = D$$

a diagonal matrix. (The essential content of this result, as explained in a
course in linear algebra, is that the linear transformation associated with
the matrix A is a simple diagonal matrix when the underlying coordinate
system is determined by the eigenvectors of the matrix.)

27.   *(Formulas for the Characteristic Equation when $n = 2$ and $n = 3$)* For
any $n \times n$ matrix A the trace of A, denoted $\mathrm{Tr}\,(A)$, is the sum of its main
diagonal entries.

(a) Show that a 2×2 matrix A has characteristic equation

$$\lambda^2 - \mathrm{Tr}\,(A)\,\lambda + \det(A) = 0$$

(b) For a 3×3 matrix A whose element in row i and column j is a_{ij}
define

$$E(A) = \begin{vmatrix} a_{22} & a_{23} \\ a_{32} & a_{33} \end{vmatrix} + \begin{vmatrix} a_{11} & a_{13} \\ a_{31} & a_{33} \end{vmatrix} + \begin{vmatrix} a_{11} & a_{12} \\ a_{21} & a_{22} \end{vmatrix}$$

How can you obtain $E(A)$ from the 3×3 matrix A by a crossing
out of rows and columns procedure? Show that A has characteristic
equation

$$-\lambda^3 + \mathrm{Tr}\,(A)\,\lambda^2 - E(A)\,\lambda + \det(A) = 0$$

28.   Why is $\mathcal{E}_k = \{\mathbf{v} : A\mathbf{v} = \lambda_k \mathbf{v}\}$ called an eigenspace of the eigenvalue λ_k?

29.   Let $\mathbf{v} = c_1 \mathbf{v}_1 + c_2 \mathbf{v}_2 + c_3 \mathbf{v}_3$, $T(\mathbf{v}) = c_1 \mathbf{v}_1 + c_2 \mathbf{v}_2$ and $U(\mathbf{v}) = c_3 \mathbf{v}_3$ be
as in the discussion of Example 5 related to symmetric matrices. Find
the matrix P_1 of T and the matrix P_3 of U relative to the standard bases
and verify that they satisfy $I = P_1 + P_3$, $A = \lambda_1 P_1 + \lambda_3 P_3$, and that
$P_1 P_3 = 0$. *Hint.* First show that $c_1 = (\mathbf{v} \cdot \mathbf{v}_1) / |\mathbf{v}_1|^2$ and similarly for the
other coefficients.

30.   Let A be the matrix in Example 5.

(a) Expand $\det(A - \lambda I)$, without attempting to factor it, to express the
characteristic equation of A as $\lambda^3 - 6\lambda^2 - 15\lambda - 8 = 0$.

(b) What are the only *possibilities* for integer roots of this equation? Are
any of the possibilities actually roots?

(c) Use this fact and (b) to factor the characteristic equation for A.

Lesson 8

Catch Up and Review

This is a self-study lesson. Now is the time to go back and clear up any points of confusion in Lessons 1–7. Get help if you need it. Ask your instructor, your GTA, and your fellow classmates for help. Don't forget the MLC! Review the goals given in Lessons 1–7. Have you achieved all of them? Have you solved *all* the assigned problems? If not, finish the unsolved problems from earlier lessons before you start on the additional problems below. Also, be sure that you really understand how you solved each problem. Could you clearly explain how to solve the problem to a confused classmate? Good luck with your review. A little extra effort here will really pay off.

Review Problems

1. Review all previously assigned problems on homeworks, quizzes, and tests!

2. Do the following:

   (a) Find the real and imaginary parts of the complex number $z = \dfrac{2-i}{1+i}$.

   (b) Describe the set of points in the complex plane satisfying the inequality $|z + i| \le 1$.

   (c) Find the domain of the function $f(z) = \dfrac{z+1}{\operatorname{Re}(z) + \operatorname{Im}(z)}$.

3. Find the eigenvalues and eigenvectors of the matrices.

   (a)
$$A = \begin{bmatrix} 1 & 2 \\ 3 & -2 \end{bmatrix}$$

   (b)
$$B = \begin{bmatrix} 1 & -2 \\ 3 & -2 \end{bmatrix}$$

4. Are the vectors $\mathbf{u} = \langle 1, 2, -2 \rangle$, $\mathbf{v} = \langle 3, 1, 0 \rangle$, $\mathbf{w} = \langle 2, -1, 1 \rangle$ linearly independent?

5. Solve the system of equations
$$\begin{cases} 2x + 3y & = -6 \\ -x + 2y & = 1 \end{cases}$$

   by the Gaussian (systematic) elimination using an augmented matrix.

6. Use an augmented matrix and systematic elimination of unknowns to find the general solution of the system
$$\begin{cases} x_1 - 2x_2 - x_3 + 3x_4 & = & 0 \\ -2x_1 + 4x_2 + 5x_3 - 5x_4 & = & 3 \\ 3x_1 - 6x_2 - 6x_3 + 8x_4 & = & -3 \end{cases}$$

7. Let A be the 2×2 matrix
$$A = \begin{bmatrix} 7 & 6 \\ 6 & -2 \end{bmatrix}$$

   (a) Find the eigenvalues of A.
   (b) Find all eigenvectors of A.
   (c) Is the matrix A diagonalizable? Why or why not?

8. Let A be the 3×3 matrix
$$A = \begin{bmatrix} 2 & -5 & 1 \\ -6 & 0 & 10 \\ 3 & 10 & h \end{bmatrix}$$

   where h is a real number.

   (a) Find $\det A$.
   (b) For what values of h is the matrix invertible?

9. Suppose the matrices C and D have inverses given by

$$C^{-1} = \begin{bmatrix} 7 & 6 \\ 6 & -2 \end{bmatrix} \text{ and } D^{-1} = \begin{bmatrix} -1 & 6 \\ 2 & -2 \end{bmatrix}.$$

(a) Find C.

(b) Find $(DC)^{-1}$

(c) Find $(CD)^{-1}$

10. Let $\mathbb{F}$ be the vector space of all functions from $\mathbb{R}$ to $\mathbb{R}$. Let $T : \mathbb{F} \to \mathbb{R}^3$ be the mapping

$$T(f) = \begin{bmatrix} f(-1) \\ f(0) \\ f(1) \end{bmatrix}.$$

Is T a linear transformation? Justify your answer.

11. Let A be an $n \times n$ matrix and suppose that there is an $n \times n$ matrix C so that $CA = I$, where I is the identity matrix.

(a) Show that the matrix equation $A\mathbf{x} = \mathbf{0}$ has only the trivial solution.

(b) Next explain why the result of part (a) implies that A can be reduced to the identity matrix I by a repeated application of row operations.

(c) Finally use the result of part (b) to show that A is an invertible matrix.

12. Find the standard matrix of the linear transformation $T : \mathbb{R}^2 \to \mathbb{R}^2$ that first performs a vertical shear mapping $\mathbf{e}_1$ to $\mathbf{e}_1 - 3\mathbf{e}_2$ and leaving $\mathbf{e}_2$ unchanged and then reflects the result about the x_2-axis.

13. Let $T : \mathbb{R}^2 \to \mathbb{R}^3$ be a linear transformation such that

$$T(\mathbf{u}) = \begin{bmatrix} 1 \\ -1 \\ 3 \end{bmatrix} \text{ and } T(\mathbf{v}) = \begin{bmatrix} 0 \\ 2 \\ -3 \end{bmatrix}. \text{ Find } T(2\mathbf{u} - \mathbf{v}).$$

14. Give a geometric description of the linear transformation associated with the matrix

$$A = \begin{bmatrix} 0 & 1 \\ 1 & 0 \\ 2 & 1 \end{bmatrix}.$$

15. Let T_A and T_B be the linear transformations with the standard matrices

$$A = \begin{bmatrix} 0 & 3 & 1 \\ 2 & 2 & 1 \end{bmatrix} \text{ and } B = \begin{bmatrix} 0 & 3 \\ 2 & 1 \\ 5 & 1 \end{bmatrix}.$$

Find the matrix associated with the composition $T_A \circ T_B$ (in which T_B acts first and T_A acts second on any input vector).

16. Let A be the 1×3 matrix $[2 \ 3 \ -1]$. Compute the products AA^T and $A^T A$.

17. Let A be an invertible $n \times n$ matrix. Prove that the linear transformation T_A associated with A must be one-to-one and onto.

18. Find the inverse of the matrix

$$A = \begin{bmatrix} 2 & 6 \\ 3 & 1 \end{bmatrix}$$

by row reducing the augmented matrix $[A|I]$, where I is the identity matrix.

19. Determine whether the functions $f_0(x) = 1$, $f_1(x) = e^{2x}$, and $f_2(x) = e^{3x}$ are linearly independent or dependent.

20. Determine whether the vectors

$$\mathbf{v}_1 = \langle 1, 1, 2 \rangle, \ \mathbf{v}_2 = \langle 2, -1, 1 \rangle, \ \mathbf{v}_3 = \langle -4, 5, 1 \rangle$$

are linearly independent or dependent. If they are dependent, exhibit a nontrivial linear combination of the vectors with sum $\mathbf{0}$.

21. Let A be a symmetric matrix.

   (a) Show that the eigenvalues of A must be real. *Hint.* Consider the expression $(A\mathbf{v}) \cdot \bar{\mathbf{v}}$, where the bar stands for complex conjugation.

   (b) Show that the eigenvectors corresponding to distinct eigenvalues must the orthogonal to each other.

   (c) Let $\mathbf{v}$ be an eigenvector of A and let $\mathbf{w}$ be perpendicular to $\mathbf{v}$. Show that $A\mathbf{w}$ is also perpendicular to $\mathbf{v}$.

22. Evaluate the determinant

$$\begin{vmatrix} 1 & 2 & 2 & 1 \\ -1 & 2 & -2 & 1 \\ 1 & -2 & 2 & -1 \\ 2 & 1 & 2 & 1 \end{vmatrix}.$$

Part III

Series Methods

Part III

Series Methods

Lesson 9

Taylor Polynomial Approximation

9.1 Goals

- Describe and understand the general qualitative properties of Taylor polynomial approximations

- Find Taylor polynomials and use them in approximation calculations

- Use the error estimate for Taylor polynomial approximation to approximate a given function at a specific point or on a given interval to within a prescribed error

9.2 Overview and a Glance Ahead

Lesson 9 sets the stage for our study of infinite series. The primary emphasis will be on power series and related polynomial approximations, called Taylor polynomials.

The group project on special limits in Appendix A.1 is usually covered in your recitation section as Lessons 9 and 10 are covered in lecture. In the project you develop some numerical and graphical evidence in support of some special limits that you will be using from now on.

In everyday language, an infinite series is a sum with an infinite number of terms. Infinite series arose early in the development of calculus. Solutions to a great many mathematical and physical problems are represented as sums of infinite series. For example, the shape of a vibrating string can be expressed as an infinite series involving sines and cosines. Such series are called Fourier series. In the final analysis, all numerical calculations reduce to additions, subtractions, multiplications, and divisions. In particular, this is true for the evaluation of complicated functions like $f(x) = \sin x$, $\cos x$, e^x, $\ln x$, and $\sqrt{x}$. (If you do

119

not regard these functions as complicated, turn off your calculator or computer and try to evaluate any one of these functions to two decimals when $x = 7$.) To evaluate these and other functions, we approximate $f(x)$ by a function $p(x)$ which can be evaluated by a finite number of the four basic algebraic operations. The simplest and most widely used approximations $p(x)$ are polynomials. Then

$$p(x) = a_0 + a_1 x + a_2 x^2 + \cdots + a_n x^n.$$

For many complicated functions, there are polynomials of higher and higher degree that approximate the given function with increasing accuracy. This suggests that perhaps a polynomial-like expression with infinitely many terms

$$a_0 + a_1 x + a_2 x^2 + \cdots + a_n x^n + \cdots$$

might exactly equal a function such as $f(x) = \sin x$, $\cos x$, e^x, $\ln x$, and $\sqrt{x}$. The expression above is called a **power series** and the possibility of expressing complicated functions by power series and using those expansions to approximate the functions to any desired degree of precision is the central theme of the next several lessons.

In Lesson 11 we shall confirm the following power series expansions:

$$
\begin{aligned}
e^x &= \sum_{n=0}^{\infty} \frac{x^n}{n!} = 1 + x + \frac{x^2}{2!} + \frac{x^3}{3!} + \frac{x^4}{4!} + \cdots + \frac{x^n}{n!} + \cdots, \\
\sin x &= \sum_{n=0}^{\infty} \frac{(-1)^n x^{2n+1}}{(2n+1)!} = x - \frac{x^3}{3!} + \frac{x^5}{5!} - \frac{x^7}{7!} + - \cdots, \\
\cos x &= \sum_{n=0}^{\infty} \frac{(-1)^n x^{2n}}{(2n)!} = 1 - \frac{x^2}{2!} + \frac{x^4}{4!} - \frac{x^6}{6!} + - \cdots.
\end{aligned}
$$

To be sure, it is not obvious that e^x, $\sin x$, and $\cos x$ are equal to the given infinite series. Nevertheless, the Taylor polynomial approximations you will study in this lesson will enable you to find such power series expansions with relative ease.

Our focus will be on power series but much of what we shall learn can be applied to other useful series, like the Fourier series mentioned earlier.

9.3   Taylor Polynomials

There are several strategies for approximating a given function $f(x)$ by a polynomial. One approach, that leads to Taylor polynomial approximations, is to choose polynomials that match $f(x)$ and more and more of its derivatives at a particular point, say the point $x = a$, called the **base point**. Typically the Taylor polynomials approximate the function rather well near $x = a$ and the accuracy increases as the number of derivatives matched goes up. We shall deal mainly with the case $a = 0$. Thus, for the time being, the Taylor polynomials match the function and its successive derivatives at the base point 0.

Let $f(x)$ be a function defined on an open interval containing 0 and with as many derivatives as we need. We want to determine a polynomial $P(x)$ that matches $f(x)$ and several of its derivatives at $x = 0$. How do we find such a polynomial? The key is to notice a simple relationship between the coefficients of a polynomial in x and its derivatives at 0. The case of a polynomial of degree 4 will make the pattern clear:

$$
\begin{aligned}
P(x) &= a_0 + a_1 x + a_2 x^2 + a_3 x^3 + a_4 x^4, & P(0) &= a_0, \\
P'(x) &= a_1 + 2a_2 x + 3a_3 x^2 + 4a_4 x^3, & P'(0) &= a_1, \\
P''(x) &= 2a_2 + 3 \cdot 2a_3 x + 4 \cdot 3a_4 x^2, & P''(0) &= 2a_2, \\
P'''(x) &= 3 \cdot 2a_3 + 4 \cdot 3 \cdot 2a_4 x, & P'''(0) &= 3 \cdot 2a_3, \\
P^{(4)}(x) &= 4 \cdot 3 \cdot 2a_4, & P^{(4)}(0) &= 4 \cdot 3 \cdot 2a_4.
\end{aligned}
$$

Therefore,

$$
a_0 = P(0), \quad a_1 = P'(0), \quad a_2 = \frac{P''(0)}{2}, \quad a_3 = \frac{P'''(0)}{3!}, \quad a_4 = \frac{P^{(4)}(0)}{4!}.
$$

Since $0! = 1$, $1! = 1$, and $2! = 2$,

$$
a_k = \frac{P^{(k)}(0)}{k!} \qquad k = 0, 1, 2, 3, 4.
$$

It follows that

$$
P(x) = P(0) + P'(0) x + \frac{P''(0)}{2} x^2 + \frac{P'''(0)}{3!} x^3 + \frac{P^{(4)}(0)}{4!} x^4.
$$

Thus, any polynomial of degree 4 is *uniquely determined* by $P(0)$ and its first four derivatives at 0.

Example 1 *Find the polynomial of degree* 4 *with*

$$
P(0) = 6, \quad P'(0) = -4, \quad P''(0) = 12, \quad P'''(0) = 30, \quad P^{(4)}(0) = 72.
$$

Solution. The polynomial is

$$
\begin{aligned}
P(x) &= P(0) + P'(0) x + \frac{P''(0)}{2} x^2 + \frac{P'''(0)}{3!} x^3 + \frac{P^{(4)}(0)}{4!} x^4 \\
&= 6 - 4x + \frac{12}{2} x^2 + \frac{30}{3!} x^3 + \frac{72}{4!} x^4 = 6 - 4x + 6x^2 + 5x^3 + 3x^4. \quad \square
\end{aligned}
$$

The reasoning used for a polynomial of degree $n = 4$ extends to any degree and yields

---

The coefficients a_0, a_1, ..., a_n of any polynomial
$$P(x) = a_0 + a_1 x + a_2 x^2 + \cdots + a_n x^n$$
of degree n satisfy
$$a_k = \frac{P^{(k)}(0)}{k!} \qquad k = 0, 1, ..., n.$$
Consequently, $P(x)$ can be expressed as
$$P(x) = \sum_{k=0}^{n} \frac{P^{(k)}(0)}{k!} x^k$$
$$= P(0) + P'(0)x + \frac{P''(0)}{2!}x^2 + \cdots + \frac{P^{(n)}(0)}{n!}x^n.$$

Example 2 *A ball is thrown vertically upward with speed 96 ft/sec from a roof top 42 feet above the ground. If the ball is subject only to the force of gravity (with gravitational acceleration 32 ft/sec^2) its position s at time t is a polynomial of degree 2 in t. Assume $t = 0$ is the time the ball is thrown, that ground level is $s = 0$, and that the s-axis is positive upward. Find s.*

Solution. Since $s(0) = 42$, $s'(0) = 96$, and $s''(0) = -32$ the position at any time is
$$s(t) = s(0) + s'(0)t + \frac{s''(0)}{2}t^2 = 42 + 96t - 16t^2. \quad \square$$

Remember the basic idea behind Taylor polynomials (about 0): successive polynomials match more and more derivatives of a given function at $x = 0$. An immediate consequence of the foregoing representation of polynomials is:

Assume $f(x)$ has derivatives up to order n at $x = 0$.
Then there is a unique polynomial $T_n(x)$ of degree $\leq n$ that satisfies
$$T_n(0) = f(0), \quad T_n'(0) = f'(0), ..., \quad T_n^{(n)}(0) = f^{(n)}(0).$$
It is given by
$$T_n(x) = \sum_{k=0}^{n} \frac{f^{(k)}(0)}{k!} x^k$$
$$= f(0) + f'(0)x + \frac{f''(0)}{2}x^2 + \cdots + \frac{f^{(n)}(0)}{n!}x^n.$$

The polynomial $T_n(x)$ is called the **nth Taylor polynomial of f about 0**. Compare the two boxed results to see that an nth degree polynomial is its own nth Taylor polynomial.

Example 3 *Find and graph the Taylor Polynomials (about 0) $T_1(x)$, $T_2(x)$, and $T_3(x)$ for $f(x) = \ln(1+x)$ and compare the graphs of these functions.*

Solution. Since $f'(x) = (1+x)^{-1}$, $f''(x) = -(1+x)^{-2}$, and $f'''(x) = 2(1+x)^{-3}$, we have $f(0) = 0$, $f'(0) = 1$, $f''(0) = -1$, $f'''(0) = 2$ and

$$\begin{aligned} T_1(x) &= f(0) + f'(0)x = x \\ T_2(x) &= f(0) + f'(0)x + \frac{f''(0)}{2}x^2 = x - \frac{1}{2}x^2 \\ T_3(x) &= f(0) + f'(0)x + \frac{f''(0)}{2}x^2 + \frac{f'''(0)}{3!}x^3 = x - \frac{1}{2}x^2 + \frac{1}{3}x^3. \end{aligned}$$

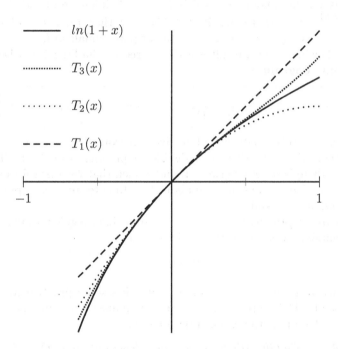

Figure 9.1: Polynomial approximations of $y = ln(1+x)$ near $x = 0$

Apparently $T_1(x)$, $T_2(x)$, and $T_3(x)$ provide rather good approximations to $\ln(1+x)$ for x near zero. The length of the interval about 0 over which the approximations seem quite good increases as the degree of the Taylor polynomial increases. Notice however that all three approximations deviate substantially from $\ln(1+x)$ for values of x "far" from 0. □

9.4 Error in Taylor Polynomial Approximation

Since $T_n(x)$ matches more and more derivatives of $f(x)$ at $x = 0$, it is reasonable to expect that $T_n(x)$ should approximate $f(x)$ reasonably well near $x = 0$. For example, the graphs of $T_2(x)$ and $f(x)$ have the same slope, the same bending (curvature), and pass through the same point when $x = 0$. So the graphs should be much the same near $x = 0$. To determine how close the graphs are, in other words how well the Taylor polynomial approximates the function, we introduce the **error (remainder)**

$$R_n(x) = f(x) - T_n(x).$$

Since $T_n(x)$ and $f(x)$ agree together with their first n derivatives at 0, it should seem reasonable that the error $R_n(x) = f(x) - T_n(x)$ should depend in some way on the amount by which $f^{(n+1)}(x)$ differs from $T_n^{(n+1)}(x) = 0$. (Why is $T_n^{(n+1)}(x) = 0$?) In fact, if $f^{(n+1)}(x) = 0$, then $f(x)$ is a polynomial of degree n and is exactly equal to its nth Taylor polynomial; so $R_n(x) = 0$ in this case. The following general result was discovered by the French mathematician **Joseph Louis Lagrange**:

$$\boxed{R_n(x) = f^{(n+1)}(c) \frac{x^{n+1}}{(n+1)!} \qquad \text{for some } c \text{ between } 0 \text{ and } x.}$$

A nice feature of this result is that it gives an exact formula for the error of approximation. However, there is a significant practical drawback. The error formula says there is some c between 0 and x such that the error formula holds but it does not give any information about how to determine c. In practice this determination is impossible.

In order to get practical error estimates from Lagrange's formula, we must find a computable upper estimate on the size of

$$\left| f^{(n+1)}(c) \right|$$

no matter where c lies between 0 and x. It takes some practice to find such upper bounds for $\left| f^{(n+1)}(c) \right|$. The next example illustrates how such an upper bound can be found for the exponential function.

Example 4 *(a) Find the nth degree Taylor polynomial for $f(x) = e^x$ about $x = 0$. (b) What degree Taylor polynomial for e^x (about 0) is needed to approximate e^x for $-1 \le x \le 1$ to within an error of $10^{-4} = 0.0001$?*

Solution. (a) Since $f(x) = e^x$, $f'(x) = e^x$, $f''(x) = e^x$, ... and in general $f^{(n)}(x) = e^x$ for all n,

$$f(0) = 1, \ f'(0) = 1, \ f''(0) = 1, \ f'''(0) = 1, \ ...$$

and the successive Taylor polynomials of e^x are

$$
\begin{aligned}
T_0(x) &= f(0) = 1, \\
T_1(x) &= f(0) + f'(0)x = 1 + x, \\
T_2(x) &= f(0) + f'(0)x + \frac{f''(0)}{2!}x^2 = 1 + x + \frac{1}{2}x^2, \\
T_3(x) &= f(0) + f'(0)x + \frac{f''(0)}{2!}x^2 + \frac{f'''(0)}{3!}x^3 = 1 + x + \frac{1}{2!}x^2 + \frac{1}{3!}x^3,
\end{aligned}
$$

and, in general,

$$T_n(x) = \sum_{k=0}^{n} \frac{f^{(k)}(0)}{k!} x^k = \sum_{k=0}^{n} \frac{1}{k!} x^k$$

$$= 1 + x + \frac{1}{2!}x^2 + \frac{1}{3!}x^3 + \cdots + \frac{1}{n!}x^n.$$

(b) Since $f^{(n+1)}(x) = e^x$ for all x and all n, $\left|f^{(n+1)}(c)\right| = |e^c| = e^c$ and the Lagrange formula gives

$$|R_n(x)| \le e^c \frac{|x|^{n+1}}{(n+1)!} \qquad \text{for some } c \text{ between } 0 \text{ and } x.$$

In this example, the values of x all satisfy $-1 \le x \le 1$ and c is always between 0 and x. The following figure illustrates the situation.

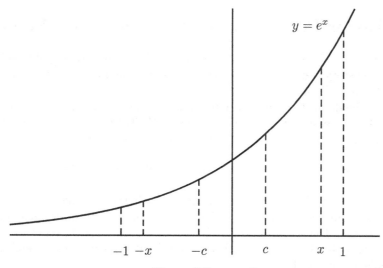

Figure 9.2: $y = e^x$

Since the natural exponential function is increasing, no matter what value of c actually occurs in Lagrange's error formula, $e^c \le e^1 = e$ for all x with $-1 \le x \le 1$. With this upper bound for e^c we obtain

$$|R_n(x)| \le e \frac{|x|^{n+1}}{(n+1)!} \le 3 \frac{1}{(n+1)!}$$

for all x in $[-1, 1]$. The required accuracy is attained for all x in $[-1, 1]$ if n is chosen so that

$$\frac{3}{(n+1)!} < 10^{-4} \Leftrightarrow (n+1)! > 30,000.$$

Since $7! = 5,040$ and $8! = 40,320$, we can take $n = 7$. Then the Taylor polynomial

$$T_7(x) = \sum_{k=0}^{7} x^k / k! = 1 + x + \frac{x^2}{2!} + \frac{x^3}{3!} + \frac{x^4}{4!} + \frac{x^5}{5!} + \frac{x^6}{6!} + \frac{x^7}{7!}$$

does the job. □

Remark. In the context of Example 4(b) we saw that the best possible upper estimate we could make for e^c was e. Then we replace e by the slightly larger value 3 for the convenience of the last calculation leading to $(n + 1)! > 30,000$. This is rather typical in practical error estimation in the sense that what is needed is a convenient upper bound that is reasonably close to the best possible upper bound. In the case of Taylor polynomial approximation, such upper bounds can often be inferred from a graph of an appropriate derivative of the function in question.

9.5   Taylor Polynomials with other Base Points

Up until now, we have approximated functions by their Taylor polynomials about 0. The story is essentially the same for approximations about any other base point, say a. So we shall be brief.

Let $f(x)$ be defined on an open interval containing the point a and assume that $f(x)$ has at least n derivatives at a. The **nth Taylor polynomial of f about a** is the unique polynomial of degree at most n that satisfies

$$T_n(a) = f(a), \quad T_n'(a) = f'(a), ..., \quad T_n^{(n)}(a) = f^{(n)}(a).$$

Thus, $T_0(x) = f(a)$ is constant and graphs as a horizontal line through the point $(a, f(a))$ and $T_1(x) = f(a) + f'(a)(x - a)$ is the linear (tangent line) approximation to f at a.

In dealing with a base point a different from 0, it is convenient to represent polynomials in powers of $x - a$:

$$P(x) = b_0 + b_1(x - a) + b_2(x - a)^2 + \cdots + b_n(x - a)^n$$

which is called a **polynomial in $x - a$**. (By expanding out and collecting terms, it also could be written as an ordinary polynomial in x.) Reasoning just as we did when a was 0, we find that

$$b_k = \frac{P^{(k)}(a)}{k!} \qquad \text{for} \quad k = 0, 1, ..., n,$$

and

$$P(x) = \sum_{k=0}^{n} \frac{P^{(k)}(a)}{k!} (x - a)^k.$$

It follows that the nth Taylor polynomial of f about a is

$$T_n\left(x\right) = \sum_{k=0}^{n} \frac{f^{(k)}\left(a\right)}{k!}\left(x-a\right)^k.$$

As before, the error $R_n\left(x\right) = f\left(x\right) - T_n\left(x\right)$ is given exactly by

$$R_n\left(x\right) = \frac{f^{(n+1)}\left(c\right)}{\left(n+1\right)!}\left(x-a\right)^{n+1} \qquad \text{for some } c \text{ between } a \text{ and } x.$$

and computable error estimates follow from the Lagrange formula by lines of reasoning similar to those used for base point 0.

Alternatively, the foregoing results can be obtained directly from the corresponding results for base point 0 by means of the chain rule and the change of variable $y = x - a$.

For historical reasons, some authors refer to Taylor polynomials about 0 as **Maclaurin polynomials**.

9.6   Suggested Problems

Find the Taylor polynomial $T_n(x)$ about a for the given function $f(x)$. Then graph $T_n(x)$ and $f(x)$ on the same screen centered horizontally at $x = a$.

1. $f(x) = \ln x$ $a = 1$ $n = 5$

2. $f(x) = \tan x$ $a = 0$ $n = 5$

3. $f(x) = \tan x$ $a = \pi/4$ $n = 4$

4. $f(x) = \sqrt{x}$ $a = 4$ $n = 3$

   Find the Taylor polynomial of order 5 about 0 for the given function $f(x)$ and use it to approximate $f(0.25)$.

5. $f(x) = \sin 2x$

6. $f(x) = \arctan x$

7. A car travels down a straight road. Let $s(t)$ be the position of the car at time t seconds. At time $t = 0$ the car has position $s(0) = 50$ ft, velocity $v(0) = -30$ ft/sec, and acceleration $a(0) = 16$ ft/sec^2. Find a Taylor polynomial that approximates $s(t)$ for t near 0.

8. The car in the preceding problem is known to accelerate gradually; specifically, its acceleration satisfies $|a'(t)| \leq 0.35$ (ft/sec^2)/sec for all t during the trip. Use the second Taylor polynomial of $s(t)$ to approximate the car's position at time $t = 1$ second. Give the best error estimate you can for your approximation of the car's position at time $t = 1$.

9. You need to approximate the position of the car in the preceding problem to within an error of at most 5 feet. Over what time interval $0 \leq t \leq T$ will the second Taylor polynomial of $s(t)$ estimate the car's position to within the required accuracy?

10. The motion of a pendulum bob with mass m is governed by the differential equation
$$mL\theta'' + mg\sin\theta = 0$$
where L is the length of the pendulum arm, g is the acceleration due to gravity, and θ, in radians, is the angle between the pendulum arm and the vertical. (Forces other than gravity have been neglected.) At time $t = 0$, the pendulum bob is set in motion with $\theta(0) = 1$ and $\theta'(0) = -3$. Assume that $L = 16$ ft and $g = 32$ ft/sec^2. Find the second degree Taylor polynomial that approximates the angular position $\theta(t)$ of the bob near $t = 0$. The Taylor polynomial provides an approximation to the solution of the nonlinear differential equation for the pendulum.

11. In the previous problem, find the third order Taylor polynomial that approximates $\theta(t)$ for t near 0.

12. For $f(x) = \sqrt{1+x}$ do the following.

   (a) Derive the Taylor polynomial approximation

$$\sqrt{1+x} \approx 1 + \frac{1}{2}x - \frac{1}{8}x^2.$$

   (b) Sketch the graph of the function and its Taylor polynomial for $-1 \leq x \leq 1$ on the same coordinate axes.

   (c) If the approximation is used for x in the interval $-0.6 \leq x \leq 0.6$, estimate the error as accurately as you can.

13. Suppose, in the previous problem, that you only need the approximation for x in the interval $0 \leq x \leq 0.6$. Estimate the error in the approximation as accurately as you can.

14. Find the Taylor polynomials about 0 for $f(x) = 1/(1-x)$ for $n = 1, 2, 3, 4$. Then find $T_n(x)$ for any positive integer n.

15. *(Taylor Polynomials for $\sin x$)*

   (a) Find the Taylor polynomials about 0 for $f(x) = \sin x$ for $n = 1, 2, 3, 4, 5, 6, 7, 8$.

   (b) Based on the pattern in part (a), if n is an *odd* number what is the relation between $T_n(x)$ and $T_{n+1}(x)$?

16. You want to approximate $\sin x$ for all x in $0 \leq x \leq \pi/2$ to within 0.0001 by a Taylor polynomial about 0. Based on the error estimates in the text, what Taylor polynomial should you use? *Hint.* For n odd, $T_n(x) = T_{n+1}(x) \Rightarrow R_n(x) = R_{n+1}(x)$. Why?

17. *(Taylor Polynomials for $\cos x$)*

   (a) Find the Taylor polynomials about 0 for $f(x) = \cos x$ for $n = 0, 1, 2, 3, 4, 5, 6, 7$.

   (b) Based on the pattern in part (a), if n is an *even* number what is the relation between $T_n(x)$ and $T_{n+1}(x)$?

18. *(Taylor Polynomials for $\ln x$ about 1)*

   (a) Find the Taylor polynomials about 1 for $f(x) = \ln x$ for $n = 1, 2, 3, 4, 5, 6$.

   (b) Find $T_n(x)$ for any positive integer n.

19. A central angle $\angle BOC$ with radian measure t is inscribed in circle with center O and radius 2. Let A be the area bounded by the chord $\overline{BC}$ and the arc BC. Use a Taylor polynomial to obtain the approximation $A \approx t^3/3$. *Hint.* First find an exact expression for A.

20. According to the theory of special relativity, an object with rest mass m_0 moving at speed v will have a relativistic mass $m = m_0/\sqrt{1 - v^2/c^2}$, where c is the speed of light in a vacuum. Physicists often approximate m by $m \approx m_0 + \frac{1}{2}m_0 (v/c)^2$. Justify this approximation.

21. *(Chain rule problem relating base point 0 and base point a.)* Let $f(x)$ be a function defined near the base point a and with as many derivatives as you wish. Introduce a new variable y by setting $x = a + y$. Then the composite function $g(y) = f(x)$ where $x = a + y$ is defined for all y near the base point 0 and has as many derivatives as you wish.

   (a) Use the chain rule to relate the successive derivatives of g evaluated at 0 to the successive derivatives of f evaluated at a.

   (b) Show that the nth Taylor polynomial of f about a can be obtained by setting $y = x - a$ in the nth Taylor polynomial of g about 0.

Lesson 10

Infinite Series

10.1 Goals

- Define, illustrate, and understand the terms sum, partial sum, convergence, and divergence of an infinite series

- Learn the properties of the basic geometric series and be able to use changes of variables to obtain variants of this series

- Learn the algebraic properties for sums, differences, and constant multiples of convergent series

- Solve applied problems involving geometric series

10.2 Overview

This lesson prepares the way for understanding clearly what an infinite series expansion like

$$e^x = 1 + x + \frac{x^2}{2!} + \cdots + \frac{x^n}{n!} + \cdots$$

means. There are two important points to address. First, what sense can we make of the implied addition of infinitely many terms. Second, how do we know (in this case) that the sum is e^x?

10.3 Convergence, Divergence, and Sum

Let's look at an example that leads naturally to an infinite series and the meaning of its sum. Take a mile walk along a straight road. Walk from milepost 0 toward milepost 1 in stages as follows. Walk halfway and stop; then walk half the remaining distance and stop; then walk half the remaining distance and stop; and so on and on.

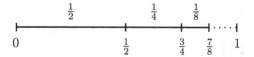

Figure 10.1: The first three stages of a one mile walk

After many stages, you are very close to 1. The figure suggests that

$$\frac{1}{2} + \frac{1}{4} + \frac{1}{8} + \frac{1}{16} + \cdots = 1$$

The expression on the left is called an infinite series. Our intuition suggests that its sum should be 1. However, there is a problem. The rules of arithmetic assign a sum only when a finite number of terms are added. What sense can we make of a sum with an infinite number of terms?

The mode of travel suggests what to do. The total distance traveled after completion of the successive stages of the trip in the figure are

$$S_1 = \frac{1}{2} = 1 - \frac{1}{2},$$

$$S_2 = \frac{1}{2} + \frac{1}{4} = 1 - \frac{1}{4},$$

$$S_3 = \frac{1}{2} + \frac{1}{4} + \frac{1}{8} = 1 - \frac{1}{8},$$

and so forth. In general,

$$S_n = \frac{1}{2} + \frac{1}{4} + \frac{1}{8} + \cdots + \frac{1}{2^n} = 1 - \frac{1}{2^n}.$$

One way to obtain the shorter formula for S_n is to observe that distance remaining to reach 1 after each stage of the trip is equal to the last distance traveled. (Why?) The distance traveled during the entire trip ought to be the limit of S_n as $n \to \infty$, which is given by

$$\lim_{n\to\infty} S_n = \lim_{n\to\infty} \left(1 - \frac{1}{2^n}\right) = 1.$$

In view of the definition of S_n,

$$\lim_{n\to\infty} \left(\frac{1}{2} + \frac{1}{4} + \frac{1}{8} + \cdots + \frac{1}{2^n}\right) = 1.$$

This limit statement is what is meant by

$$\frac{1}{2} + \frac{1}{4} + \frac{1}{8} + \cdots + \frac{1}{2^n} + \cdots = 1$$

or, more briefly, in summation notation by

$$\sum_{n=1}^{\infty} \frac{1}{2^n} = 1.$$

In general, an expression of the form

$$\sum_{n=1}^{\infty} a_n = a_1 + a_2 + \cdots + a_n + \cdots$$

is called an **infinite series**, or just a **series**. The **nth term** of the series is a_n. The **nth partial sum** is

$$S_n = a_1 + a_2 + \cdots + a_n = \sum_{k=1}^{n} a_k.$$

If $\lim_{n \to \infty} S_n = S$ *(finite or infinite)*, then S is the **sum** of the series and we write

$$\sum_{n=1}^{\infty} a_n = S \quad \text{or} \quad a_1 + a_2 + \cdots + a_n + \cdots = S.$$

We say that a series **converges** if it has a *finite* sum. From the introductory discussion,

$$\sum_{n=1}^{\infty} \frac{1}{2^n} = 1.$$

So this series converges and has sum 1.

A series **diverges** if it has an infinite sum or no sum at all. A series with the sum ∞ or $-\infty$ is said to *diverge to* ∞ or $-\infty$. Examples of divergent series are

$$\sum_{n=1}^{\infty} n^2 = 1 + 4 + 9 + \cdots = \infty,$$

and

$$\sum_{n=0}^{\infty} (-1)^n = 1 - 1 + 1 - 1 + \cdots.$$

The partial sums of the last series are 1, 0, 1, 0, 1, 0, ... which obviously have no limit. So the series $\sum_{n=0}^{\infty} (-1)^n$ has no sum and, hence, diverges.

In the last example, the summation index n started with $n = 0$ instead of $n = 1$. From time to time, we shall use other starting values and other summation indices besides n. The symbol used for the index of summation really doesn't matter because it is a dummy variable, much like a variable of integration.

It should seem reasonable that for a series to converge its nth term should tend to zero. This is indeed the case because $a_n = S_n - S_{n-1}$; hence, if a series converges, then $a_n = S_n - S_{n-1} \to S - S = 0$. This simple observation is quite useful. We state it in two ways:

$$\begin{array}{l} \sum a_n \quad \text{converges} \quad \Rightarrow \quad a_n \to 0. \\ a_n \not\to 0 \quad \Rightarrow \quad \sum a_n \quad \text{diverges.} \end{array}$$

We refer to the second statement as the **basic divergence test**.

Example 1 *What can you conclude from the boxed result about the convergence or divergence of the series*

$$(a) \quad \sum_{n=1}^{\infty} \sin \frac{\pi n}{2n+1} \qquad (b) \quad \sum_{n=1}^{\infty} \frac{1}{n}.$$

Solution. (a) Since

$$\frac{\pi n}{2n+1} = \frac{n}{n} \frac{\pi}{2 + 1/n} = \frac{\pi}{2 + 1/n} \to \frac{\pi}{2} \quad \text{as} \quad n \to \infty,$$

the nth term of the series

$$a_n = \sin \frac{\pi n}{2n+1} \to \sin \frac{\pi}{2} = 1 \neq 0 \quad \text{as} \quad n \to \infty.$$

Hence, the series in (a) diverges by the basic divergence test.

(b) The nth term of the series is $a_n = 1/n$ and $1/n \to 0$ as $n \to \infty$. Now be careful! You might want to conclude that the series converges because its nth term tends to zero. That is NOT what either part of the boxed result says. The first statement in the box says that if you *already know* the series converges, then you can conclude that its nth term tends to zero. It does NOT say that if the nth term of a series tends to zero, then the series must converge! So at this point all we can say is that the boxed result gives us no information about the convergence or divergence of the series $\sum_{n=1}^{\infty} \frac{1}{n}$. Stay tuned. $\square$

Here are a few simple but very important observations. The bottom line is that changing, adding, or deleting a finite number of terms from a series does not affect whether the series converges or diverges. (Of course, it may affect its sum, if the series has one.) Consider the two series

$$\frac{1}{2} + \frac{1}{4} + \frac{1}{8} + \cdots + \frac{1}{2^n} + \cdots \quad \text{and} \quad 7 + \frac{1}{2} + \frac{1}{4} + \frac{1}{8} + \cdots + \frac{1}{2^n} + \cdots.$$

We know that the first series converges (and its sum is 1). What about the second series? The $(n+1)$-st partial sum of the second series is 7 more than the n-th partial sum of the first series. So the partial sums of the second series converge to $7 + 1 = 8$. It follows that the second series also converges. By the same reasoning, the series

$$1 + 4 + 9 + 16 + \cdots \quad \text{and} \quad 7 + 1 + 4 + 9 + 16 + \cdots$$

both diverge. Similar arguments show that, for any m,

$$\sum_{n=1}^{\infty} a_n \quad \text{and} \quad \sum_{n=m}^{\infty} a_n \quad \text{both converge or both diverge.}$$

A very important conclusion follows:

> Any finite number of terms of a series can be changed, removed, or added without any affect on the convergence or divergence of the series.

Of course, in the case of convergence, changes of the foregoing type will very likely change the sum of the series (but will not affect its convergence).

10.4 Geometric Series

The most important series in calculus and its applications is the **geometric series**

$$\sum_{n=0}^{\infty} x^n = 1 + x + x^2 + \cdots + x^n + \cdots.$$

Since the ratio of any two consecutive terms in the geometric series is x, we call x the **common ratio** of the series. Here are the basic facts about the geometric series:

> $$\sum_{n=0}^{\infty} x^n = \frac{1}{1-x} \quad \text{for } |x| < 1.$$
> The series diverges if $|x| \geq 1$.

To see why, form the nth partial sum of the geometric series

$$S_n = 1 + x + x^2 + \cdots + x^n.$$

It is easy to express this sum more compactly. Multiply the foregoing expression by x and subtract to obtain

$$\begin{aligned} S_n - xS_n &= 1 + x + x^2 + \cdots + x^n \\ &\quad -x - x^2 - \cdots - x^n - x^{n+1}. \end{aligned}$$

Consequently,

$$\begin{aligned} (1-x)\,S_n &= 1 - x^{n+1}, \\ S_n &= \frac{1 - x^{n+1}}{1-x} \quad \text{for} \quad x \neq 1. \end{aligned}$$

If $|x| < 1$, x^{n+1} has limit 0 as $n \to \infty$ and, hence, $\lim_{n \to \infty} S_n = 1/(1-x)$; otherwise, there is no finite limit, which confirms the results in the box.

The formula for S_n is important in its own right. Here are two ways to express it that we will used later for estimating errors:

$$1 + x + x^2 + \cdots + x^n = \frac{1 - x^{n+1}}{1-x} \quad \text{for} \quad x \neq 1,$$

$$\frac{1}{1-x} = 1 + x + x^2 + \cdots + x^n + \frac{x^{n+1}}{1-x} \quad \text{for} \quad x \neq 1.$$

Variants of Geometric Series

The geometric series

$$\sum_{n=0}^{\infty} x^n = 1 + x + x^2 + \cdots + x^n + \cdots = \frac{1}{1-x} \quad \text{for} \quad |x| < 1$$

is often used with other indices and with various changes of variable. Such variants of the geometric series will become increasingly important as we go along. For the moment, we just give a few examples to illustrate the possibilities.

First, observe that

$$\sum_{n=1}^{\infty} x^n = x + x^2 + \cdots + x^n + \cdots = x\left(1 + x + x^2 + \cdots + x^n + \cdots\right)$$

$$= \frac{x}{1-x} \quad \text{for} \quad |x| < 1.$$

What is the sum if the starting index is $n = 2$?

Replace x by $-x$ in the geometric series and use $|-x| = |x|$ to obtain

$$\sum_{n=0}^{\infty} (-1)^n x^n = 1 - x + x^2 - x^3 + \cdots = \frac{1}{1+x} \quad \text{for} \quad |x| < 1.$$

Set $x = 1/2$ to obtain

$$\sum_{n=0}^{\infty} \frac{(-1)^n}{2^n} = 1 - \frac{1}{2} + \frac{1}{4} - \frac{1}{8} + \cdots = \frac{1}{1 + (1/2)} = \frac{2}{3}.$$

In the series with sums $1/(1-x)$ and $1/(1+x)$ let $x = t^2$ and use the fact that $|t^2| < 1$ if and only if $|t| < 1$ to obtain

$$\sum_{n=0}^{\infty} t^{2n} = 1 + t^2 + t^4 + t^6 + \cdots = \frac{1}{1-t^2} \quad \text{for} \quad |t| < 1,$$

$$\sum_{n=0}^{\infty} (-1)^n t^{2n} = 1 - t^2 + t^4 - t^6 + \cdots = \frac{1}{1+t^2} \quad \text{for} \quad |t| < 1.$$

There is no need to memorize formulas such as these. They can be recovered from the basic geometric series by simple changes of variable whenever you need them.

Example 2 *Find an infinite series expansion, similar to a geometric series, for the function*

$$\frac{x^3}{5-x^2}.$$

Solution. The key is to "see" the geometric series hidden in the term $1/\left(5-x^2\right)$:

$$\frac{x^3}{5-x^2} = \frac{x^3}{5}\frac{1}{1-x^2/5}.$$

Let $t = x^2/5$, a step you will quickly learn to do in your head with a little practice, to get

$$\frac{1}{1-x^2/5} = \frac{1}{1-t} = \sum_{n=0}^{\infty} t^n = \sum_{n=0}^{\infty}\left(\frac{x^2}{5}\right)^n = \sum_{n=0}^{\infty}\frac{x^{2n}}{5^n} \quad \text{for} \quad |t| = \left|\frac{x^2}{5}\right| < 1.$$

Finally, since $\left|x^2/5\right| < 1$ if and only if $|x| < \sqrt{5}$,

$$\begin{aligned}
\frac{x^3}{5-x^2} &= \frac{x^3}{5}\frac{1}{1-x^2/5} = \frac{x^3}{5}\sum_{n=0}^{\infty}\frac{x^{2n}}{5^n} = \sum_{n=0}^{\infty}\frac{x^{2n+3}}{5^{n+1}} \\
&= \frac{x^3}{5} + \frac{x^5}{5^2} + \frac{x^7}{5^3} + \cdots \quad \text{for} \quad |x| < \sqrt{5}. \quad \square
\end{aligned}$$

10.5 Series of Functions

The geometric series is a series whose terms are functions, namely the functions x^n. For each x with $|x| < 1$ the series converges and the sum of the series is the function

$$\sum_{n=0}^{\infty} x^n = \frac{1}{1-x}$$

with domain all x with $|x| < 1$. The most important series in applications are series of functions.

Earlier when we defined the sum S of a series by

$$\sum_{n=1}^{\infty} a_n = S \quad \text{if} \quad \lim_{n\to\infty} S_n = S$$

you were probably thinking of each a_n as a number. Then S_n and S are numbers. *We use the same definitions when the a_n are functions.* In the case of the geometric series, the functions are $a_n\left(x\right) = x^n$. The partial sums S_n and sum S also are functions of x. Specifically,

$$S_n\left(x\right) = \frac{1-x^{n+1}}{1-x} \quad \text{for } x \neq 1.$$

These partial sums have a finite limit if and only if $|x| < 1$ in which case

$$\lim_{n \to \infty} S_n(x) = S(x) = \frac{1}{1-x}.$$

10.6   Series With Complex Terms

So far we have only displayed series whose terms are real numbers or functions. Nevertheless, the reasoning we have used applies verbatim to series whose terms are complex numbers or functions; the absolute value signs above need only be interpreted as the absolute values of complex numbers. The variable x in the geometric series is usually replaced by z when we are dealing with a problem where complex numbers are in use. Thus,

$$\boxed{\begin{array}{l} \sum_{n=0}^{\infty} z^n = \dfrac{1}{1-z} \qquad \text{for } |z| < 1. \\ \text{The series diverges if } |z| \geq 1. \end{array}}$$

For example, $z = i/2$ has $|z| = 1/2$ and

$$\sum_{n=0}^{\infty} \left(\frac{i}{2}\right)^n = 1 + \frac{i}{2} - \frac{1}{4} - \frac{i}{8} + \frac{1}{16} - \frac{i}{32} + \cdots = \frac{1}{1 - i/2} = \frac{2}{2-i}.$$

What is the sum expressed in standard form?

10.7   Power Series

The geometric series is a particular power series. An infinite series of the form

$$\sum_{n=0}^{\infty} a_n x^n = a_0 + a_1 x + a_2 x^2 + \cdots + a_n x^n + \cdots$$

is called a **power series** *in powers of* x (or *about* $x = 0$). Here the *coefficients* can be real or complex numbers (although normally they are real). In the geometric series $a_n = 1$ for all n. Likewise, an infinite series of the form

$$\sum_{n=0}^{\infty} c_n z^n = c_0 + c_1 z + c_2 z^2 + \cdots + c_n z^n + \cdots$$

is called a **power series** *in powers of* z (or *about* $z = 0$). In many respects (but not always) power series behave like "infinite degree" polynomials. Stay tuned.

10.8 Algebraic Properties of Series

There are some natural and useful properties of sums of convergent series that follow immediately from the algebraic limit laws of calculus. They are just like familiar properties of finite sums:

$$\sum (a_n + b_n) = \sum a_n + \sum b_n,$$
$$\sum (a_n - b_n) = \sum a_n - \sum b_n,$$
$$\sum c a_n = c \sum a_n.$$

In these expressions a_n, b_n, and c can be real or complex numbers or functions. Each property holds whenever the series on the right-hand side converge. We have used a customary shorthand notation in which the limits of summation are suppressed in the sigma-notation. It is understood that all series are summed over the same values of n.

10.9   Suggested Problems

Determine whether the series is convergent or divergent. If convergent find its sum.

1. $\sum_{n=1}^{\infty} 4\left(\frac{2}{3}\right)^{n-1}$

2. $\sum_{n=0}^{\infty} 4\left(-1\right)^n \left(\frac{2}{3}\right)^n$

3. $\sum_{n=0}^{\infty} 3^{-n}8^{n+1}$

4. $\sum_{n=0}^{\infty} 3^n 8^{-n+1}$

5. $\sum_{n=1}^{\infty} \frac{3^n + 2^n}{6^n}$

6. $\sum_{n=0}^{\infty} \left(2\left(\frac{1}{3}\right)^n + 3\left(-\frac{1}{5}\right)^n\right)$

(a) Find the sum of the following series and (b) state the values of x for which the series converges to its sum.

7. $\sum_{n=3}^{\infty} x^n$

8. $\sum_{n=1}^{\infty} \left(x - 3\right)^n$

9. $\sum_{n=1}^{\infty} \frac{x^n}{4^n}$

10. $\sum_{n=0}^{\infty} \tan^n x$

11. $\sum_{n=0}^{\infty} \frac{x^n}{1+x^2}$

12. $\sum_{n=0}^{\infty} \frac{x^n+(1-x)^n}{1+x}$

13. $\sum_{n=0}^{\infty} \frac{x^{2n}}{(1+x^2)^n}$

(a) Find a power series, similar to the geometric series expansion for the function $1/(1-x)$, for each of the following functions. (b) State the values of x for which the expansion is valid.

14. $x^2/(1-x)$

15. $x/(1-2x)$

16. $1/(1+9x^2)$

17. $x^2 / \left(1 - 4x^2\right)$

   (a) Make the indicated change of variables $x = f(t)$ in the geometric series $\sum_{n=0}^{\infty} x^n = 1/(1-x)$ for $|x| < 1$ to obtain a related series in t.

   (b) State the t values for which the new expansion is valid.

   (c) Express the result in part (a) in the $\cdots$ notation including enough terms so the general pattern is clear.

18. $x = -3t$

19. $x = \sqrt{t}$

20. $x = e^{-t}$

21. $x = 2\sin t$

22. Let c be a fixed complex number. For which z does the series $\sum_{n=0}^{\infty} cz^n$ converge? What is its sum? Give a geometric description of the region of convergence.

23. *(The basic divergence test)*

   (a) What conclusion can you draw about convergence or divergence of the series $\sum_{n=1}^{\infty} \cos(1/n)$ from the basic divergence test? Explain briefly.

   (b) What conclusion can you draw about convergence or divergence of the series $\sum_{n=1}^{\infty} \sin(1/n)$ from the basic divergence test? Explain briefly.

   (c) What conclusion can you draw about convergence or divergence of the series $\sum_{n=1}^{\infty} 1/n^2$ from the basic divergence test? Explain briefly.

24. Take a walk starting at mile post 0. First, walk 1/2 mile toward mile post 1 and stop. Second, walk 1/4 mile back toward mile post 0 and stop. Third, walk 1/8 mile toward mile post 1 and stop. Fourth, walk 1/16 mile back toward mile post 0 and stop. Continue walking indefinitely in this back and forth manner.

   (a) Find the total distance that you walk.

   (b) How far from mile post 0 do you end up?

25. Revisit the mile walk in this lesson. Instead of walking 1/2 the remaining distance at each stage of the trip, walk a fixed fraction x with $0 < x < 1$ of the remaining distance at each stage. In this walk, show that

$$S_n = x + x(1-x) + x(1-x)^2 + \cdots + x(1-x)^n$$

and explain why the distance remaining to milepost 1 after the nth stage of the trip is $(1-x)^n$. Use this information to show that $\sum_{n=0}^{\infty} x(1-x)^n = 1$ as expected. Reconfirm the sum by using the result of Prob. 22.

26. What is c if $\sum_{n=0}^{\infty} \frac{3^n + c^n}{6^n} = 2$?

27. If $0 < r < 2$, then $\sum_{n=0}^{\infty} r(1-r)^n =$?

28. If $-1 < x < 1$, then $\sum_{n=0}^{\infty} (-1)^n x^n =$?

29. Start with a square of side length 1. Join the midpoints of its four sides to form a smaller square and 4 right triangles. Let A_1 be the area of one of the right triangles. Now, join the midpoints of each side of the smaller square to form a new even smaller square and 4 new right triangles. Let A_2 be the area of one of the new right triangles. Continue with the process for ever. Find $\sum_{n=1}^{\infty} A_n$.

30. *(The Multiplier Effect)* The federal government pumps an extra $1 billion into the economy in hopes of stimulating growth. Assume each business and individual saves 15% of its income and spends the rest. So initially, the $1 billion results in $0.85 billion in new spending. The businesses and individuals who receive this new income likewise save 15% of the new income and spend the rest. This process continues on and on indefinitely. Find the total increase in spending due to governmental pump priming.

31. A ball is dropped vertically and bounces up and down. Assume that, on subsequent bounces, the ball always rebounds a fixed fraction r ($0 < r < 1$) of its previous height. If the ball is initially dropped from a height of H feet, find the total distance the ball travels assuming it bounces up and down forever.

Lesson 11

Taylor Series
Representations

11.1 Goals

- Define a Taylor series and explain its relationship to Taylor polynomials

- Find Taylor series of given functions

- Use the remainder (error) estimates from Lesson 9 to show that particular functions have Taylor series representations

11.2 Overview

We know from the examples and homework in Lesson 9 that for several functions $f(x)$ it is true that

$$f(x) \approx T_n(x) = \sum_{k=0}^{n} \frac{f^{(k)}(0)}{k!} x^k$$

at least for certain values of x, where $T_n(x)$ is the nth Taylor polynomial of f. Moreover, the accuracy of the approximation often improves as n increases. It is natural to ask if

$$f(x) = \lim_{n \to \infty} T_n(x) = \lim_{n \to \infty} \sum_{k=0}^{n} \frac{f^{(k)}(0)}{k!} x^k.$$

In this lesson we address this question and find means for confirming it for most of the functions that you have met so far in calculus.

143

11.3   Taylor Series

We call the infinite series

$$\sum_{k=0}^{\infty} \frac{f^{(k)}(0)}{k!} x^k$$

whose nth partial sum is $T_n(x)$ the **Taylor series of f about 0**. The question posed above is when is $f(x)$ the sum of its Taylor series; that is, when is

$$f(x) = \sum_{k=0}^{\infty} \frac{f^{(k)}(0)}{k!} x^k.$$

We will return to this question several times in subsequent lessons. For now we take some important first steps. Notice that for $f(x)$ to have a Taylor series about 0 it must have derivatives of all orders at 0. Since the index of summation is a dummy variable (just like a variable of integration), it is useful to observe that any convenient letter can be used for that index. Thus,

$$\sum_{k=0}^{\infty} \frac{f^{(k)}(0)}{k!} x^k = \sum_{n=0}^{\infty} \frac{f^{(n)}(0)}{n!} x^n = \sum_{r=0}^{\infty} \frac{f^{(r)}(0)}{r!} x^r.$$

For historical reasons, the Taylor series for f *about 0* also is called the **Maclaurin series of f**. We will refer only to Taylor series and normally we will suppress the qualification "about 0" or some other point when the base point is clear from the context.

It is worth observing that we have already established that the function $f(x) = 1/(1-x)$ is the sum of its Taylor series; however, we arrived at this result from quite a different point of view.

Example 1 *Show that $f(x) = 1/(1-x)$ is the sum of its Taylor series (about 0).*

Solution. The Taylor series is

$$\sum_{n=0}^{\infty} \frac{f^{(n)}(0)}{n!} x^n$$

and

$$
\begin{aligned}
&f(x) = (1-x)^{-1}, && f(0) = 1 = 0!, \\
&f'(x) = (1)(1-x)^{-2}, && f'(0) = 1 = 1!, \\
&f''(x) = (1)(2)(1-x)^{-3}, && f''(0) = (1)(2) = 2!, \\
&f'''(x) = (1)(2)(3)(1-x)^{-4}, && f'''(0) = (1)(2)(3) = 3!, \\
&\cdots && \cdots \\
&f^{(n)}(x) = (1)(2)(3)\cdots(n)(1-x)^{-n-1}, && f^{(n)}(0) = (1)(2)(3)\cdots(n) = n!.
\end{aligned}
$$

Consequently, for $f(x) = 1/(1-x)$,

$$\sum_{n=0}^{\infty} \frac{f^{(n)}(0)}{n!} x^n = \sum_{n=0}^{\infty} \frac{n!}{n!} x^n = \sum_{n=0}^{\infty} x^n = \frac{1}{1-x} \quad \text{for} \quad |x| < 1$$

from our knowledge about the geometric series. So the function $f(x) = 1/(1-x)$ is the sum of its Taylor series about 0 for $|x| < 1$.   □

Example 2 *Find the Taylor series of $f(x) = e^x$.*

Solution. Since $f(x) = e^x$, $f'(x) = e^x$, $f''(x) = e^x$, and so on, we find that $f(0) = 1$, $f'(0) = 1$, $f''(0) = 1$, and in general $f^{(n)}(0) = 1$ for all n. Therefore, $f(x) = e^x$ has Taylor series

$$\sum_{n=0}^{\infty} \frac{f^{(n)}(0)}{n!} x^n = \sum_{n=0}^{\infty} \frac{1}{n!} x^n. \quad □$$

Notice an important point: Example 2 tells us that the Taylor series of e^x about 0 is $\sum_{n=0}^{\infty} \frac{1}{n!} x^n$ but it *does not tell us that the sum of the series is e^x.*

11.4   When is $f(x)$ the Sum of its Taylor Series?

To begin to answer this question, we start with the Taylor series

$$\sum_{n=0}^{\infty} \frac{f^{(n)}(0)}{n!} x^n$$

of $f(x)$ and its nth partial sum

$$T_n(x) = \sum_{k=0}^{n} \frac{f^{(k)}(0)}{k!} x^k = f(0) + \frac{f'(0)}{1!} x + \frac{f''(0)}{2!} x^2 + \cdots + \frac{f^{(n)}(0)}{n!} x^n,$$

which is the nth Taylor polynomial of $f(x)$. The error or remainder in approximation of $f(x)$ by this partial sum is

$$R_n(x) = f(x) - T_n(x).$$

Since the sum of a series is the limit of its sequence of partial sums,

$$\boxed{\begin{array}{lll} f(x) = \sum_{n=0}^{\infty} \frac{f^{(n)}(0)}{n!} x^n & \Leftrightarrow & T_n(x) \to f(x) \quad \text{as} \quad n \to \infty \\ & \Leftrightarrow & R_n(x) \to 0 \quad \text{as} \quad n \to \infty \end{array}}$$

For this result to be useful, we must have a reasonable expression for $R_n(x)$ that enables us to estimate its size for large n. The Lagrange form for the error in Taylor polynomial approximation given in Lesson 9 is just such an expression.

$$R_n(x) = f^{(n+1)}(c)\frac{x^{n+1}}{(n+1)!} \qquad \text{for some } c \text{ between 0 and } x.$$

This estimate is often used with the special limit

$$\lim_{m\to\infty} \frac{|x|^m}{m!} = 0$$

for any fixed value of x.

Example 3 *Use the Lagrange formula for the error to show that $f(x) = e^x$ is the sum of its Taylor series for all x.*

Solution. Fix a value of x. Then

$$R_n(x) = f^{(n+1)}(c)\frac{x^{n+1}}{(n+1)!} = e^c\frac{x^{n+1}}{(n+1)!}$$

for some c between 0 and x. Since the exponential function is increasing and $c \leq |x|$, $e^c \leq e^{|x|}$ and

$$|R_n(x)| \leq e^{|x|}\frac{x^{n+1}}{(n+1)!} \to 0$$

as $n \to \infty$. (We have used the special limit above with $m = n+1$.) Since $R_n(x) \to 0$ as as $n \to \infty$, we have established that

$$e^x = \sum_{n=0}^{\infty} \frac{x^n}{n!}. \quad \square$$

Reasoning similar to that used in Example 3 can be applied to $\sin x$ and $\cos x$ (see the problems) to establish that these functions are the sums of their Taylor series. As we have mentioned earlier and now have established:

$$e^x = \sum_{n=0}^{\infty} \frac{x^n}{n!} = 1 + x + \frac{x^2}{2!} + \frac{x^3}{3!} + \frac{x^4}{4!} + \cdots \qquad \text{for all } x.$$

$$\sin x = \sum_{n=0}^{\infty} \frac{(-1)^n x^{2n+1}}{(2n+1)!} = x - \frac{x^3}{3!} + \frac{x^5}{5!} - \frac{x^7}{7!} + - \cdots \qquad \text{for all } x.$$

$$\cos x = \sum_{n=0}^{\infty} \frac{(-1)^n x^{2n}}{(2n)!} = 1 - \frac{x^2}{2!} + \frac{x^4}{4!} - \frac{x^6}{6!} + - \cdots \quad \text{for all } x.$$

Another notation for the exponential function is $\exp(x)$; that is,

$$\exp(x) = e^x.$$

This notation is convenient typographically when the power to which e is raised is itself a complicated expression. For instance compare the ease with which both sides of the following equation can be read:

$$\exp\left(\frac{x}{1-x^2}\right) = e^{\frac{x}{1-x^2}}.$$

With this new notation, the power series for the exponential function can be written as

$$\exp(x) = \sum_{n=0}^{\infty} \frac{x^n}{n!} = 1 + x + \frac{x^2}{2!} + \frac{x^3}{3!} + \frac{x^4}{4!} + \cdots \quad \text{for all } x.$$

In order to use Taylor series expansions effectively, we need a better understanding of infinite series in general and power series in particular. Stay tuned.

11.5 Other Base Points

As for Taylor polynomials, the story for Taylor series about a base point, say a, other than 0 is essentially the same as for the base point 0. So we shall be brief.

Let $f(x)$ be defined on an open interval containing the point a and assume that $f(x)$ has derivatives of all orders at a. The **Taylor series of f about a** is

$$\sum_{n=0}^{\infty} \frac{f^{(n)}(a)}{n!} (x-a)^n$$

which also is called a **power series in $x - a$**. From Lesson 9, the error $R_n(x) = f(x) - T_n(x)$ can be expressed in Lagrange form as follows:

$$R_n(x) = \frac{f^{(n+1)}(c)}{(n+1)!} (x-a)^{n+1} \quad \text{for some } c \text{ between } a \text{ and } x.$$

Example 4 *Find the Taylor series of* $\cos x$ *about the base point* 1.

Solution. The derivatives of the cosine repeat in a cycle of length four:

$$
\begin{aligned}
f(x) &= \cos x, & f^{(4)}(x) &= \cos x, \\
f'(x) &= -\sin x, & f^{(5)}(x) &= -\sin x, \\
f''(x) &= -\cos x, & f^{(6)}(x) &= -\cos x, \\
f'''(x) &= \sin x, & f^{(7)}(x) &= \sin x,
\end{aligned}
$$

and so on. Thus, the Taylor series for $\cos x$ about 1 is

$$
\sum_{n=0}^{\infty} \frac{\cos^{(n)}(1)}{n!} (x-1)^n =
$$

$$
(\cos 1) - (\sin 1)(x-1) - \frac{\cos 1}{2!}(x-1)^2 + \frac{\sin 1}{3!}(x-1)^3 + - - + \cdots. \quad \square
$$

Reasoning as in Example 3 you can show that the Taylor series about 1 for $\cos x$ has sum $\cos x$ for all x.

11.6 Suggested Problems

1. Find the Taylor series about 0 of the following functions.

   (a) $\sin x$

   (b) $\cos x$

   (c) xe^x

   (d) $\ln(1-x)$

   (e) $(1+x)^{1/2}$

2. Show that $\sin x$ is the sum of its Taylor series about 0.

3. Show that $\cos x$ is the sum of its Taylor series about 0.

4. Show that $\ln(1-x)$ is the sum of its Taylor series about 0 for $-1/2 \leq x \leq 1/2$.

5. Find the Taylor series about a of the following functions.

   (a) $\sin x$ $a = \pi/6$

   (b) $\cos x$ $a = \pi/4$

   (c) $\ln x$ $a = 1$

   (d) $\sqrt{x}$ $a = 4$

6. Show that $\sin x$ is the sum of its Taylor series expansion about $a = \pi/6$.

7. Show that $\cos x$ is the sum of its Taylor series expansion about $a = \pi/4$.

   For problems 8 - 15, use the Taylor series expansions given in this lesson to find the (exact) sum of the series.

8. $\sum_{n=0}^{\infty} \frac{1}{n!}$

9. $\sum_{n=2}^{\infty} \frac{1}{n!}$

10. $\sum_{n=0}^{\infty} \frac{2^n}{n!}$

11. $\sum_{n=1}^{\infty} (-1)^n \frac{3^n}{n!}$

12. $\sum_{n=0}^{\infty} (-1)^n \frac{\pi^{2n+1}}{6^{2n+1}(2n+1)!}$

13. $\sum_{n=0}^{\infty} (-1)^n \frac{\pi^{2n}}{2^{2n}(2n)!}$

14. $\sum_{n=0}^{\infty} \frac{x^{2n}}{n!}$

15. $\sum_{n=0}^{\infty} (-1)^n \frac{x^n}{n!}$

It is not always easy to write down Taylor series expansions by computing all the successive derivatives of a function. The next examples should convince you of this. (Later we will find new ways to find Taylor series that can sometimes avoid unpleasant calculations.) Find, by evaluating derivatives at 0, the first three *nonzero* terms in the Taylor series about 0 for the given function.

16. $\cos x^2$

17. e^{-x^2}

18. $\tan x$

19. $\sec x$

Use the series expansions given in this or in earlier lessons and appropriate changes of variable to find infinite series representations for:

20. e^{-x^2}

21. $\sin x^2$

22. $\cos \sqrt{x}$

23. $xe^{-x} + \cos x$

24. $1/(1 + x^2)$

25. $x/(1 - x^4)$

Since $e^x = \sum_{n=0}^{\infty} \frac{x^n}{n!}$ for each x, there is a Taylor polynomial $T_n(x)$ that approximates e^x as accurately as desired. However, based on the reasoning used in Example 3, if you change x you may also have to change the Taylor polynomial to achieve a given accuracy. The next Problem shows that you can find a single Taylor polynomial that does the job for all x provided you restrict x to a bounded interval.

26. Restrict x to the interval $[a,b]$ and let $g = \max(|a|, |b|)$. Adjust the reasoning in Example 3 to show that

$$|R_n(x)| \leq e^g \frac{g^{n+1}}{(n+1)!} \qquad \text{for all } x \text{ in } [a,b].$$

Now explain why you can find a single Taylor polynomial $T_n(x)$ that approximates e^x as accurately as desired for all x in the interval $[a,b]$.

Lesson 12

Series With
Nonnegative Terms
The Integral Test

12.1 Goals

- Explain how the sum of a series with nonnegative terms is related to the area of an infinite system of rectangles

- Learn and apply the integral test

- Know when a p-series converges and when it diverges

- Approximate the sum of a series that converges by the integral test to within a prescribed tolerance using the error estimates associated with the test

12.2 Overview

Frequently an infinite series is obtained from calculations intended to solve a problem of interest. We expect the series obtained to converge and that its sum is the solution of the problem. When we get a series in this way, the first step in checking that it really does solve the problem at hand is to check that it converges. Then it has a finite sum and hopefully the sum really does solve the problem. If all this works out, the series itself gives us a means of approximating the solution to any desired degree of precision.

In this lesson, which is restricted to series with nonnegative terms, you will learn the integral test for convergence or divergence of particular series. This test and others you will learn are helpful in the foregoing scenario. Area comparisons make it easy to understand the integral test and also lead to effective means for estimating the sum of a series that converges by the integral test.

12.3   Series with Nonnegative Terms

Two series with nonnegative terms are

$$\sum_{n=1}^{\infty} \frac{1}{2^n} = 1 \quad \text{and} \quad \sum_{n=1}^{\infty} n = 1 + 2 + 3 + \cdots = \infty.$$

The first series converges and has a finite sum. The second series diverges and has an infinite sum. These results are typical of the general situation for series with nonnegative terms. A series with nonnegative terms always has a sum, finite or infinite.

It is easy to understand why this is so. Let

$$\sum_{n=1}^{\infty} a_n$$

be a series with nonnegative terms; so each $a_n \geq 0$. The partial sums of the series satisfy

$$S_1 \leq S_2 \leq S_3 \leq \cdots \leq S_n \leq \cdots$$

because each partial sum is gotten from its predecessor by adding a nonnegative term. The partial sums are a nondecreasing sequence of real numbers. There are two possibilities for such a sequence. Either the sequence is **bounded above**, which means there is a number M that is greater than all the S_n or the sequence is not bounded above. If the sequence S_n is bounded above by M, then it is a fundamental property of the real number system that S_n converges and $\lim_{n\to\infty} S_n = S \leq M$. If the sequence S_n is not bounded above, then its terms ultimately becomes larger than any positive real number and $\lim_{n\to\infty} S_n = S = \infty$. Since S is the sum of the series, we have established:

Every series $\sum a_n$ with $a_n \geq 0$ has a finite or infinite sum.

The following figure shows how to interpret the sum of a series $\sum_{n=1}^{\infty} a_n$ with each $a_n \geq 0$ as an area. The nth rectangle has height a_n, width 1, and area a_n. The sum S of the series is the sum of the areas (finite or infinite) of the infinite system of rectangles in the figure.

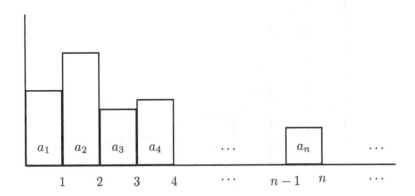

Figure 12.1: Area interpretation of $S = \sum_{n=1}^{\infty} a_n$ with $a_n \geq 0$

12.4 The Harmonic Series

The area interpretation of the sum of a series enables us to use integral calculus to study the convergence or divergence of certain infinite series. In the next example we do just that. In Example 1 of Lesson 10 we tried to decide whether the series $\sum_{n=1}^{\infty} \frac{1}{n}$ converged or diverged. This series came up early in the study of infinite series and some prominent mathematicians of the 17th century believed that the series converged because its terms $1/n$ got steadily smaller and tended to zero. Let's see if they were correct in that belief.

Example 1 *Determine whether the **harmonic series** $\sum_{n=1}^{\infty} \frac{1}{n}$ converges or diverges.*

Solution. Let

$$S_n = 1 + \frac{1}{2} + \frac{1}{3} + \cdots + \frac{1}{n}$$

be the nth partial sum of the series. The harmonic series converges if the partial sums have a finite limit and the series diverges if the partial sums have an infinite limit. The figure that follows

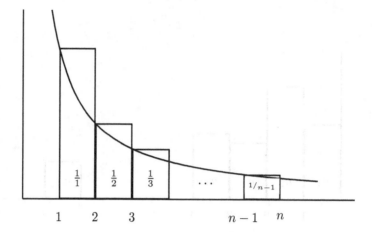

Figure 12.2: Graph of $y = \frac{1}{x}$

shows that

$$S_n = \left(1 + \frac{1}{2} + \frac{1}{3} + \cdots + \frac{1}{n-1}\right) + \frac{1}{n} > \left(\int_1^n \frac{1}{x}\,dx\right) + \frac{1}{n},$$

$$S_n > \ln n + \frac{1}{n} \to \infty \quad \text{as } n \to \infty,$$

where we have used the basic fact (see the problems) that

$$\boxed{\lim_{n \to \infty} \ln n = \infty.}$$

Therefore, the partial sums of the harmonic series grow without bound and the harmonic series diverges to ∞ :

$$\sum_{n=1}^{\infty} \frac{1}{n} = \infty. \quad \square$$

Were you inclined to believe that the harmonic series should converge? It is intuitively appealing to believe that if the terms of a series tend to zero then the series must converge. THIS STATEMENT IS JUST PLAIN FALSE as the foregoing example shows. It is important that you understand the reasoning in the example and that you begin to adjust your intuition and understanding of infinite series accordingly.

12.5 Improper Integrals

The area comparison used in our discussion of the harmonic series is worth pursuing further and leads to the integral test for the convergence or divergence of certain positive-termed series. The test is expressed most conveniently in terms of improper integrals, which are closely related to the definite integrals you already know. The definite integrals, $\int_a^b f(x)\,dx$, you have studied earlier are sometimes called *proper integrals*. This means a and b are finite and the integrand $f(x)$ is bounded for $a \le x \le b$. These integrals give the (signed) area between the graph of $y = f(x)$ and the x-axis. They have numerous applications. All this is familiar.

Integrals for which $a = -\infty$ and/or $b = \infty$ are examples of **improper integrals**. Such integrals are defined as limits of proper integrals and have rather evident area interpretations. In this lesson, we only need improper integrals of the form $\int_a^\infty f(x)\,dx$ with a finite. These improper integrals are defined by

$$\int_a^\infty f(x)\,dx = \lim_{b \to \infty} \int_a^b f(x)\,dx$$

provided there is a limit, finite or infinite. (Stop and draw a figure that illustrates this definition in terms of areas.) The improper integral is said to *converge (exist)* if the limit exists and is finite; otherwise, the improper integral *diverges (does not exist)*. If the limit is $-\infty$ or ∞, we say the integral diverges to $-\infty$ or ∞. This terminology matches the language we are using for infinite series.

Example 2 *By definition*

$$\begin{aligned} \int_1^\infty \frac{1}{x^2}\,dx &= \lim_{b \to \infty} \int_1^b \frac{1}{x^2}\,dx = \lim_{b \to \infty} \left[-\frac{1}{x} \right]_1^b \\ &= \lim_{b \to \infty} \left[-\frac{1}{b} + 1 \right] = 1. \end{aligned}$$

The improper integral converges and is equal to 1. Draw a figure that illustrates this limit calculation in terms of areas. □

Example 3 *By definition*

$$\begin{aligned} \int_1^\infty \frac{1}{x}\,dx &= \lim_{b \to \infty} \int_1^b \frac{1}{x}\,dx = \lim_{b \to \infty} \left[\ln x \right]_1^b \\ &= \lim_{b \to \infty} \ln b = \infty. \end{aligned}$$

The improper integral diverges to ∞. Draw a figure that illustrates this limit calculation in terms of areas. □

12.6   The Integral Test

Remember that a series $\sum_{n=1}^\infty a_n$ with $a_n \ge 0$ always has a sum S, finite or infinite,

$$\sum_{n=1}^\infty a_n = S \qquad 0 \le S \le \infty.$$

The sum can be interpreted as the area of an infinite system of rectangles as illustrated earlier in the lesson. This area point of view links positive-termed series with improper integrals. One such connection is illustrated in the next two figures in which the function $y = f(x)$ is positive, decreasing, and continuous and $f(n) = a_n$, the nth term of the series.

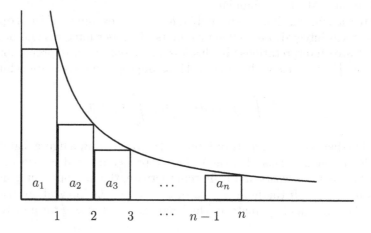

Figure 12.3: Area Comparison I

An area comparison in the foregoing figure shows that

$$S_n = a_1 + a_2 + a_3 + \cdots + a_n \leq a_1 + \int_1^n f(x)\,dx.$$

A similar area comparison in the following figure

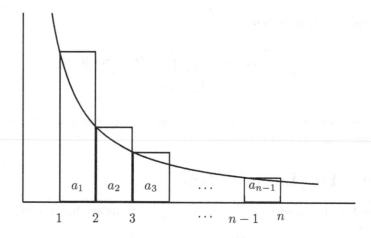

Figure 12.4: Area Comparison II

yields

$$\int_1^n f(x)\ dx \le a_1 + a_2 + a_3 + \cdots + a_{n-1} \le S_n.$$

Combining these estimates gives

$$\int_1^n f(x)\ dx \le S_n \le a_1 + \int_1^n f(x)\ dx.$$

Finally let $n \to \infty$ to obtain

$$\int_1^\infty f(x)\ dx \le S \le a_1 + \int_1^\infty f(x)\ dx. \tag{12.1}$$

Now it is apparent that S and $\int_1^\infty f(x)\ dx$ are either both finite or both infinite. This is the integral test:

The Integral Test
Let $f(x)$ be a positive, decreasing, and continuous for $x \ge 1$. Let $a_n = f(n)$. Then
$\sum_{n=1}^\infty a_n$ converges $\quad\Longleftrightarrow\quad$ $\int_1^\infty f(x)\ dx$ converges.

The conclusion of the integral test also can be expressed as

$$\sum_{n=1}^\infty a_n < \infty \quad\Longleftrightarrow\quad \int_1^\infty f(x)\ dx < \infty.$$

Useful variants of the integral test are obtained by replacing 1 by other integers.

Example 4 *From Example 2,*

$$\int_1^\infty \frac{1}{x^2}\ dx = 1.$$

Since $f(x) = \frac{1}{x^2}$ is positive, decreasing, and continuous for $x \ge 1$, and $f(n) = \frac{1}{n^2}$, the integral test tells us that $\sum_{n=1}^\infty \frac{1}{n^2}$ converges. $\square$

Example 5 *From Example 3,*

$$\int_1^\infty \frac{1}{x}\ dx = \infty.$$

Since $f(x) = \frac{1}{x}$ is positive, decreasing, and continuous for $x \ge 1$, and $f(n) = \frac{1}{n}$, the integral test tells us that the harmonic series $\sum_{n=1}^\infty \frac{1}{n}$ diverges (as we already know). $\square$

Use of the integral test as in Examples 4 and 5 when $p > 0$ and the basic divergence test when $p \le 0$ leads to the useful result:

The **p-series** $\quad \sum_{n=1}^\infty \frac{1}{n^p}$ converges $\quad\Longleftrightarrow\quad p > 1.$

12.7   Approximating Sums Of Series That Converge By The Integral Test

Assume that the series $\sum_{n=1}^{\infty} a_n$ converges by the integral test applied to the positive, decreasing, continuous function $f(x)$ with $f(n) = a_n$. As usual, let

$$S = \sum_{n=1}^{\infty} a_n \quad \text{and} \quad S_N = \sum_{n=1}^{N} a_n.$$

The area comparisons that led to (12.1) when applied to the series

$$a_{N+1} + a_{N+2} + a_{N+3} + \cdots,$$

whose first term is a_{N+1} and which is sometimes referred to as the "tail" of the series $\sum_{n=1}^{\infty} a_n$, gives

$$\int_{N+1}^{\infty} f(x)\, dx \le a_{N+1} + a_{N+2} + a_{N+3} + \cdots \le a_{N+1} + \int_{N+1}^{\infty} f(x)\, dx.$$

Since the middle term in this inequality is $S - S_N$,

$$\int_{N+1}^{\infty} f(x)\, dx \le S - S_N \le a_{N+1} + \int_{N+1}^{\infty} f(x)\, dx.$$

These inequalities indicate how good and how bad S_N can be as an approximation to S.

If the series converges very slowly, then the partial sums S_N have little practical value in approximating S. In such cases, we can often do much better with virtually no extra work if we know an antiderivative of $f(x)$. Indeed, define

$$U_N = S_N + \int_{N+1}^{\infty} f(x)\, dx.$$

Then adding S_N to all members of the foregoing inequality yields

$$\boxed{U_N < S < U_N + a_{N+1} \quad \text{and} \quad 0 < S - U_N < a_{N+1}.}$$

In words, *the approximation U_N is less than the sum S of the series by at most the first term omitted from the full series.*

In view of the area comparisons that led to U_N, we sometimes refer to U_N as the *area corrected approximation* to S.

Example 6 *Find $S = \sum_{n=1}^{\infty} 1/n^3$ accurate to within 0.001.*

Solution. The series converges by the integral test; it is the p-series with $p = 3$. The exact sum of this series is unknown. We shall use U_N to approximate S. Here $a_n = 1/n^3$, $f(x) = 1/x^3$, and from the preceding displayed results,

$$U_N = S_N + \int_{N+1}^{\infty} \frac{1}{x^3}\, dx = S_N + \frac{1}{2(N+1)^2},$$

$$0 < S - U_N < \frac{1}{(N+1)^3}.$$

So U_N approximates S to within 0.001 if

$$\frac{1}{(N+1)^3} < 0.001 \Longleftrightarrow (N+1)^3 > 10^3 \Longleftrightarrow N > 9.$$

Let $N = 10$. Then $0 < S - U_{10} < 0.001$. Use a calculator to find

$$S_{10} = \sum_{n=1}^{10} \frac{1}{n^3} \approx 1.1975, \qquad U_{10} = S_{10} + \frac{1}{2\,(11)^2} \approx 1.2016.$$

The approximation $S \approx 1.2016$ is accurate to within 0.001. $\;\square$

In the foregoing example, to approximate S to within 0.001 with S_N you would need to use $N \geq 23$; see the problems. This may help you to appreciate the advantage of using the area corrected approximation U_N instead of S_N as an approximation to S. This point is driven home more forcefully in one of the suggested problems.

12.8   Suggested Problems

1. Let $f(x)$ be positive, decreasing, and continuous for $x \geq 1$ and let $a_n = f(n)$. Let A, B, and C be $\int_1^7 f(x)\, dx$, $\sum_{n=1}^6 a_n$, and $\sum_{n=2}^7 a_n$, in some order. If $A \leq B \leq C$, find A, B, and C. Use a sketch to justify your answer.

Use the integral test to determine whether the series converges or diverges:

2. $\sum_{n=1}^\infty \dfrac{n}{n^2 + 3}$

3. $\sum_{k=1}^\infty k e^{-3k^2}$

4. $\sum_{n=1}^\infty \dfrac{\arctan n}{n^2 + 1}$

5. $\dfrac{1}{3} + \dfrac{1}{7} + \dfrac{1}{11} + \dfrac{1}{15} + \cdots$

6. $\dfrac{1}{3^2} + \dfrac{1}{7^2} + \dfrac{1}{11^2} + \dfrac{1}{15^2} + \cdots$

7. $\dfrac{1}{\sqrt{2}} + \dfrac{1}{2\sqrt{4}} + \dfrac{1}{3\sqrt{6}} + \dfrac{1}{4\sqrt{8}} + \cdots$

Find the values of p for which the series is convergent:

8. $\sum_{n=1}^\infty n\left(1 + n^2\right)^p$

9. $\sum_{n=1}^\infty \dfrac{\ln n}{n^p}$

10. $\sum_{n=2}^\infty \dfrac{1}{n (\ln n)^p}$

Check that the following series converge by the integral test. Then use $U_N = S_N + \int_{N+1}^\infty f(x)\, dx$ to approximate the sum S of the series to within 0.001.

11. $\sum_{n=1}^\infty 1/n^2$

12. $\sum_{n=1}^\infty 1/n^4$

13. $\sum_{n=1}^\infty n e^{-n^2}$

14. $\sum_{n=1}^\infty n^{-1/2} e^{-\sqrt{n}}$

15. Numerical experiments on *any computer* will suggest that the harmonic series *appears* to converge. In fact, if the computer runs long enough all the partial sums calculated after a certain point will be equal.

    (a) Explain *briefly* why the foregoing statement is true. *Hint.* How does a computer store any number that is sufficiently small.

    (b) The integral test shows that the harmonic series diverges; hence, $S_n \to \infty$ as $n \to \infty$. However, the divergence of the partial sums to infinity is exceedingly slow. For the harmonic series use area comparisons to show that $\ln(N+1) < S_N < 1 + \ln N$; hence, $0 < S_N - \ln N < 1$. Use these results to estimate reasonably well how large N must be to make S_N exceed 10, 20, and 100. (Got the point?)

16. *(Comparison of U_N and S_N as approximations to S.)* In the context of Example 6, use the inequality $\int_{N+1}^{\infty} f(x)\, dx < S - S_N$ to show that $S - S_N > 0.001$ for all $N < 23$. Hence, to approximate $S = \sum_{n=1}^{\infty} 1/n^3$ to within 0.001 by S_N requires a choice for N that will be greater than or equal to 23.

17. *(Comparison of U_N and S_N as approximations to S.)* (a) Show that the series $\sum_{n=2}^{\infty} 1/\left(n(\ln n)^2\right)$ converges by the integral test. (b) Find N so that U_N approximates the sum S of the series to with 0.01. (c) As in Problem 14 find at least how large N must be so that S_N approximates the sum S of the series to with 0.01. *Remark.* The sizes of N in (b) and (c) are astronomically different! The value of N you should find in (c) is so large that no current computer could even come close to carrying out the computations to produce S_N, even if it could have started to compute when the universe was born.

18. Show that $\lim_{n \to \infty} \ln n = \infty$. *Hint.* For any positive integer m show that $\lim_{m \to \infty} \ln 2^m = \infty$. If $n > 2^m$, then $\ln n > \ln 2^m$.

19. *(The Harmonic Series)* Show that the harmonic series diverges using the following line of reasoning.

    (a) First show that the partial sums of the harmonic series satisfy

    $$S_2 \ge S_1 + \frac{1}{2}, \quad S_4 \ge S_2 + \frac{1}{2}, \quad S_8 \ge S_4 + \frac{1}{2}, \quad S_{16} \ge S_8 + \frac{1}{2}, \dots .$$

    (b) Second, deduce from part (a) that $S_{2^m} \ge S_1 + m/2$ for any positive integer m.

    (c) Finally, observe that for $n > 2^m$, $S_n > S_{2^m}$ and conclude that $S_n \to \infty$ as $n \to \infty$.

Lesson 13

Comparison Tests

13.1 Goals

- Learn and apply the basic comparison test

- Learn and apply the limit comparison test

13.2 Overview

The integral test and other tests you will learn give specific ways to test particular series for convergence or divergence. Once you know the convergence and divergence properties of a batch of "test" series, it is natural to expect that you can use these series to test other series for convergence or divergence. A series that is "close enough" to a convergent series should converge and a series that is "close enough" to a divergent series should diverge. Comparison tests are the vehicles that put these plausible expectations on a firm foundation.

In this lesson we continue to treat only series with nonnegative terms.

13.3 Basic Comparison Test

We know that the geometric series $\sum_{n=1}^{\infty} \frac{1}{2^n}$ converges. In fact, we even know its sum

$$\sum_{n=1}^{\infty} \frac{1}{2^n} = 1.$$

So what can we say about the series

$$\sum_{n=1}^{\infty} \frac{1}{2^n + 7}?$$

163

Since

$$\frac{1}{2^n + 7} \leq \frac{1}{2^n}$$

each partial sum of $\sum_{n=1}^{\infty} \frac{1}{2^n+7}$ is less than the corresponding partial sum of $\sum_{n=1}^{\infty} \frac{1}{2^n}$. Consequently, the limits of the partial sums, which are the sums of the series, satisfy

$$\sum_{n=1}^{\infty} \frac{1}{2^n + 7} \leq \sum_{n=1}^{\infty} \frac{1}{2^n}.$$

Since $\sum_{n=1}^{\infty} \frac{1}{2^n}$ converges (has a finite sum), it follows that $\sum_{n=1}^{\infty} \frac{1}{2^n+7}$ converges.

In the same way,

$$0 \leq a_n \leq b_n \quad \text{for all} \quad n \quad \Rightarrow \quad \sum a_n \leq \sum b_n.$$

where the sums may be finite or infinite. An immediate consequence is

---

Basic Comparison Test
Let $0 \leq a_n \leq b_n$ for all n. Then
$\sum b_n < \infty \quad \Rightarrow \quad \sum a_n < \infty;$
$\sum a_n = \infty \quad \Rightarrow \quad \sum b_n = \infty.$

In other words,

If $0 \leq a_n \leq b_n$ for all n then
$\sum b_n$ converges $\quad \Rightarrow \quad \sum a_n$ converges;
$\sum a_n$ diverges $\quad \Rightarrow \quad \sum b_n$ diverges.

The basic comparison test remains valid if the inequalities $0 \leq a_n \leq b_n$ hold only for all large n because the behavior of a finite number of terms of a series has no effect on its convergence or divergence.

Example 1 *Determine whether the series $\sum_{n=1}^{\infty} \frac{1}{n^2+5n+1}$ converges or diverges.*

Solution. Since

$$0 \leq \frac{1}{n^2 + 5n + 1} \leq \frac{1}{n^2} \text{ and } \sum_{n=1}^{\infty} \frac{1}{n^2} \text{ converges}$$

the series $\sum_{n=1}^{\infty} \frac{1}{n^2+5n+1}$ is convergent. $\square$

13.4 Limit Comparison Test

Although the basic comparison test is easy to understand, it can be challenging to apply. This is so because even if the test is applicable to a particular pair of series $\sum a_n$ and $\sum b_n$, it may not be easy to establish that the inequalities $0 \le a_n \le b_n$ are in fact true (at least for all large n). Fortunately, in such cases, the inequalities often can be inferred from a simple limit comparison. An example will illustrate how this works.

Example 2 *Determine whether the series $\sum_{n=1}^{\infty} \frac{\sqrt{n}}{n^2-5n+1}$ converges or diverges.*

Solution. The series has positive terms for $n \ge 5$. Since, for large n, n^2 is very much larger than n, it follows that

$$\frac{\sqrt{n}}{n^2-5n+1} \approx \frac{n^{1/2}}{n^2} = \frac{1}{n^{3/2}}.$$

Since convergence or divergence of a series depends only upon the behavior of its terms for all large n, it is reasonable to expect that the given series converges because it should behave like the convergent (p-series) $\sum 1/n^{3/2}$ with $p = 3/2 > 1$. This plausible expectation is correct and follows from the basic comparison test as you can see as follows: The approximate equality $\frac{\sqrt{n}}{n^2-5n+1} \approx \frac{1}{n^{3/2}}$ becomes more nearly an equality as n increases. In fact,

$$\lim_{n \to \infty} \frac{\sqrt{n}/(n^2-5n+1)}{1/n^{3/2}} = \lim_{n \to \infty} \frac{n^{1/2} n^{3/2}}{n^2-5n+1} = \lim_{n \to \infty} \frac{n^2}{n^2(1-5/n+1/n^2)}$$

$$= \lim_{n \to \infty} \frac{1}{1-5/n+1/n^2} = 1.$$

By the meaning of a limit, the ratio $\frac{\sqrt{n}/(n^2-5n+1)}{1/n^{3/2}}$ will be as close to 1 as desired for all n large enough. In particular, the ratio will be less than 2 for all n large enough. That is,

$$\frac{\sqrt{n}/(n^2-5n+1)}{1/n^{3/2}} < 2 \quad \text{for all large } n,$$

$$\frac{\sqrt{n}}{n^2-5n+1} < \frac{2}{n^{3/2}} \quad \text{for all large } n.$$

Now, the basic comparison test tells us that the series $\sum \frac{\sqrt{n}}{n^2-5n+1}$ converges because the series $\sum \frac{2}{n^{3/2}} = 2\sum \frac{1}{n^{3/2}}$ converges. $\square$

The reasoning used in the foregoing example can be used to establish the following variant of the basic comparison test.

Limit Comparison Test
If a_n and b_n are positive for all large n and $\lim_{n \to \infty} a_n/b_n$ is positive and finite, then $\sum a_n$ and $\sum b_n$ either both converge or both diverge.

There are "one-way" versions of the limit comparison test that apply when $\lim_{n \to \infty} a_n/b_n = 0$ or ∞; see the problems.

Example 3 *Determine whether the series* $\sum_{n=1}^{\infty} \frac{n\sqrt{n}}{n^2+n-1}$ *converges or diverges.*

Solution. For large n, the terms of this series $a_n = n\sqrt{n}/\left(n^2 + n - 1\right)$ behave like the terms $b_n = n\sqrt{n}/n^2 = 1/n^{1/2}$. In fact,

$$\lim_{n \to \infty} \frac{n\sqrt{n}/\left(n^2+n-1\right)}{1/n^{1/2}} = \lim_{n \to \infty} \frac{nn^{1/2}n^{1/2}}{n^2+n-1}$$

$$= \lim_{n \to \infty} \frac{n^2}{n^2\left(1 + 1/n - 1/n^2\right)} = 1.$$

Since the p-series $\sum 1/n^{1/2}$ diverges, it follows that the given series diverges by the limit comparison test. $\square$

Variations on a Theme

Comparison tests also can be used to test series of functions for convergence or divergence. Here is an example using the basic comparison test that hints of things to come.

Example 4 *Let* $x \geq 0$. *Determine whether the series* $\sum_{n=1}^{\infty} \frac{x^n}{\sqrt{n}}$ *converges or diverges.*

Solution. The series now depends on x and the convergence or divergence does too. Since

$$0 \leq \frac{x^n}{\sqrt{n}} \leq x^n \text{ and the geometric series } \sum_{n=1}^{\infty} x^n \text{ converges for } 0 \leq x < 1$$

the series $\sum_{n=1}^{\infty} \frac{x^n}{\sqrt{n}}$ converges for $0 \leq x < 1$ (by the basic comparison test.) On the other hand, since for $x \geq 1$

$$\frac{x^n}{\sqrt{n}} \geq \frac{1}{\sqrt{n}} > 0 \text{ and the series } \sum_{n=1}^{\infty} \frac{1}{\sqrt{n}} \text{ diverges,}$$

it follows by comparison that the series $\sum_{n=1}^{\infty} \frac{x^n}{\sqrt{n}}$ diverges for $x \geq 1$. $\square$

13.5   Suggested Problems

Determine whether the given series converges or diverges.

1. $\sum \frac{1}{n^2+n+2}$

2. $\sum \frac{1}{n^2+2n-2}$

3. $\sum \frac{n}{n^2+2n+3}$

4. $\sum \frac{3}{5+2^n}$

5. $\sum \frac{3^n}{4^n+2^n}$

6. $\sum \frac{n^2+3n}{n^5+4}$

7. $\sum \frac{\sqrt{n}}{n+4}$

8. $\sum \frac{\sqrt{2n+3}}{1+n^2}$

9. $\sum \frac{n\ln n}{n^3+n}$

10. $\sum \frac{\sin^2 n}{n\sqrt{n}}$

11. $\sum \sin\left(\frac{1}{n}\right)$

12. $\sum \frac{4+\cos n^5}{n^3}$

13. $\sum \frac{1}{n!}$

14. $\sum \frac{n^2}{n!}$

15. $\sum \frac{n^n}{n!}$

16. $\sum \frac{n^n}{(2n)!}$

In the series that follow $x \geq 0$. Determine the values of x for which the series converges and those for which it diverges.

17. $\sum_{n=0}^{\infty} \frac{x^n}{n^2+n+1}$

18. $\sum_{n=1}^{\infty} \frac{3+\cos nx}{n^2}$

19. $\sum_{n=0}^{\infty} e^{-nx}$

20. $\sum_{n=0}^{\infty} x^n e^{-nx}$ *Hint.* For $x \geq 0$, what is the max of $x^n e^{-nx}$?

21. $\sum_{n=1}^{\infty} \frac{\sin^2 nx}{n^2}$

22. Justify the conclusions of the basic comparison test by making area comparisons using systems of rectangles. Illustrate your discussion with sketches.

23. Explain why $\sum \frac{1}{n^{1+1/n}}$ is not a p-series. Then determine whether the series converges or diverges.

24. Explain why $\sum \frac{1}{n^{1-1/n}}$ is not a p-series. Then determine whether the series converges or diverges.

25. *(Variants of the Limit Comparison Test)* Use the basic comparison test to justify the following convergence tests in which a_n and b_n are positive for all large n.

   (a) If $\sum b_n$ converges and $\lim_{n\to\infty} a_n/b_n = 0$, then $\sum a_n$ also converges.

   (b) If $\sum a_n$ converges and $\lim_{n\to\infty} a_n/b_n = \infty$, then $\sum b_n$ also converges.

Lesson 14

Alternating Series and Absolute Convergence

14.1   Goals

- Learn and apply the alternating series test

- If a series converges by the alternating series test, use the associated error estimate to approximate the sum to any desired accuracy

- Distinguish between absolute convergence and conditional convergence and understand the practical significance of the distinction

14.2   Overview

Previous lessons dealt mainly with series with nonnegative terms. However, series whose terms change sign have important applications, especially alternating series, whose terms alternate in sign. Such series often arise by a successive approximation scheme for solving a complicated problem. A first approximation overestimates the solution, then a correction term is calculated that when subtracted from the first approximation leads to a better approximation that underestimates the solution, then another correction term is added to the current approximation leading to a still better approximation that now over shoots the solution, and so on. Sometimes convergence of a series whose terms vary in sign can be deduced by examining the related series of absolute values of the terms in the original series. This enables us to use indirectly tests for positive-termed series on some series whose terms are not all positive or whose terms may be complex numbers or functions.

169

14.3   Alternating Series

A series of real numbers whose terms alternate in sign is called an **alternating series**. For example, the series

$$1 - \frac{1}{2} + \frac{1}{3} - \frac{1}{4} + \frac{1}{5} - \frac{1}{6} + - \cdots$$

is called the **alternating harmonic series**. It can be written in sigma-notation in two natural ways:

$$\sum_{n=1}^{\infty} (-1)^{n+1} \frac{1}{n} \quad \text{and} \quad \sum_{n=0}^{\infty} (-1)^n \frac{1}{n+1}.$$

Write out several terms in each series to confirm this.

Quite generally there are two convenient ways to express an alternating series in sigma-notation, namely,

$$\sum_{n=1}^{\infty} (-1)^{n+1} b_n \;\; = \;\; b_1 - b_2 + b_3 - b_4 + - \cdots ,$$

$$\sum_{n=0}^{\infty} (-1)^n b_{n+1} \;\; = \;\; b_1 - b_2 + b_3 - b_4 + - \cdots .$$

where in each case $b_n \geq 0$. You need to become comfortable with both ways.

There is a simple convergence test for alternating series, that often can be applied by inspection:

Alternating Series Test
If the numerical size of the terms in an alternating series decrease and tend to zero, then the series converges.

The following figure motivates the alternating series test.

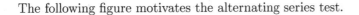

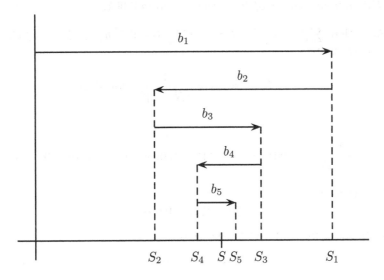

Figure 14.1: Partial Sums of an Alternating Series

Example 1 *Obviously the numerical size of the terms in the alternating harmonic series decrease and tend to zero. So the alternating harmonic series converges.* $\square$

By comparison, recall that the harmonic series diverges. We will learn later that the alternating harmonic series has sum $\ln 2$:

$$1 - \frac{1}{2} + \frac{1}{3} - \frac{1}{4} + \frac{1}{5} - \frac{1}{6} + - \cdots = \ln 2.$$

As displayed in the foregoing figure, the consecutive partial sums of an alternating series successively overshoot and undershoot the sum S of the series. Moreover, the sum of the series is trapped between the partial sums S_N and S_{N+1} which are b_{N+1} units apart. These observations give the following very easy way to approximate the sum of a series that converges by the alternating series test.

> *Error of Approximation in an Alternating Series*
> If a series converges by the alternating series test, then
> any partial sum S_N ending with a positive term is greater than S
> any partial sum S_N ending with a negative term is less than S
> and in either case
> $$|S - S_N| < b_{N+1}.$$

Example 2 *The series $\sum_{n=1}^{\infty} (-1)^{n+1}/n^2$ converges by the alternating series test. Estimate the sum S of the series to within 0.001.*

Solution. Here $\sum_{n=1}^{\infty} (-1)^{n+1}/n^2 = \sum_{n=1}^{\infty} (-1)^{n+1} b_n$ for $b_n = 1/n^2$. By the foregoing estimate

$$|S - S_N| < b_{N+1} = \frac{1}{(N+1)^2} \quad \text{for all } N.$$

Now

$$\frac{1}{(N+1)^2} < 0.001 \Leftrightarrow (N+1)^2 > 1000 \Leftrightarrow N+1 > 10\sqrt{10} > 31.$$

Let $N = 31$ to get

$$|S - S_{31}| < 0.001.$$

Use a calculator or computer to find that

$$S_{31} \approx 0.82297$$

which approximates S to within 0.001. For the record, it is known that the series has sum $\pi^2/12 \approx 0.82247$. $\square$

Variations on a Theme

Recall that convergence is not affected by any finite number of terms of a series. Consequently, if a series *ultimately* satisfies the conditions of the alternating series test, then the series converges. Likewise, the error estimate associated with the test holds for all N beyond the point where the hypotheses of the alternating series test are satisfied.

In some cases where the alternating series test (or its variants) apply it may not be obvious that the numerical size of the terms decrease (or ultimately decrease). In such cases, if $b_n = f(n)$ for a differentiable function $f(x)$, then you can often use the first derivative test to determine if $f(x)$, and hence b_n, ultimately decreases.

14.4 Absolute Convergence

A series $\sum a_n$ is said to be **absolutely convergent (converge absolutely)** if $\sum |a_n|$ is convergent. It is reasonable to expect that an absolutely convergent series converges. This is true:

$$\boxed{\sum |a_n| \quad \text{convergent} \Rightarrow \sum a_n \quad \text{convergent.}}$$

This result holds for series with real or complex terms. The next example will help explain why this result is true for series with real terms.

Example 3 *(a) Show that the series*

$$\sum_{n=1}^{\infty} \frac{(-1)^{n+1}}{n^2} = 1 - \frac{1}{2^2} + \frac{1}{3^2} - \frac{1}{4^2} + \frac{1}{5^2} - \frac{1}{6^2} + -\cdots$$

converges absolutely. (b) Then show that it converges.

Solution. (a)

$$\sum_{n=1}^{\infty} \left| \frac{(-1)^n}{n^2} \right| = \sum_{n=1}^{\infty} \frac{1}{n^2}$$

and we know that $\sum 1/n^2$ converges. So the series $\sum (-1)^{n+1}/n^2$ is absolutely convergent. (b) To show that $\sum_{n=1}^{\infty} (-1)^n/n^2$ converges use the basic comparison test twice: Both series

$$1 + 0 + \frac{1}{3^2} + 0 + \frac{1}{5^2} + 0 + \cdots$$

$$0 + \frac{1}{2^2} + 0 + \frac{1}{4^2} + 0 + \frac{1}{6^2} + \cdots$$

converge by comparison with the convergent series $\sum 1/n^2$. Therefore, the difference of these two series

$$1 - \frac{1}{2^2} + \frac{1}{3^2} - \frac{1}{4^2} + \frac{1}{5^2} - \frac{1}{6^2} + -\cdots$$

converges. $\square$

Of course the convergence of $\sum (-1)^{n+1}/n^2$ in (b) of Example 3 follows directly from the alternating series test, but the reasoning used in (b) is important because it can be used to establish the general principal that absolute convergence implies convergence for series of real numbers.

Example 4 *Show that the series $\sum_{n=0}^{\infty} z^n/(n+1)$ converges absolutely for any complex number z with $|z| < 1$.*

Solution. Since

$$\left| \frac{z^n}{n+1} \right| \le \frac{|z|^n}{n+1} \le |z|^n$$

and the geometric series

$$\sum_{n=0}^{\infty} |z|^n \text{ converges for any } |z| < 1,$$

the series $\sum_{n=0}^{\infty} z^n/(n+1)$ converges absolutely for $|z| < 1$. (Which test was used without mention in this solution?) $\square$

Example 5 *Discuss the convergence properties of $\sum_{n=1}^{\infty} \frac{\cos nx}{n^2}$.*

Solution. Since $|\cos nx| \leq 1$ for any choice of n and any x,

$$\sum_{n=1}^{\infty} \left| \frac{\cos nx}{n^2} \right| \leq \sum_{n=1}^{\infty} \frac{1}{n^2} < \infty.$$

The given series is absolutely convergent for all x; hence, it is convergent for all x. $\square$

Example 6 *Determine when the power series $\sum_{n=1}^{\infty} (-1)^{n+1} x^n/n$ converges.*

Solution. The series converges for some x and diverges for others. If $|x| > 1$ then $(-1)^{n+1} x^n/n \nrightarrow 0$; hence, the series diverges for such x. If $|x| < 1$, the geometric series $\sum |x|^n$ converges and, since $\left| \frac{x^n}{n} \right| \leq |x|^n$, the series $\sum \left| \frac{x^n}{n} \right|$ converges. So $\sum (-1)^{n+1} \frac{x^n}{n}$ is absolutely convergent (hence convergent) for $|x| < 1$. For $x = 1$, the series is the alternating harmonic series which converges. For $x = -1$, the series is the negative of the harmonic series which diverges. In summary, the power series

$$\sum_{n=1}^{\infty} (-1)^{n+1} \frac{x^n}{n} \quad \text{converges} \iff -1 < x \leq 1. \quad \square$$

In the solution to Example 6 the following basic limit was used:

If $b > 1$ and $p > 0$, then

$$\lim_{n \to \infty} \frac{b^n}{n^p} = \infty,$$

equivalently,

$$\lim_{n \to \infty} \frac{n^p}{b^n} = 0.$$

These limits express the fact that an exponential function with base greater than 1 grows incredibly more rapidly than any power function.

Example 7 *The alternating harmonic series $\sum_{n=1}^{\infty} (-1)^{n+1}/n$ is convergent, but the corresponding series of absolute values $\sum_{n=1}^{\infty} 1/n$ is divergent; it is the harmonic series. So the alternating harmonic series is not absolutely convergent.* $\square$

Series, such as the alternating harmonic series, that converge but are not absolutely convergent are called **conditionally convergent**.

14.5 Conditional Versus Absolute Convergence

What's all the fuss about? If we are interested in the series $\sum a_n$ and its convergence or divergence, then why do we care whether the series $\sum |a_n|$ converges or not? There are two important reasons.

1. First, we know several tests (and will learn others) for establishing convergence of a series with nonnegative terms. If we use one of those tests to establish convergence of $\sum |a_n|$, then we get the convergence of $\sum a_n$ free of charge.

2. Second, the distinction is important because conditionally convergent series and absolutely convergent series behave quite differently under familiar algebraic operations. The terms of an absolutely convergent series can be added in any order without changing the sum of the series or the fact that it converges. Also, parentheses can be inserted into an absolutely convergent series without changing its sum.

You say of course, but read on. The sum of a conditionally convergent series may change and the series may even become divergent if its terms are rearranged. For example,

$$1 - \frac{1}{2} + \frac{1}{3} - \frac{1}{4} + \frac{1}{5} - \frac{1}{6} + \frac{1}{7} - \frac{1}{8} + \cdots = \ln 2$$

and the rearranged series

$$1 + \frac{1}{3} - \frac{1}{2} + \frac{1}{5} + \frac{1}{7} - \frac{1}{4} + \frac{1}{9} + \frac{1}{11} - \frac{1}{6} \cdots = \frac{3}{2} \ln 2.$$

The famous German mathematician Bernhard Riemann (1826-1866) proved that the terms of a conditionally convergent series can be rearranged so that the rearranged series has *any prescribed sum S*, including ∞ and $-\infty$. A conditionally convergent series can also be rearranged so that the resulting series does not have a sum.

14.6   Suggested Problems

1. Give brief clear answers to the following questions:

   (a) What is an alternating series?

   (b) To which alternating series does the alternating series test apply?

   (c) Suppose the hypotheses of the alternating series test are met. What can you say about the error when the alternating sum of the first n terms of the series are used to approximate the sum of the series?

   Show that each alternating series converges. Then estimate the error made when the partial sum S_{10} is used to approximate the sum of the series.

2. $\sum_{n=1}^{\infty} (-1)^{n+1} \frac{1}{\ln(n+1)}$

3. $\sum_{n=1}^{\infty} (-1)^{n+1} \frac{n}{n^2+1}$

4. $\sum_{n=1}^{\infty} \left(-\frac{4}{5}\right)^n$

5. $\sum_{n=1}^{\infty} \frac{(-1)^{n+1} n}{2^n}$

6. $\sum_{n=0}^{\infty} \frac{(-1)^n}{\sqrt{n(n+1)}}$

   For problems 7 - 14, determine whether the series is absolutely convergent, conditionally convergent, or divergent.

7. $\sum_{n=1}^{\infty} (-1)^{n-1} \frac{1}{n\sqrt{n}}$

8. $\sum_{n=1}^{\infty} (-1)^{n+1} \frac{1}{5+n}$

9. $\sum_{n=1}^{\infty} (-1)^{n+1} \frac{n}{5+n}$

10. $\sum_{n=1}^{\infty} \frac{\cos n\pi}{n}$

11. $\sum_{n=1}^{\infty} \frac{\sin(n\pi/2)}{n}$

12. $\sum_{n=1}^{\infty} (-1)^{n+1} \frac{\sin(n)}{n\sqrt{n}}$

13. $\sum_{n=1}^{\infty} (-1)^{n+1} \frac{1}{\sqrt{n(n+1)}}$

14. $\sum_{n=1}^{\infty} \frac{(-2)^{n-1}}{n^2}$

For problems 15 - 18,

(a) Determine the values of x for which the series converges.

(b) Determine where the convergence is absolute.

(c) Draw a figure that illustrates the domain of convergence.

15. $\sum_{n=1}^{\infty} x^n / n^2$

16. $\sum_{n=1}^{\infty} x^n / n$

17. $\sum_{n=1}^{\infty} (\sin nx) / n^3$

18. $\sum_{n=1}^{\infty} x^n / \sqrt{n}$

For problems 19 - 21,

(a) Verify that the series converges by the alternating series test.

(b) Find the smallest N such that the error estimate $|S - S_N| < 0.001$ is guaranteed to hold in connection with the alternating series test.

(c) Calculate the corresponding S_N correct to five decimal places. (d) Is $S_N > S$ or is $S_N < S$? Explain briefly.

19. $\sum_{n=1}^{\infty} (-1)^{n+1} / n^3$

20. $\sum_{n=1}^{\infty} (-1)^{n+1} / n^n$

21. $\sum_{n=1}^{\infty} (-1)^{n+1} (\sin (1/n)) / n^2$

For problems 22 - 25, let z be a complex variable. Determine where each series is absolutely convergent. Describe the domain of absolute convergence geometrically.

22. $\sum_{n=1}^{\infty} z^n / n^2$

23. $\sum_{n=1}^{\infty} z^n / n$

24. $\sum_{n=1}^{\infty} z^n / \sqrt{n}$

25. $\sum_{n=0}^{\infty} (-1)^n z^n / n\sqrt{n}$

26. Is the 75th partial sum S_{75} of the series $\sum_{n=1}^{\infty} (-1)^{n+1} / (n^2 + 1)$ an overestimate or an underestimate for the sum S of the series? Explain.

27. Is the 56th partial sum S_{56} of the series $\sum_{n=1}^{\infty} (-1)^{n+1} / (n^2 + 1)$ an overestimate or an underestimate for the sum S of the series? Explain.

Lesson 15

Root and Ratio Tests

15.1 Goals

- Learn and apply the ratio test

- Learn and apply the root test

- Approximate sums of series using comparisons with geometric series

15.2 Overview

The root and ratio tests are two of the most widely applicable tests for the convergence or divergence of a series, especially power series. Both tests are based on comparisons with geometric series and both tests apply to series with real or complex terms. Further comparisons yield numerical approximations for the sum of a series that converges by these tests. In applying the root or ratio test it is useful to know several basic limits that come up in calculus. They are listed at the end of this lesson. Don't overlook them!

15.3 The Root Test

The root test is a little simpler for series with positive terms. So we start with that case. Let $\sum a_n$ be a series with every $a_n \geq 0$. Compare $\sum a_n$ with the geometric series $\sum r^n$ to obtain

$$\sum a_n \text{ converges if } a_n \leq r^n \text{ for all large } n \text{ and some } r < 1,$$
$$\sum a_n \text{ diverges if } a_n \geq r^n \text{ for all large } n \text{ and some } r \geq 1.$$

These results are expressed more conveniently in the following form.

Let $a_n \geq 0$. Then:

$\sum a_n$ converges if $a_n^{1/n} \leq r$ for all large n and some $r < 1$.

$\sum a_n$ diverges if $a_n^{1/n} \geq r$ for all large n and some $r \geq 1$.

Example 1 *Does $\sum_{n=1}^{\infty} \left(\frac{n+2}{3n-1} \right)^n$ converge or diverge?*

Solution. Here $a_n = \left(\frac{n+2}{3n-1} \right)^n$ and

$$a_n^{1/n} = \frac{n+2}{3n-1} \to \frac{1}{3} \text{ as } n \to \infty.$$

Consequently, $a_n^{1/n}$ can be made as near to $1/3$ as desired by taking n large enough. Since $1/3 < 2/3$, it follows that

$$a_n^{1/n} < \frac{2}{3} \text{ for all large } n$$

and by the foregoing test $\sum \left(\frac{n+2}{3n-1} \right)^n$ converges. $\square$

The reasoning just used in Example 1 stands behind

The Root Test

Assume

$$|a_n|^{1/n} \to L \text{ (finite or infinite) as } n \to \infty.$$

Then

$\sum a_n$ converges absolutely if $L < 1$,

$\sum a_n$ diverges if $L > 1$,

the test fails if $L = 1$.

By the test "fails" is meant that the root test cannot distinguish convergence from divergence when the limit $L = 1$.

Example 2 *Determine where the series $\sum_{n=1}^{\infty} (-1)^n z^n / n^2$ converges.*

Solution. As usual, z is a complex variable. Here $a_n = (-1)^n z^n / n^2$ and

$$|a_n|^{1/n} = \frac{|z|}{n^{2/n}} = \frac{|z|}{\left(n^{1/n} \right)^2} \to \frac{|z|}{1} = |z|$$

by special limit #4 at the end of this lesson. Consequently, by the root test, the series

converges absolutely if $|z| < 1$

and diverges if $|z| > 1$.

The root test gives no information if $|z| = 1$. However, if $|z| = 1$,

$$\sum_{n=1}^{\infty} \left| (-1)^n \frac{z^n}{n^2} \right| = \sum_{n=1}^{\infty} \frac{1}{n^2} < \infty$$

and the series converges absolutely when $|z| = 1$. In summary, the series

$$\text{converges absolutely if } |z| \leq 1$$
$$\text{and diverges if } |z| > 1. \quad \square$$

15.4 The Ratio Test

The ratio test also is a little simpler for series with positive terms. The geometric series $\sum r^n$ converges if $0 < r < 1$ and diverges if $r \geq 1$. Notice that the common ratio of two consecutive terms of the series is $r^{n+1}/r^n = r$. Therefore, the geometric series $\sum r^n$ converges if the common ratio $r < 1$ and diverges if the common ratio $r \geq 1$. A very similar result holds for any series of positive terms:

Let $a_n > 0$. Then:

$\sum a_n$ converges if $\dfrac{a_{n+1}}{a_n} \leq r < 1$ for all large n.

$\sum a_n$ diverges if $\dfrac{a_{n+1}}{a_n} \geq r \geq 1$ for all large n.

First we establish the test for convergence. Since the convergence of $\sum_{n=0}^{\infty} a_n$ depends only on a_n for n arbitrarily large, we can change the initial terms of the series, if necessary, so that

$$\frac{a_{n+1}}{a_n} \leq r < 1 \quad \text{for } n = 0, 1, 2, 3, \dots .$$

Then $a_{n+1} \leq a_n r$ for all n and, hence,

$$
\begin{aligned}
a_1 &\leq a_0 r, \\
a_2 &\leq a_1 r \leq a_0 r^2, \\
a_3 &\leq a_2 r \leq a_0 r^3,
\end{aligned}
$$

and, in general,

$$a_n \leq a_0 r^n.$$

Since $0 < r < 1$,

$$\sum a_n \leq \sum a_0 r^n = a_0 \sum r^n = \frac{a_0}{1-r} < \infty$$

and the basic comparison test implies that $\sum a_n$ converges. The proof of the test for divergence amounts to reversing the inequalities and noting that $\sum a_0 r^n$ diverges for $r \geq 1$.

Example 3 *Does $\sum_{n=1}^{\infty} n^2/2^n$ converge or diverge?*

Solution. Let $a_n = n^2/2^n$. Then

$$\frac{a_{n+1}}{a_n} = a_{n+1} \cdot \frac{1}{a_n} = \frac{(n+1)^2}{2^{n+1}} \cdot \frac{2^n}{n^2} = \frac{1}{2}\left(1 + \frac{1}{n}\right)^2 \to \frac{1}{2}$$

as $n \to \infty$. Consequently, a_{n+1}/a_n can be made as near to $1/2$ as desired by taking n large enough. Since $1/2 < 3/4$, it follows that

$$\frac{a_{n+1}}{a_n} \le \frac{3}{4} < 1 \quad \text{for all } n \text{ large}$$

and by the foregoing boxed result $\sum_{n=1}^{\infty} n^2/2^n$ converges. □

The line of reasoning in the previous example leads to

The Ratio Test
Let $a_n \ne 0$ for all large n and
$$\left|\frac{a_{n+1}}{a_n}\right| \to L \text{ (finite or infinite) as } n \to \infty.$$
Then
$$\sum a_n \quad \text{converges absolutely if } L < 1,$$
$$\sum a_n \quad \text{diverges if } L > 1,$$
$$\text{the test fails if } L = 1.$$

Example 4 *For what values of x does the series $\sum_{n=1}^{\infty} (-1)^n \frac{x^{2n}}{n^2}$ converge?*

Solution. Let $a_n = (-1)^n x^{2n}/n^2$. If $x = 0$, it is obvious that the series converges absolutely. (Why?) For $x \ne 0$,

$$\left|\frac{a_{n+1}}{a_n}\right| = \frac{|x|^{2(n+1)}}{(n+1)^2} \cdot \frac{n^2}{|x|^{2n}} = |x|^2 \left(\frac{n}{n+1}\right)^2 \to |x|^2$$

as $n \to \infty$. By the ratio test, the given series

$$\text{converges absolutely if } |x|^2 < 1 \iff |x| < 1$$
$$\text{and diverges if } |x|^2 > 1 \iff |x| > 1.$$

If $|x| = 1$, that is if $x = \pm 1$, the ratio test gives no information. However, for $x = \pm 1$, the series is

$$\sum_{n=1}^{\infty} (-1)^n \frac{1}{n^2}$$

which we know converges absolutely. In summary, $\sum (-1)^n \frac{x^{2n}}{n^2}$ converges absolutely for $|x| \le 1$ and diverges for $|x| > 1$. □

Example 5 *Use both the ratio test and the root test to determine if the series*

$$\sum_{n=1}^{\infty} \frac{n^2}{n!}$$

converges or diverges.

Solution. Here $a_n = n^2/n!$. First let's apply the ratio test:

$$\left| \frac{a_{n+1}}{a_n} \right| = \frac{(n+1)^2}{(n+1)!} \cdot \frac{n!}{n^2} = \left(\frac{n+1}{n} \right)^2 \frac{n!}{(n+1)!} = \left(1 + \frac{1}{n} \right)^2 \frac{1}{n+1} \to 0$$

as $n \to \infty$ and the series converges. Now let's apply the root test:

$$|a_n|^{1/n} = \frac{\left(n^{1/n} \right)^2}{(n!)^{1/n}} \to 0$$

because (as we know) $n^{1/n} \to 1$ and (see below) $(n!)^{1/n} = \sqrt[n]{n!} \to \infty$ as $n \to \infty$. So the given series converges by the root test. $\square$

The fact that

$$\sqrt[n]{n!} \to \infty \quad \text{as} \quad n \to \infty$$

is an elementary consequence of a much more useful result, called Stirling's formula, that tells how rapidly $n!$ grows with n in terms of more familiar functions:

Stirling's Formula
$$\lim_{n \to \infty} \frac{n!}{\sqrt{2\pi n}\, (n/e)^n} = 1$$

Stirling's formula often is express as

$$n! \sim \sqrt{2\pi n}\, (n/e)^n,$$

which is read $n!$ is *asymptotic* with $\sqrt{2\pi n}\, (n/e)^n$ as $n \to \infty$, and where the tilde notation means that the ratio of the two expressions has limit 1 as $n \to \infty$.

15.5 Approximation of Sums of Series That Converge by the Root or Ratio Test

Refinements of the comparisons with geometric series used to establish the ratio and root tests lead to practical numerical approximations for sums of series that converge by these tests.

Suppose for example that the terms of the series $\sum_{n=0}^{\infty} a_n$ satisfy

$$\frac{|a_{n+1}|}{|a_n|} \le r < 1 \text{ for } n \ge M.$$

Then the series converges absolutely by the ratio test. Let S be its sum and S_N be its Nth partial sum. Then

$$|S - S_N| = \left| \sum_{k=N+1}^{\infty} a_k \right| \leq \sum_{k=N+1}^{\infty} |a_k|.$$

If $N \geq M$, then comparison with the geometric series, just as we did earlier in the lesson, gives

$$|a_{N+2}| \leq |a_{N+1}|r, \quad |a_{N+3}| \leq |a_{N+1}|r^2, \quad |a_{N+4}| \leq |a_{N+1}|r^3, \quad \ldots$$

Hence, if $N \geq M$,

$$\begin{aligned}
|S - S_N| &\leq \sum_{k=N+1}^{\infty} |a_k| \leq |a_{N+1}| \left(1 + r + r^2 + r^3 + \cdots \right) \\
&= |a_{N+1}| \frac{1}{1-r}
\end{aligned}$$

In summary, we have:

$$\boxed{\begin{aligned}
&\text{Assume } \frac{|a_{n+1}|}{|a_n|} \leq r < 1 \text{ for } n \geq M. \\
&\text{If } N \geq M \text{ then the partial sum } S_N \text{ and} \\
&\text{sum } S \text{ of the series } \sum_{n=0}^{\infty} a_n \text{ satisfy} \\
&\qquad |S - S_N| \leq \frac{|a_{N+1}|}{1-r}.
\end{aligned}}$$

Some thought is required to use this error estimate effectively because you must determine an M and a corresponding r so that the hypotheses of the error test are satisfied. The name of the game is to choose M not too large but large enough so that the corresponding r you determine is reasonably less than 1. In typical applications $|a_{n+1}/a_n| \to L < 1$ and you want to pick M not too large but large enough so that r is reasonably close to L. The rub is that normally a larger M allows a relatively smaller r. You have to strike a balance. Finding a suitable pair of M and r usually requires a little numerical experimentation with a calculator or computer.

Example 6 *Find* $\sum_{n=1}^{\infty} n^2/2^n$ *accurate to within* 0.001.

Solution. Let $a_n = n^2/2^n$. From Example 3, the series converges by the ratio test. In fact,

$$\frac{a_{n+1}}{a_n} = \frac{1}{2} \left(1 + \frac{1}{n} \right)^2 \to \frac{1}{2}.$$

The formula for the ratios show that they decrease as n increases. Here are a few sample ratios:

n	1	2	3	5	10	20
$\frac{a_{n+1}}{a_n}$	2	$\frac{9}{8}$	$\frac{8}{9}$	$\frac{18}{25} = 0.72$	$\frac{121}{200} \approx 0.61$	$\frac{441}{800} \approx 0.56$

The last two decimal approximations are rounded up. Since the ratios decrease, any column in the table with $n \geq 3$ determines a pair of values M and r that satisfy the hypotheses of the error estimate. For example, we can take $M = 10$ and $r = 0.61$. Then for $N \geq M = 10$,

$$|S - S_N| < \frac{|a_{N+1}|}{1 - r} = \frac{(N+1)^2 / 2^{N+1}}{.39} = \frac{(N+1)^2}{(.39)\, 2^{N+1}}$$

and the required accuracy will be achieved if $N \geq 10$ also satisfies

$$\frac{(N+1)^2}{(.39)\, 2^{N+1}} < 0.001 \iff \frac{2^{N+1}}{(N+1)^2} > \frac{1}{0.00039} \approx 2564.1.$$

Use a graphics utility to plot graphs of $2^{x+1} / (x+1)^2$ and 2564.1 on the same screen to see that any $N \geq 20$ will satisfy the foregoing inequality. The same conclusion can be reached by trial-and-error calculations of $2^{x+1} / (x+1)^2$ for various integer values of x and comparison with 2564.1. Therefore,

$$S_{20} = \sum_{n=1}^{20} \frac{n^2}{2^n} \approx 5.9995$$

approximates the sum of the series to within 0.001. You may suspect that the sum is 6. Stay tuned. $\square$

Very similar reasoning related to the root test gives the estimate:

Assume $|a_n|^{1/n} \leq r < 1$ for $n \geq M$.
If $N \geq M$ then the partial sum S_N and
sum S of the series $\sum_{n=0}^{\infty} a_n$ satisfy
$$|S - S_N| \leq \frac{r^{N+1}}{1 - r}.$$

The following fact is often useful when using this error estimate:

$n^{1/n}$ decreases for $n \geq 3$.

You can confirm this by checking that the derivative of the function $x^{1/x}$ is negative for $x \geq 3$.

15.6   Special Limits

Here are several special limits that you may find useful when you apply the ratio
or root test to particular series. (If you did the group project on special limits
in the supplemental materials at the end of these lessons, you already have met
most of the special limits and developed some numerical evidence in support of
them. Now you can prove some of them!)

As $n \to \infty$:

1. $a^n \to 0$ provided $|a| < 1$.

2. $a^{1/n} \to 1$ provided $a > 0$.

3. $\dfrac{\ln n}{n^p} \to 0$ for any $p > 0$; in particular, $\dfrac{\ln n}{n} \to 0$.

4. $n^{1/n} \to 1$.

5. $\left(1 + \dfrac{x}{n}\right)^n \to e^x$ for all x.

6. $\dfrac{x^n}{n!} \to 0$ for all x.

A homework problem guides you through the verification of three of these
results.

15.7 Suggested Problems

What can you say about the series $\sum a_n$ in each case.

1. $\lim_{n \to \infty} \left| \frac{a_{n+1}}{a_n} \right| = 4$

2. $\lim_{n \to \infty} \left| \frac{a_{n+1}}{a_n} \right| = \frac{1}{4}$

3. $\lim_{n \to \infty} \left| \frac{a_{n+1}}{a_n} \right| = 1$

For problems 4 - 16, use either the ratio or the root test to determine (absolute) convergence, divergence, or that the test is inconclusive.

4. $\sum n \left(\frac{1}{3} \right)^n$

5. $\sum \left(\frac{1}{\ln n} \right)^n$

6. $\sum \left(\frac{n}{2n-11} \right)^n$

7. $\sum (-1)^n \left(\frac{1}{2} + \frac{2}{n} \right)^n$

8. $\sum \frac{n^2}{n!}$

9. $\sum (-1)^n \frac{n^3}{(2n)!}$

10. $\sum \frac{n^n}{(2n)!}$

11. $\sum \frac{n^n}{n!}$

12. $1 + \frac{1}{2} + \frac{1}{3} + \frac{1}{4} + \cdots$

13. $1 - \frac{1}{2^2} + \frac{1}{3^2} - \frac{1}{4^2} + \cdots$

14. $1 - \frac{1}{2\sqrt{2}} + \frac{1}{3\sqrt{3}} - \frac{1}{4\sqrt{4}} + \cdots$

15. $\frac{2}{1 \cdot 3 \cdot 4} - \frac{3}{2 \cdot 4 \cdot 5} + \frac{4}{3 \cdot 5 \cdot 6} - \frac{5}{4 \cdot 6 \cdot 7} + - \cdots$

16. $\frac{2}{1 \cdot 3 \cdot 4} + \frac{3}{2 \cdot 4 \cdot 5} + \frac{4}{3 \cdot 5 \cdot 6} + \frac{5}{4 \cdot 6 \cdot 7} + \cdots$

For problems 17 - 20, determine whether the series is absolutely convergent, conditionally convergent, or divergent.

17. $\sum_{n=1}^{\infty} \frac{(-2)^n}{n^2}$

18. $\sum_{n=0}^{\infty} \frac{(-2)^n}{n!}$

19. $\sum_{n=1}^{\infty} \left(\frac{n^2+4}{2n^2-1} \right)^n$

20. $\sum_{n=1}^{\infty} (-1)^n \left(\frac{n^2+4}{\sqrt{2n^4-1}} \right)^n$

For problems 21 - 24,

    (a) Use the ratio test to show that the series converges.

    (b) Then use the error estimate in this lesson associated with the ratio test to approximate the sum to within 0.001.

21. $\sum_{n=0}^{\infty} 1/n!$

22. $\sum_{n=0}^{\infty} n/2^n$

23. $\sum_{n=0}^{\infty} \left(n^2 + n \right) /3^n$

24. $\sum_{n=0}^{\infty} (-1)^n \left(\frac{1}{1+n} \right)^n$

For problems 25 - 28,

    (a) Use the root test to show that the series converges.

    (b) Then use the error estimate in this lesson associated with the root test to approximate the sum to within 0.001.

25. $\sum_{n=0}^{\infty} 1/n!$ *Hint.* $\sqrt[n]{n!}$ is increasing.

26. $\sum_{n=0}^{\infty} n/2^n$

27. $\sum_{n=0}^{\infty} (-1)^n \left(\frac{1}{1+n} \right)^n$

28. $\sum_{n=0}^{\infty} \left(n^2 + n \right) /3^n$

29. For real x, $\sum_{n=1}^{\infty} x^n /n3^n$ is a real power series. (a) Show that it converges absolutely by the ratio test for all $|x| < 3$. (b) Its sum $S(x)$ and partial sums $S_N(x)$ are functions of x. Determine N so that that the partial sum $S_N(x)$ will approximate $S(x)$ to within 0.001 for *all* x in the interval $-2 \le x \le 2$.

30. For real x, $\sum_{n=1}^{\infty} nx^n /3^n$ is a real power series. (a) Show that it converges absolutely by the root test for all $|x| < 3$. (b) Its sum $S(x)$ and partial sums $S_N(x)$ are functions of x. Determine N so that that the partial sum $S_N(x)$ will approximate $S(x)$ to within 0.001 for *all* x in the interval $-2 \le x \le 2$.

31. Use the ratio test to determine where the given power series converges absolutely and where it diverges. What happens at the two endpoints of the interval of convergence?

    (a) $\sum n x^n$

    (b) $\sum n^2 x^n$

    (c) $\sum n^3 x^n$

    (d) What general result is suggested by (a), (b), and (c)? State and confirm it.

32. Use the root test to determine where the given power series converges absolutely and where it diverges. What happens at the two endpoints of the interval of convergence?

    (a) $\sum x^n/n$

    (b) $\sum x^n/n^2$

    (c) $\sum x^n/n^3$

    (d) What general result is suggested by (a), (b), and (c)? State and confirm it.

33. Fix $|x| < 1$ and $p > 0$. Use Problem 31(d) to show that $n^p x^n \to 0$ as $n \to \infty$.

For problems 34 - 37,

    (a) Determine for which z (as usual a complex variable) the series converges absolutely and for which z it diverges.

    (b) Describe the region of absolute convergence geometrically.

34. $\sum (-1)^n n^2 z^n / 2^n$

35. $\sum (\ln n) z^n$

36. $\sum z^n / n!$

37. $\sum n! z^n / 3^n$

38. The terms of the series $\sum a_n$ are defined recursively by $a_1 = 1/2$ and $a_{n+1} = \frac{4n+1}{3n+2} a_n$ for $n \geq 1$. Determine whether the series converges or diverges.

39. The terms of the series $\sum a_n$ are defined recursively by $a_1 = 2$ and $a_{n+1} = \frac{3n+2}{4n+1} a_n$ for $n \geq 1$. Determine whether the series converges or diverges.

40. *(More Error Estimates)* Assume there is a positive integer N such that $a_n \geq a_{n+1} > 0$ for all $n > N$. Establish the following assertions:

   (a) If $0 < r < 1$, then $\sum_{n=N+1}^{\infty} a_n r^n \leq \dfrac{a_{N+1} r^{N+1}}{1 - r}$.

   (b) If $r > 0$, then $\sum_{n=N+1}^{\infty} a_n \dfrac{r^n}{n!} < a_{N+1} \dfrac{r^{N+1}}{(N+1)!} e^r$.

   (c) Moreover, in (b) if $r < N+2$, then $\sum_{n=N+1}^{\infty} a_n \dfrac{r^n}{n!} < a_{N+1} \dfrac{r^{N+1}}{(N+1)!} \dfrac{N+2}{N+2-r}$.
   Hint. Use a geometric series.

41. Let $S_N(x)$ be the Nth partial sum and $S(x)$ the sum of a given power series. Do the following:

   (a) For the power series $\sum_{n=1}^{\infty} \frac{n}{2^n} x^n$ use (a) of the previous problem to find a reasonable N so that $S_N(x)$ approximates $S(x)$ to 4 decimal places (error at most 0.00005) for all x with $-1 \leq x \leq 1$. *Hint.* For $|x| \leq 1$,
   $$\left| \frac{n}{2^n} x^n \right| \leq \frac{n}{2^n} = \frac{n}{(\sqrt{2})^n} \left(\frac{1}{\sqrt{2}} \right)^n.$$

   (b) For the power series $\sum_{n=1}^{\infty} \frac{1}{\sqrt{n}} \frac{x^n}{n!}$ use (b) of the previous problem to find a reasonable N so that $S_N(x)$ approximates $S(x)$ to 4 decimal places (error at most 0.00005) for all x with $-2 \leq x \leq 2$.

   (c) For the power series $\sum_{n=1}^{\infty} \frac{1}{\sqrt{n}} \frac{x^n}{n!}$ use (c) of the previous problem to find a reasonable N so that $S_N(x)$ approximates $S(x)$ to 4 decimal places (error at most 0.00005) for all x with $-2 \leq x \leq 2$.

42. Use Stirling's formula to deduce that $\sqrt[n]{n!} \to \infty$ as $n \to \infty$.

43. *(The Special Limits)* Recall that $e^x \to 0$ as $x \to -\infty$, $e^x \to 1$ as $x \to 0$, and $a^x = e^{x \ln a}$ for any $a > 0$.

   (a) Verify special limit #1. *Hint.* $|a^n| = |a|^n = e^{n \ln |a|}$

   (b) Verify special limit #2. *Hint.* $a^{1/n} = e^{(1/n) \ln a}$

   (c) Verify special limit #4. *Hint.* $n^{1/n} = e^{(1/n) \ln n}$ and special limit #3

Lesson 16

Power Series

16.1 Goals

- Learn the general convergence properties of power series

- Find the radius of convergence of particular power series

- Know that a power series converges absolutely inside its interval of convergence (real case) and inside its circle of convergence (complex case)

- Establish convergence or divergence at the end points of the interval of convergence (or on the circle of convergence in simple cases)

- Learn and apply the algebraic properties for addition, subtraction, multiplication, and division of power series and how to determine intervals (disks) in which the resulting series converge absolutely.

16.2 Overview

Recall that a **power series** (in powers of x or about $x = 0$) is an infinite series of the form

$$\sum a_n x^n = a_0 + a_1 x + a_2 x^2 + \cdots + a_n x^n + \cdots.$$

As always, x is understood to be a real variable and in this context the coefficients are (usually) real numbers. We also have met power series in z

$$\sum a_n z^n = a_0 + a_1 z + a_2 z^2 + \cdots + a_n z^n + \cdots,$$

where z is understood to be a complex variable. The coefficients of a complex power series may be either real or complex numbers. You have worked with several examples of such power series in earlier lessons. We will take a closer

191

look at power series in the next two lessons. In certain respects power series behave like "infinite degree" polynomials and it is important to know when this is the case. In Lesson 11 we saw that some complicated functions of calculus can be expressed as power series. In particular,

$$e^x = 1 + x + \frac{x^2}{2!} + \frac{x^3}{3!} + \cdots + \frac{x^n}{n!} + \cdots,$$

$$\sin x = x - \frac{x^3}{3!} + \frac{x^5}{5!} - \frac{x^7}{7!} + - \cdots,$$

$$\cos x = 1 - \frac{x^2}{2!} + \frac{x^4}{4!} - \frac{x^6}{6!} + - \cdots,$$

for all real x. Indeed, virtually all the functions you have met in calculus have power series expansions. Power series expansions such as these have important theoretical and computational uses.

In this lesson and the next one, we shall concentrate successively on the convergence properties of power series, the algebraic properties of power series, the analytic properties of power series, on new ways to obtain power series expansions, and finally on some applications. This lesson deals primarily with convergence properties and algebraic properties of power series.

16.3   Convergence of Power Series

Did you notice a common convergence property of the power series in all the examples given in earlier lessons and in the homework? In each case, there was a number $r > 0$ such that the power series converged absolutely for $|x| < r$ and diverged for $|x| > r$. This behavior is typical, as we explain next. The following results should seem quite plausible based on your experience with particular power series. The proofs of these results and other general results about power series discussed later will be skipped. They can be found in most books on advanced calculus.

> For any power series $\sum a_n x^n$ there are three possibilities:
> (a) $\sum a_n x^n$ converges only for $x = 0$;
> (b) $\sum a_n x^n$ converges absolutely for all x;
> (c) There is a number $r > 0$ such that
> $\qquad \sum a_n x^n$ converges absolutely for $|x| < r$
> $\qquad$ and $\sum a_n x^n$ diverges for $|x| > r$.

Let C be the set of values x for which the power series $\sum a_n x^n$ converges. By the foregoing theorem, C is one of six intervals

$$[0,0], \quad [-r,r], \quad (-r,r] \quad [-r,r), \quad (-r,r) \quad (-\infty,\infty)$$

for some $r > 0$. We call C the **interval of convergence** of the power series. Define $r = 0$ if $C = [0,0]$ and $r = \infty$ if $C = (-\infty, \infty)$. Then r is called the **radius of convergence** of the power series.

The terminology radius of convergence comes from the corresponding theorem for complex power series:

> For any power series $\sum a_n z^n$ there are three possibilities:
> (a) $\sum a_n z^n$ converges only for $z = 0$;
> (b) $\sum a_n z^n$ converges absolutely for all z;
> (c) There is a number $r > 0$ such that
> $\sum a_n z^n$ converges absolutely for $|z| < r$
>   and $\sum a_n z^n$ diverges for $|z| > r$

Let D be the set of values z for which the power series $\sum a_n z^n$ converges. We call D the **domain of convergence** of the power series. In case (c), the power series converges absolutely inside the circle $|z| = r$ in the complex plane, diverges outside the circle $|z| = r$, and may converge or diverge at points on the circle $|z| = r$. Define $r = 0$ if $D = \{0\}$ and $r = \infty$ if $D = \mathbb{C}$, the entire complex plane. Then r is called the **radius of convergence** of the power series and the circle $|z| = r$ the **circle of convergence** of the power series. The domain of convergence D consists of all points z inside the circle $|z| < r$ together with any points on the circle at which the series converges.

Example 1 *Find the radius and interval of convergence of the power series* $\sum_{n=0}^{\infty} n! x^n / (2n)!$

Solution. We try the ratio test because of the factorials. As usual the base point must be treated separately. The series is obviously absolutely convergent when $x = 0$. Let $b_n = n! x^n / (2n)!$ For $x \neq 0$,

$$\left| \frac{b_{n+1}}{b_n} \right| = \left| \frac{(n+1)! x^{n+1}}{[2(n+1)]!} \cdot \frac{(2n)!}{n! x^n} \right| = \frac{(n+1)|x|}{(2n+2)(2n+1)} = \frac{|x|}{2(2n+1)} \to 0$$

as $n \to \infty$. (Be sure you understand why $(2n)! / [2(n+1)]!$ simplifies to $1/(2n+2)(2n+1)$.) By the ratio test, the series converges for all $x \neq 0$; consequently, the interval of convergence is $(-\infty, \infty)$ and the radius of convergence is $r = \infty$. $\square$

Example 2 *Find the circle of convergence of the power series* $\sum (-1)^n z^n / n^2$. *What is the domain of convergence?*

Solution. This time we apply the root test. (Try the ratio test for yourself.) Let $c_n = (-1)^n z^n / n^2$. Then

$$|c_n|^{1/n} = \left| \frac{(-1)^n z^n}{n^2} \right|^{1/n} = \frac{|z|}{n^{2/n}} = \frac{|z|}{\left(n^{1/n} \right)^2} \to \frac{|z|}{1^2} = |z| \quad \text{as } n \to \infty.$$

By the root test, the series

converges absolutely for $|z| < 1$
and diverges for $|z| > 1$.

So the radius of convergence is $r = 1$, the circle of convergence is $|z| = 1$, the unit circle in the complex plane. We know the series converges absolutely in the open unit disk $|z| < 1$. If $|z| = 1$,

$$\sum \left| \frac{(-1)^n z^n}{n^2} \right| = \sum \frac{1}{n^2} < \infty.$$

So the series also converges absolutely at each point on the circle $|z| = 1$. The domain of convergence is the closed unit disk $|z| \leq 1$. $\square$

For a given complex power series it can be quite difficult to decide whether or not the series converges at a particular point on its circle of convergence. Fortunately, in most practical situations, what happens on the circle of convergence is not especially important. The action usually takes place inside the circle of convergence (where the convergence is absolute).

Example 3 *Fix a real number $\alpha \neq 0$. The Taylor series of $(1 + x)^\alpha$ is (see the suggested problems)*

$$1 + \sum_{n=1}^{\infty} \binom{\alpha}{n} x^n = 1 + \alpha x + \frac{\alpha(\alpha - 1)}{1 \cdot 2} x^2 + \frac{\alpha(\alpha - 1)(\alpha - 2)}{1 \cdot 2 \cdot 3} x^3 +$$

$$\frac{\alpha(\alpha - 1)(\alpha - 2)(\alpha - 3)}{1 \cdot 2 \cdot 3 \cdot 4} x^4 + \cdots$$

*where the coefficient of x^n, called a **binomial coefficient**, is*

$$\binom{\alpha}{n} = \frac{\alpha(\alpha - 1)(\alpha - 2) \cdots (\alpha - n + 1)}{1 \cdot 2 \cdot 3 \cdots \cdot n}.$$

*Find the radius of convergence of this power series, called the **binomial series**.*

Solution. Observe that two consecutive binomial coefficients satisfy

$$\binom{\alpha}{n+1} = \frac{\alpha(\alpha - 1)(\alpha - 2) \cdots (\alpha - n + 1)(\alpha - n)}{1 \cdot 2 \cdot 3 \cdots \cdot n \cdot (n+1)} = \binom{\alpha}{n} \frac{\alpha - n}{n+1}$$

Now, it is easy to find the radius of convergence of the binomial series using the ratio test:

$$\left| \frac{\binom{\alpha}{n+1} x^{n+1}}{\binom{\alpha}{n} x^n} \right| = \left| \frac{\alpha - n}{n+1} \right| |x| \to |x| \qquad \text{as } n \to \infty.$$

By the ratio test, the binomial series

converges absolutely for $|x| < 1$

and diverges for $|x| > 1$

Consequently, the binomial series has radius of convergence 1 and converges absolutely for $-1 < x < 1$. $\square$

The binomial series is most useful for fractional powers such as $(1 + x)^{1/2}$, $(1 + x)^{-1/2}$, and $(1 + x)^{1/3}$. Newton, who used the binomial series in approximate calculation of roots, is often credited with discovering the binomial series; however, it also was known to Leibniz. As you probably have guessed, the binomial series has the expected sum:

$$
\begin{aligned}
(1 + x)^\alpha \;=\; & 1 + \alpha x + \frac{\alpha\,(\alpha - 1)}{1 \cdot 2} x^2 + \frac{\alpha\,(\alpha - 1)\,(\alpha - 2)}{1 \cdot 2 \cdot 3} x^3 + \\
& \frac{\alpha\,(\alpha - 1)\,(\alpha - 2)\,(\alpha - 3)}{1 \cdot 2 \cdot 3 \cdot 4} x^4 + \cdots
\end{aligned}
$$

for $-1 < x < 1$. See the group projects for one way to establish this binomial expansion.

As the foregoing examples suggest, the radius and domain of convergence of a power series often may be found using either the ratio or the root test.

16.4   Algebraic Properties

Real or complex power series can be added, subtracted, multiplied, and divided in the same way that polynomials are. We summarize these useful facts below.

Let $\sum_{n=0}^\infty a_n z^n$ be a power series with radius of convergence $r_a > 0$ and let $\sum_{n=0}^\infty b_n z^n$ be power series with radius of convergence $r_b > 0$. Let

$$
r = \min\left(r_a, r_b\right).
$$

Then

$$
\sum_{n=0}^\infty a_n z^n \pm \sum_{n=0}^\infty b_n z^n = \sum_{n=0}^\infty \left(a_n \pm b_n\right) z^n \qquad \text{for} \quad |z| < r
$$

If the two power series are multiplied as if they were ordinary polynomials and like powers are collected in the usual way, then the formula obtained for the product is

$$
\left(\sum_{n=0}^\infty a_n z^n\right)\left(\sum_{n=0}^\infty b_n z^n\right) = \sum_{n=0}^\infty c_n z^n \qquad \text{where} \quad c_n = \sum_{k=0}^n a_k b_{n-k}.
$$

This multiplication formula is valid for $|z| < r$. To understand the formula for c_n, notice that to get one of the terms in the product that is a multiple of z^n you must multiply together two terms on the left side of the product whose exponents add to n. Such terms have the form $a_k z^k$ and $b_{n-k} z^{n-k}$ and each pair contributes the term $a_k z^k b_{n-k} z^{n-k} = a_k b_{n-k} z^n$ to the product.

The sum, difference, and product power series each convergence absolutely for $|z| < r = \min(r_a, r_b)$.

Division of $\sum_{n=0}^{\infty} a_n z^n$ by $\sum_{n=0}^{\infty} b_n z^n$ can be carried out formally just as if the power series were polynomials (provided that $b_0 \neq 0$) to yield

$$\frac{\sum_{n=0}^{\infty} a_n z^n}{\sum_{n=0}^{\infty} b_n z^n} = \sum_{n=0}^{\infty} d_n z^n$$

and the quotient power series converges absolutely for $|z| < r = \min(r_a, r_b, s)$ where s is the minimum distance from the base point (here 0) to the nearest zero of the the power series in denominator.

In practice, except in special cases, only the first few terms of the product or quotient series can be calculated by hand. The algebra required to compute even a few terms is often unpleasant and best done with the aid of a CAS. No matter how the algebraic steps above are carried out, you can determine an interval (disk) in which the resulting power series converges absolutely even without knowing all the terms of that series!

16.5   General Power Series

$\sum a_n x^n$ is a power series in x or a power series about $x = 0$. A general power series of the form $\sum a_n (x - c)^n$ is called a **power series in $x - c$ or a power series about c**. The change of variables $t = x - c$ replaces the power series $\sum a_n (x - c)^n$ by the power series $\sum_{n=0}^{\infty} a_n t^n$. In this way, any question concerning a power series about c can be recast as a question concerning a power series about 0. In particular, the change of variables enables us to transfer the basic convergence results of power series about 0 to power series about any point c:

For any power series $\sum a_n (x - c)^n$ there are three possibilities:
  (a) $\sum a_n (x - c)^n$ converges only for $x = c$;
  (b) $\sum a_n (x - c)^n$ converges absolutely for all x;
  (c) There is a number $r > 0$ such that
        $\sum a_n (x - c)^n$ converges absolutely for $|x - c| < r$
      and $\sum a_n (x - c)^n$ diverges for $|x - c| > r$.

The corresponding result holds for complex power series in $z - c$. Radius of convergence, interval of convergence (real case), circle of convergence and domain of convergence (complex case) are defined as expected.

Example 4 *Find the radius and circle of convergence of* $\sum_{n=1}^{\infty} (-1)^n \frac{(z-2)^n}{n3^n}$.

Solution. Since

$$\left| (-1)^n \frac{(z-2)^n}{n3^n} \right|^{1/n} = \frac{|z-2|}{3n^{1/n}} \to \frac{|z-2|}{3} \qquad \text{as } n \to \infty,$$

it follows from the root test that the series

$$\text{converges absolutely for } \tfrac{1}{3}|z-2| < 1 \quad \text{or} \quad |z-2| < 3$$
$$\text{and diverges for } \tfrac{1}{3}|z-2| > 1 \quad \text{or} \quad |z-2| > 3$$

Since $|z-2| < 3$ is the open disk in the complex plane with center 2 and radius 3, the radius of convergence is $r = 3$ and the circle of convergence has equation $|z-2| = 3$. $\square$

16.6   Suggested Problems

1. What is a power series?

2. What is the radius of convergence of a power series?

3. What is the interval of convergence of a real power series?

Find the radius of convergence and interval of convergence of each power series.

4. $\sum_{n=0}^{\infty} \frac{x^n}{n!}$

5. $\sum_{n=1}^{\infty} \frac{(3x)^n}{n2^n}$

6. $\sum_{n=0}^{\infty} \sqrt{n}\,(x-2)^n$

7. $\sum_{n=1}^{\infty} \frac{(2x-1)^n}{n4^n}$

8. $\sum_{n=0}^{\infty} n^2\,(x-4)^{2n}$

9. $\sum_{n=1}^{\infty} (-1)^{n+1} \frac{(2x+3)^n}{2^{2n}n^{1/2}}$

10. $\frac{x}{1\cdot 2} - \frac{x^2}{2\cdot 3} + \frac{x^3}{3\cdot 4} - \frac{x^4}{4\cdot 5} + - \cdots$

11. $\frac{x-4}{1\cdot 2} - \frac{(x-4)^2}{2\cdot 3} + \frac{(x-4)^3}{3\cdot 4} - \frac{(x-4)^4}{4\cdot 5} + - \cdots$

12. $x - \frac{x^3}{3!} + \frac{x^5}{5!} - \frac{x^7}{7!} + - \cdots$

Find the radius of convergence and circle of convergence of the power series.

13. $\sum z^n / n!$

14. $\sum (z+i)^n / n$

15. $\sum (3z-2)^n / \sqrt{n}2^n$

16. $\sum n!\,(2z-1)^n$

17. The Bessel function of order 1,

$$J_1(x) = \sum_{n=0}^{\infty} (-1)^n \frac{x^{2n+1}}{n!\,(n+1)!2^{2n+1}},$$

has important applications in mathematics, physics, and engineering. Find the domain of $J_1(x)$; that is determine its interval of convergence.

18. Suppose $\sum a_n x^n$ has radius of convergence 2 and $\sum b_n x^n$ has radius of convergence 5. What can you say about the radius of convergence of $\sum (a_n + b_n) x^n$?

19. The series $\sum_{n=0}^{\infty} a_n x^n$ is given by $a_0 = 1$, $a_1 = 0$, $a_2 = -1$, and $a_{n+3} = a_n$ for $n \geq 0$. Explain why the series must converge for all $|x| < 1$. Then find the sum of the series.

(a) Use algebraic manipulations and the power series expansions for e^x, $\sin x$, $\cos x$, and geometric series to find the first three nonzero terms in the power series expansion of the given function. (b) For what values of x can you guarantee that the power series converges absolutely? Why?

(If you have a CAS, you can easily find several more nonzero terms in the power series expansions of the functions.)

20. $\sin 2x$

21. $e^x + 3 \cos x$

22. $e^x \sin x$

23. $\cos x \sin x$

24. $e^x / \cos x$

25. $\tan x$

26. $\cos x / e^x$

27. $(\sin x) / (1 - x)$

28. Suppose you need to calculate the first several coefficients c_0, c_1,..., c_N of the product series

$$\left(\sum_{n=0}^{\infty} a_n x^n \right) \left(\sum_{n=0}^{\infty} b_n x^n \right) = \sum_{n=0}^{\infty} c_n x^n.$$

Explain why c_0, c_1,..., c_N also are the coefficients of 1, x,..., x^N in the product of the two polynomials $\sum_{n=0}^{N} a_n x^n$ and $\sum_{n=0}^{N} b_n x^n$.

29. Show that $\sum z^n / n!$ has radius of convergence infinity. Conclude that for any z

$$\frac{|z|^n}{n!} \to 0 \quad \text{as} \quad n \to \infty$$

30. Fix $\alpha \neq 0$. If $f(x) = (1 + x)^\alpha$ verify by direct calculation that

$$\frac{f^{(n)}(0)}{n!} = \frac{\alpha (\alpha - 1) (\alpha - 2) \cdots (\alpha - n + 1)}{1 \cdot 2 \cdot 3 \cdots \cdot n} = \left(\begin{array}{c} \alpha \\ n \end{array} \right).$$

Lesson 17

Analytic Properties of Power Series

17.1 Goals

- Learn and apply the fact that a power series is continuous inside its interval or circle of convergence

- Learn and apply term-by-term differentiation and integration properties of power series to obtain new power series representations from known ones

- Use changes of variable to obtain new power series representations from known ones

- Use power series methods and error estimates for sums of series to approximate definite integrals to a prescribed accuracy

- Learn the uniqueness property of power series representations and its significance for finding Taylor series expansions

17.2 Overview

In many respects, a power series behaves like an "infinite degree polynomial" inside its interval of convergence. This is true not only for addition, subtraction, multiplication, and division but also for differentiation and integration. Any polynomial can be differentiated or integrated term-by-term. Similarly, any power series can be differentiated or integrated term-by-term inside its interval of convergence. This is an important practical and theoretical property of power series.

We will not prove the facts concerning continuity and term-by-term differentiation and integration of power series, but Examples 5 and 6 of this lesson illustrate the type of reasoning that lies behind the general proofs. Our first order of business is to learn how to apply these important properties of power series.

17.3   Calculus and Power Series

Suppose a power series $\sum_{n=0}^{\infty} a_n x^n$ has radius of convergence $r > 0$. Then the sum of the series, call it $f(x)$, is a function of x for $|x| < r$:

$$f(x) = \sum_{n=0}^{\infty} a_n x^n \quad \text{for} \quad |x| < r.$$

Several basic properties of sums of power series follow.

Continuity of Power Series
Let $f(x) = \sum_{n=0}^{\infty} a_n x^n$ with radius of convergence $r > 0$ and interval of convergence I.
Then $f(x) = \sum_{n=0}^{\infty} a_n x^n$ is continuous on I.
Consequently, for any c in I
$$\lim_{x \to c} \sum_{n=0}^{\infty} a_n x^n = \sum_{n=0}^{\infty} a_n c^n$$
with the understanding that $x \to c$ with x in I.

Continuity of the sum of a power series inside its interval of convergence is relatively easy to establish using a related geometric series. Continuity at end points of the interval of convergence that belong to that interval is more subtle; that result is known as Abel's theorem. You will find some applications in the problems.

Example 1 *Use power series to establish that* $\lim_{x \to 0} \frac{\sin x}{x} = 1$.

Solution.

$$\lim_{x \to 0} \frac{\sin x}{x} = \lim_{x \to 0} \frac{1}{x} \left(x - \frac{x^3}{3!} + \frac{x^5}{5!} - \frac{x^7}{7!} + - \cdots \right)$$

$$= \lim_{x \to 0} \left(1 - \frac{x^2}{3!} + \frac{x^4}{5!} - \frac{x^6}{7!} + - \cdots \right) = 1. \quad \square$$

Differentiation and Integration of Power Series

Let $f(x) = \sum_{n=0}^{\infty} a_n x^n$ with radius of convergence $r > 0$. Then:

(1) $\int_a^b f(x)\,dx = \int_a^b \sum_{n=0}^{\infty} a_n x^n\,dx = \sum_{n=0}^{\infty} a_n \left[\dfrac{x^{n+1}}{n+1}\right]_a^b$ for $-r < a, b < r$.

(2) $f(x)$ is differentiable and
$$f'(x) = \frac{d}{dx}\sum_{n=0}^{\infty} a_n x^n = \sum_{n=1}^{\infty} n a_n x^{n-1} \quad \text{for} \quad -r < x < r.$$
(3) The differentiated and integrated series have the same radius of convergence as the original power series.
(4) The interval of convergence for the differentiated series is the same or smaller than for the original series. The interval of convergence for the integrated series is the same or larger than for the original series.

Property (1) also has the indefinite integral formulation

$$\int f(x)\,dx = \sum_{n=0}^{\infty} a_n \frac{x^{n+1}}{n+1} + C$$

with C a constant of integration and where x varies inside the interval of convergence of the original power series. In words, a power series can be integrated term-by-term inside its interval of convergence.

Since the differentiated series in (2) is again a power series with the same radius of convergence as the original, we can apply (2) repeatedly to differentiate term-by-term again and again:

Let $f(x) = \sum_{n=0}^{\infty} a_n x^n$ with radius of convergence $r > 0$.
Then $f(x)$ has derivatives of all orders and
the kth derivative of $f(x)$ can be obtained by
differentiating the original series k times term-by-term.

17.4 Uniqueness of Power Series Representations

Suppose that $f(x)$ has a power series representation with radius of convergence $r > 0$:

$$f(x) = \sum_{n=0}^{\infty} a_n x^n = a_0 + a_1 x + a_2 x^2 + a_3 x^3 + \cdots \quad \text{for} \quad |x| < r.$$

Evidently there must be a close connection between the function $f(x)$ and the coefficients a_n in the power series. A little reflection will reveal the precise connection. (Compare what follows with the polynomial case that was treated in Lesson 9.) Since

$$
\begin{aligned}
f\left(x\right) &= a_0 + a_1 x + a_2 x^2 + a_3 x^3 + a_4 x^4 + \cdots, \\
f'\left(x\right) &= a_1 + 2a_2 x + 3a_3 x^2 + 4a_4 x^3 + \cdots, \\
f''\left(x\right) &= 2 \cdot 1 a_2 + 3 \cdot 2 a_3 x + 4 \cdot 3 a_4 x^2 + \cdots, \\
f'''\left(x\right) &= 3 \cdot 2 \cdot 1 a_3 + 4 \cdot 3 \cdot 2 a_4 x + 5 \cdot 4 \cdot 3 a_5 x^2 + \cdots, \\
f^{(iv)}\left(x\right) &= 4 \cdot 3 \cdot 2 \cdot 1 a_4 + 5 \cdot 4 \cdot 3 \cdot 2 a_5 x + \cdots,
\end{aligned}
$$

it follows that

$$
\begin{aligned}
f\left(0\right) &= a_0, \\
f'\left(0\right) &= a_1, \\
f''\left(0\right) &= 2 \cdot 1 a_2, \\
f'''\left(0\right) &= 3 \cdot 2 \cdot 1 a_3, \\
f^{(iv)}\left(0\right) &= 4 \cdot 3 \cdot 2 \cdot 1 a_4,
\end{aligned}
$$

and, in general,

$$
f^{(n)}\left(0\right) = n \cdot (n-1) \cdots 3 \cdot 2 \cdot 1 a_n.
$$

Therefore,

$$
a_n = \frac{f^{(n)}\left(0\right)}{n!} \qquad n = 0, 1, 2, \ldots .
$$

Uniqueness of Power Series Representations
If $f\left(x\right) = \sum_{n=0}^{\infty} a_n x^n$ with radius of convergence $r > 0$, then
$$
a_n = \frac{f^{(n)}\left(0\right)}{n!} \qquad n = 0, 1, 2, \ldots,
$$
and, hence,
$$
f\left(x\right) = \sum_{n=0}^{\infty} \frac{f^{(n)}\left(0\right)}{n!} x^n \qquad \text{for} \quad |x| < r.
$$

There are two important conclusions in this uniqueness result: First, it is conceivable that a given function $f\left(x\right)$ might have more than one power series representation about 0. The uniqueness result says that this does not happen. Second, if $f\left(x\right)$ has a power series representation, then it is the Taylor series for $f\left(x\right)$. *This means that if we find a power series representation for a function by any means whatsoever, the power series we have found is the Taylor series for the function.* This gives us an important new way to obtain Taylor series without calculating the coefficients $f^{(n)}\left(0\right)/n!$ directly, as we had to do up until now. For example, all the power series representations developed in this lesson are the Taylor series for the functions on the left side of the equations. None of these series will be found by calculating $f^{(n)}\left(0\right)/n!$ directly. To see the advantage of avoiding the direct approach, try your luck on a direct calculation of the Taylor series of e^{-x^2}. Then read Example 2 of this lesson where the Taylor series expansion of e^{-x^2} is obtained by inspection from the known power series expansion of e^x.

17.5 Applications

Changes of variable in known power series expansions, such as we used in Lesson 10, algebraic manipulation, and term-by-term differentiation and integration of such series expansions can lead to a surprising variety of useful new series expansions. A few examples will hint at what is possible.

Example 2 *Evaluate $\int_0^1 e^{-x^2} dx$ correct to within 10^{-6}.*

Solution. This integral has no elementary antiderivative and consequently cannot be evaluated exactly using the fundamental theorem of calculus. Replace x by $-x^2$ in the power series expansion $e^x = \sum_{n=0}^{\infty} x^n/n!$ which holds for all x to obtain

$$e^{-x^2} = \sum_{n=0}^{\infty} \frac{\left(-x^2\right)^n}{n!} = \sum_{n=0}^{\infty} \frac{(-1)^n x^{2n}}{n!}$$

for all x. Integrate term-by-term to find

$$\int_0^1 e^{-x^2} dx = \sum_{n=0}^{\infty} \frac{(-1)^n}{n!} \left. \frac{x^{2n+1}}{2n+1} \right|_0^1 = \sum_{n=0}^{\infty} \frac{(-1)^n}{(2n+1)\,n!} = 1 - \frac{1}{3 \cdot 1!} + \frac{1}{5 \cdot 2!} - \frac{1}{7 \cdot 3!} + - \cdots.$$

Since the series on the right satisfies the conditions of the alternating series test, the error committed by cutting of the series at the term $(-1)^N / (2N+1)\,N!$ is at most the magnitude of the next term in the series. Consequently, we want to choose the smallest N such that

$$\frac{1}{(2(N+1)+1)(N+1)!} = \frac{1}{(2N+3)(N+1)!} < 10^{-6},$$

equivalently,

$$(2N+3)(N+1)! > 10^6.$$

A little experimentation with a calculator shows that $N = 8$ does the job and that

$$\int_0^1 e^{-x^2} dx \approx \sum_{n=0}^{8} \frac{(-1)^n}{(2n+1)\,n!} = 0.746824$$

with error less than 10^{-6}. $\square$

Example 3 *Find power series expansions for* $\ln(1-x)$ *and* $\ln x$.

Solution. The key here is to recognize that $\ln(1-x)$ has derivative $-1/(1-x)$, which apart from the minus sign is the sum of the basic geometric series. So we can get a power series for $\ln(1-x)$ by integrating the geometric series expansion term-by-term. Here are the details:

$$-\frac{1}{1-x} = -\sum_{n=0}^{\infty} x^n \quad \text{for} \quad -1 < x < 1,$$

$$\ln(1-x) = -\sum_{n=0}^{\infty} \frac{x^{n+1}}{n+1} + C,$$

for some constant C. Set $x = 0$ to find that $C = 0$; hence,

$$\ln(1-x) = -\sum_{n=0}^{\infty} \frac{x^{n+1}}{n+1} = -\left(x + \frac{x^2}{2} + \frac{x^3}{3} + \frac{x^4}{4} + \cdots\right) \quad \text{for} \quad -1 < x < 1.$$

Now simply make the change of variable $u = 1 - x$ and observe that

$$-1 < x < 1 \text{ if and only if } 0 < u < 2 \text{ (check this)}$$

to obtain

$$\ln u = -\left((1-u) + \frac{(1-u)^2}{2} + \frac{(1-u)^3}{3} + \frac{(1-u)^4}{4} + \cdots\right)$$

$$= (u-1) - \frac{(u-1)^2}{2} + \frac{(u-1)^3}{3} - \frac{(u-1)^4}{4} + - \cdots$$

for $0 < u < 2$, which is a power series expansion for $\ln u$ about 1. If you prefer to use x as the independent variable, simply replace u by x to get

$$\ln x = (x-1) - \frac{(x-1)^2}{2} + \frac{(x-1)^3}{3} - \frac{(x-1)^4}{4} + - \cdots$$

for $0 < x < 2$. This is the power series expansion about 1 (in powers of $x-1$) of $\ln x$. $\square$

Example 4 *Use term-by-term differentiation of the geometric series to find the sum of the power series* $\sum_{n=1}^{\infty} n^2 x^n$.

Solution. The critical observation needed to get started here (and in similar problems) is that term-by-term differentiation of the geometric series ultimately produces new series with terms that are very nearly $n^2 x^n$. Indeed, two term-by-term differentiations of

$$\frac{1}{1-x} = \sum_{n=0}^{\infty} x^n \quad \text{for} \quad -1 < x < 1$$

yield

$$\frac{1}{(1-x)^2} = \sum_{n=1}^{\infty} n x^{n-1} \quad \text{for} \quad -1 < x < 1,$$

$$\frac{2}{(1-x)^3} = \sum_{n=2}^{\infty} n(n-1) x^{n-2} \quad \text{for} \quad -1 < x < 1.$$

Notice that we get close to the series $\sum_{n=1}^{\infty} n^2 x^n$ if we multiple the last equation by x^2 :

$$\frac{2x^2}{(1-x)^3} = \sum_{n=2}^{\infty} n(n-1) x^n = \sum_{n=2}^{\infty} n^2 x^n - \sum_{n=2}^{\infty} n x^n,$$

$$\sum_{n=2}^{\infty} n^2 x^n = \frac{2x^2}{(1-x)^3} + \sum_{n=2}^{\infty} n x^n.$$

The series we seek starts with $n = 1$ not $n = 2$. To get the desired additional term, add x to both sides to get

$$x + \sum_{n=2}^{\infty} n^2 x^n = \frac{2x^2}{(1-x)^3} + x + \sum_{n=2}^{\infty} n x^n,$$

$$\sum_{n=1}^{\infty} n^2 x^n = \frac{2x^2}{(1-x)^3} + \sum_{n=1}^{\infty} n x^n = \frac{2x^2}{(1-x)^3} + x \sum_{n=1}^{\infty} n x^{n-1},$$

$$= \frac{2x^2}{(1-x)^3} + x \cdot \frac{1}{(1-x)^2} = \frac{x^2 + x}{(1-x)^3}.$$

So

$$\sum_{n=1}^{\infty} n^2 x^n = \frac{x^2 + x}{(1-x)^3} \quad \text{for} \quad -1 < x < 1. \quad \square$$

Let $x = 1/2$ in the last formula to find $\sum_{n=1}^{\infty} n^2/2^n = 6$. Compare this with Example 6 in Lesson 15 where we approximated the sum of this series.

17.6 Variations on a Theme

All of the foregoing results about real power series $\sum a_n x^n$, with one exception, apply to complex power series $\sum a_n z^n$. The exception is the analogue of Abel's theorem, which is more delicate in the complex domain. Otherwise, the only change needed is to replace interval of convergence by domain of convergence in the complex case. For example, the reasoning used in Example 4 yields

$$\sum_{n=1}^{\infty} n^2 z^n = \frac{z^2 + z}{(1-z)^3} \quad \text{for} \quad |z| < 1$$

in the complex domain.

Likewise, analogs of the results above hold for both real and complex power series of the form $\sum a_n (x - c)^n$ and $\sum a_n (z - c)^n$. For example, if $f(x) = \sum_{n=0}^{\infty} a_n (x - c)^n$ for $|x - c| < r$, and limits of integration a and b are chosen inside the interval of convergence, then

$$\int_a^b f(x)\, dx = \int_a^b \sum_{n=0}^{\infty} a_n (x - c)^n\, dx = \sum_{n=0}^{\infty} a_n \left[\frac{(x - c)^{n+1}}{n + 1} \right]_a^b.$$

There is an indefinite integral formulation of term-by-term integration. What is it?

17.7   Term-by-Term Operations Revisited

The next two examples confirm, in two special cases, the general results about term-by-term differentiation and integration stated earlier. The reasoning used in the examples is very much like the reasoning used to establish the general results.

Example 5 *Show that the geometric series*

$$\frac{1}{1 - x} = 1 + x + x^2 + \cdots + x^n + \cdots \quad for \quad |x| < 1$$

can be differentiated term-by-term to obtain

$$\frac{1}{(1 - x)^2} = 1 + 2x + 3x^2 + \cdots + nx^{n-1} + \cdots \quad for \quad |x| < 1.$$

Solution. We start (see Lesson 10) with the finite geometric series with remainder

$$\frac{1}{1 - x} = 1 + x + x^2 + \cdots + x^n + \frac{x^{n+1}}{1 - x} \quad for \quad x \neq 1$$

and differentiate both sides to obtain

$$\frac{1}{(1 - x)^2} = 1 + 2x + 3x^2 + \cdots + nx^{n-1} + \frac{x^n + (1 - x) nx^n}{(1 - x)^2} \quad for \quad x \neq 1.$$

Fix x with $|x| < 1$ and let $n \to \infty$. Then $x^n \to 0$ and $nx^n \to 0$ (see the problems). Therefore,

$$\frac{x^n + (1 - x) nx^n}{(1 - x)^2} \to 0 \quad as \quad n \to \infty$$

and, from the previous equation,

$$\frac{1}{(1 - x)^2} = 1 + 2x + 3x^2 + \cdots + nx^{n-1} + \cdots \quad for \quad |x| < 1. \quad \square$$

Example 6 *Replace x by $-x^2$ in the geometric series to get*

$$\frac{1}{1+x^2} = 1 - x^2 + x^4 - x^6 + - \cdots \quad \text{for} \quad -1 < x < 1.$$

Show that this series can be integrated term-by-term to yield

$$\arctan x = x - \frac{x^3}{3} + \frac{x^5}{5} - \frac{x^7}{7} + - \cdots \quad \text{for} \quad -1 \le x \le 1.$$

Solution. We begin again with

$$\frac{1}{1-x} = 1 + x + x^2 + \cdots + x^n + \frac{x^{n+1}}{1-x} \quad \text{for} \quad x \ne 1$$

and let $x = -t^2$ to obtain

$$\frac{1}{1+t^2} = 1 - t^2 + t^4 - t^6 + \cdots + (-1)^n t^{2n} + \frac{(-1)^{n+1} t^{2n+2}}{1+t^2} \quad \text{for all } t.$$

Integrate from 0 to x to find

$$
\begin{aligned}
\arctan x &= \int_0^x \frac{1}{1+t^2}\, dt \\
&= x - \frac{x^3}{3} + \frac{x^5}{5} - \frac{x^7}{7} + \cdots + (-1)^n \frac{x^{2n+1}}{2n+1} + (-1)^{n+1} \int_0^x \frac{t^{2n+2}}{1+t^2}\, dt.
\end{aligned}
$$

Now, for $-1 \le x \le 1$,

$$\left| \int_0^x \frac{t^{2n+2}}{1+t^2}\, dt \right| \le \int_0^1 t^{2n+2}\, dt = \frac{1}{2n+3} \to 0 \quad \text{as} \quad n \to \infty.$$

It follows that

$$\arctan x = x - \frac{x^3}{3} + \frac{x^5}{5} - \frac{x^7}{7} + - \cdots \quad \text{for} \quad -1 \le x \le 1. \quad \square$$

17.8   Power Series and Differential Equations

Power series often provide solutions to differential equations that cannot be solved by more elementary means. Conversely, knowledge about solutions of particular differential equations can enable you to find the sum of certain power series. The following examples give a glimpse of the interplay between power series and differential equations.

The first example takes advantage of your knowledge of solutions to the exponential growth equation $y' = y$ to sum a particular power series.

Example 7 *Find an explicit formula for the sum of the series*

$$S(x) = \sum_{n=0}^{\infty} \frac{x^n}{n!} = 1 + x + \frac{x^2}{2!} + \frac{x^3}{3!} + \frac{x^4}{4!} + \cdots .$$

Solution. Of course, you know the sum is e^x. But the point here is the method. So forget you know the answer. The series converges for all x by the ratio test. First, notice that $S(0) = 1$. Next, differentiate the series for $S(x)$ term-by-term to obtain

$$S'(x) = 0 + 1 + x + \frac{x^2}{2!} + \frac{x^3}{3!} + \cdots = S(x)$$

for all x. The same calculation, expressed in summation notation, is

$$S'(x) = \sum_{n=1}^{\infty} \frac{nx^{n-1}}{n!} = \sum_{n=1}^{\infty} \frac{x^{n-1}}{(n-1)!} = \sum_{n=0}^{\infty} \frac{x^n}{n!} = S(x)$$

where n was replaced everywhere by $n+1$ in passing from the middle to the last summation. (Changes of variable like this will be very helpful when the going gets tougher. Stay tuned.) Either way,

$$S'(x) = S(x) \quad \text{and} \quad S(0) = 1.$$

In MTH 252 you learned that the initial value problem

$$y' = y \quad \text{and} \quad y(0) = 1$$

has the *unique* solution $y = e^x$. But we just showed that $S(x) = \sum_{n=0}^{\infty} \frac{x^n}{n!}$ solves this initial value problem. So $S(x) = e^x$ and we have a new derivation of the power series expansion

$$e^x = \sum_{n=0}^{\infty} \frac{x^n}{n!}$$

for all x. $\square$

Now, let's turn the tables. Suppose you have not met the exponential growth equation before.

Example 8 *Show that the initial value problem*

$$y' = y, \quad y(0) = 1,$$

has a power series solution.

Solution. Let

$$y = \sum_{n=0}^{\infty} a_n x^n.$$

We seek to determine the coefficients a_n so that the series solves the initial value problem. First, set $x = 0$ in the series to see that $y(0) = a_0$. So we choose $a_0 = 1$ to satisfy the initial condition. Second, substitute the series for y into the differential equation $y' = y$ and differentiate term-by-term to obtain

$$\frac{d}{dx}\left(\sum_{n=0}^{\infty} a_n x^n\right) = \sum_{n=0}^{\infty} a_n x^n,$$

$$\sum_{n=1}^{\infty} a_n n x^{n-1} = \sum_{n=0}^{\infty} a_n x^n. \tag{17.1}$$

To see what this means write out explicitly several terms on each side of the equation

$$1a_1 + 2a_2x + 3a_3x^2 + 4a_4x^3 + \cdots = a_0 + a_1x + a_2x^2 + a_3x^3 + \cdots .$$

This equation will clearly be satisfied (and, by the uniqueness of power series representations, can only be satisfied) if we can choose the a_n so that the powers of x on both sides have the *same* coefficients. This requires

$$1a_1 = a_0, \ 2a_2 = a_1, \ 3a_3 = a_2, \ 4a_4 = a_3, \ldots$$

and, in general,

$$(n+1)\, a_{n+1} = a_n \qquad \text{for} \quad n = 0, 1, 2, \ldots .$$

Another way to arrive at the same result, but working in summation notation, is to make a change of variable in (17.1) so that x occurs to the same power in all the summations in equation (17.1). To this end, replace n everywhere on the left side by $n+1$ and note that summing from $n+1 = 1$ to infinity means that n varies from 0 to infinity to obtain

$$\sum_{n=0}^{\infty} a_{n+1}\, (n+1)\, x^n = \sum_{n=0}^{\infty} a_n x^n .$$

Now equate coefficients of x^n on both sides to get

$$(n+1)\, a_{n+1} = a_n \qquad \text{for} \quad n = 0, 1, 2, \ldots,$$

just as before. Either way

$$a_{n+1} = \frac{1}{n+1} a_n \qquad \text{for} \quad n = 0, 1, 2, \ldots .$$

Since $a_0 = 1$,

$$
\begin{aligned}
a_1 &= \frac{1}{0+1} a_0 = 1, \\
a_2 &= \frac{1}{1+1} a_1 = \frac{1}{2}, \\
a_3 &= \frac{1}{2+1} a_2 = \frac{1}{3} \cdot \frac{1}{2} = \frac{1}{3!}, \\
a_4 &= \frac{1}{3+1} a_3 = \frac{1}{4} \cdot \frac{1}{3} \cdot \frac{1}{2} = \frac{1}{4!},
\end{aligned}
$$

and so on. In general,

$$a_n = \frac{1}{n!} \qquad \text{for} \quad n = 0, 1, 2, \ldots .$$

So

$$y = \sum_{n=0}^{\infty} a_n x^n = \sum_{n=0}^{\infty} \frac{1}{n!} x^n .$$

It is easy to check that this power series has radius of convergence $r = \infty$. Hence, the term-by-term differentiation used above is justified and y solves the initial value problem. $\square$

As in Example 7, we know that e^x is the only solution to the initial value problem in Example 8 so we have yet another derivation of the Taylor series expansion for e^x. But, what is really significant about the solution in Example 8 is the process of finding a power series solution to a given differential equation. It is most useful in cases where you cannot solve the differential equation by other means.

Example 9 *Find a power series solution to the initial value problem*

$$y' = xy, \quad y(0) = 1.$$

Solution. Let

$$y = \sum_{n=0}^{\infty} a_n x^n.$$

Since $y(0) = a_0$, we must choose $a_0 = 1$ to satisfy the initial condition. Next, substitute the series for y into the differential equation $y' = xy$ and differentiate term-by-term to obtain

$$\frac{d}{dx}\left(\sum_{n=0}^{\infty} a_n x^n\right) = x\sum_{n=0}^{\infty} a_n x^n,$$

$$\sum_{n=1}^{\infty} a_n n x^{n-1} = \sum_{n=0}^{\infty} a_n x^{n+1}. \tag{17.2}$$

Replace n by $n-2$ everywhere in the right member of the previous equation to get

$$\sum_{n=1}^{\infty} a_n n x^{n-1} = \sum_{n=2}^{\infty} a_{n-2} x^{n-1}.$$

Thus $y = \sum_{n=0}^{\infty} a_n x^n$ will satisfy the differential equation $y' = xy$ if we choose

$$a_1 = 0 \quad \text{and} \quad na_n = a_{n-2} \quad \text{for } n = 2, 3, \ldots.$$

In summary, $y = \sum_{n=0}^{\infty} a_n x^n$ will solve the given initial value problem if

$$a_0 = 1, \quad a_1 = 0, \quad \text{and} \quad a_n = \frac{1}{n}a_{n-2} \quad \text{for } n = 2, 3, \ldots.$$

Use the recurrence relation to find

$$a_2 = \frac{1}{2}a_0 = \frac{1}{2}, \ a_3 = \frac{1}{3}a_1 = 0,$$

$$a_4 = \frac{1}{4}a_2 = \frac{1}{4\cdot 2}, \ a_5 = \frac{1}{5}a_3 = 0,$$

$$a_6 = \frac{1}{6}a_4 = \frac{1}{6\cdot 4\cdot 2}, \ a_7 = \frac{1}{7}a_5 = 0,$$

$$a_8 = \frac{1}{8}a_6 = \frac{1}{8\cdot 6\cdot 4\cdot 2}, \ a_9 = \frac{1}{9}a_7 = 0,$$

and so on. In general,

$$a_{2n} = \frac{1}{2 \cdot 4 \cdot 6 \cdots \cdot 2n} = \frac{1}{2^n n!} \quad \text{and} \quad a_{2n+1} = 0.$$

for $n = 0, 1, 2, \ldots$. Since all coefficients with an odd index are zero,

$$y = \sum_{n=0}^{\infty} a_n x^n = \sum_{n=0}^{\infty} a_{2n} x^{2n} = \sum_{n=0}^{\infty} \frac{1}{2^n n!} x^{2n}.$$

This power series has infinite radius of convergence (by what test?) and, hence, solves the given initial value problem.

Once again we are in luck and can find the sum of the series

$$y = \sum_{n=0}^{\infty} \frac{1}{n!} \left(\frac{x^2}{2} \right)^n = \exp\left(x^2/2 \right). \quad \square$$

The Airy differential equation, used in the next example, is named after the English astronomer and mathematician who directed the Cambridge Observatory from 1835 to 1881. Solutions to the Airy equation cannot be expressed in terms of the standard functions of calculus that you are used to using.

Example 10 *Solve $y'' + xy = 0$, $y(0) = 1$, $y'(0) = 0$.*

Solution. We try to express the solution to this problem as a power series: $y = \sum_{n=0}^{\infty} a_n x^n$. Our goal is to determine the coefficients in the power series so that y satisfies the Airy equation and the given initial conditions $y(0) = 1$ and $y'(0) = 0$. Since $y = \sum_{n=0}^{\infty} a_n x^n$ and $y' = \sum_{n=1}^{\infty} n a_n x^{n-1}$, we have $y(0) = a_0$ and $y'(0) = a_1$. The initial conditions will be satisfied if we choose

$$a_0 = 1 \quad \text{and} \quad a_1 = 0.$$

In order to see what is required for $y = \sum_{n=0}^{\infty} a_n x^n$ to satisfy the differential equation, substitute the power series for y into the left side of the differential equation, differentiating term-by-term, to obtain

$$
\begin{aligned}
y'' + xy &= \sum_{n=2}^{\infty} n(n-1) a_n x^{n-2} + x \sum_{n=0}^{\infty} a_n x^n \\
&= \sum_{n=2}^{\infty} n(n-1) a_n x^{n-2} + \sum_{n=0}^{\infty} a_n x^{n+1}.
\end{aligned}
$$

Now, combine like powers of x by replacing n everywhere in the second sum on the right by $n - 3$ to find

$$
\begin{aligned}
y'' + xy &= \sum_{n=2}^{\infty} n(n-1) a_n x^{n-2} + \sum_{n=3}^{\infty} a_{n-3} x^{n-2} \\
&= 2a_2 + \sum_{n=3}^{\infty} [n(n-1) a_n + a_{n-3}] x^{n-2}.
\end{aligned}
$$

Evidently, the power series $y = \sum_{n=0}^{\infty} a_n x^n$ will satisfy the differential equation $y'' + xy = 0$ if we choose

$$2a_2 = 0 \quad \text{and} \quad n(n-1)a_n + a_{n-3} = 0 \quad \text{for } n = 3, 4, 5, \ldots .$$

In summary,

$$a_0 = 1, \quad a_1 = 0, \quad a_2 = 0, \quad \text{and} \quad a_n = -\frac{a_{n-3}}{n(n-1)} \quad \text{for } n = 3, 4, 5, \ldots .$$

The recursion relation $a_n = -a_{n-3}/n(n-1)$ determines $a_3, a_6, a_9, \ldots$ in terms of $a_0 = y(0) = 1$; determines $a_4, a_7, a_{10}, \ldots$ in terms of $a_1 = 0$; and determines $a_5, a_8, a_{11}, \ldots$ in terms of $a_2 = y''(0)/2$. This last equality comes from the fact that the power series for y must be its Taylor series. Set $x = 0$ in the Airy equation $y'' + xy = 0$ to find that $y''(0) = 0$. So $a_2 = 0$. Now since $a_1 = 0$, the recursion relation implies that $a_4 = 0$ which in turn yields $a_7 = 0$ and so on. In general $a_{3n+1} = 0$ for $n = 0, 1, 2, \ldots$. Similarly, since $a_2 = 0$, $a_{3n+2} = 0$ for $n = 0, 1, 2, \ldots$. The a_{3n} are obtained from $a_0 = 1$ and the recursion relation,

$$a_0 = 1, \quad a_3 = -\frac{1}{2 \cdot 3}, \quad a_6 = \frac{1}{2 \cdot 3 \cdot 5 \cdot 6}, \quad a_9 = -\frac{1}{2 \cdot 3 \cdot 5 \cdot 6 \cdot 8 \cdot 9}, \ldots .$$

Finally, the solution y to the initial value problem is

$$y(x) = \sum_{n=0}^{\infty} a_{3n} x^{3n} = 1 - \frac{1}{2 \cdot 3} x^3 + \frac{1}{2 \cdot 3 \cdot 5 \cdot 6} x^6 - \frac{1}{2 \cdot 3 \cdot 5 \cdot 6 \cdot 8 \cdot 9} x^9 + - \cdots$$

where the a_{3n} are given by repeatedly applying the recursion relation $a_n = -a_{n-3}/n(n-1)$. $\square$

17.9 Suggested Problems

1. The power series $\sum a_n x^n$ has radius of convergence 4. What can be said about the radius of convergence of the power series $\sum n a_n x^{n-1}$?

2. The power series $\sum a_n x^n$ converges for $|x| < 3$. What can be said about the convergence of the power series $\sum \frac{a_n}{n+1} x^{n+1}$?

For problems 3 - 16, find, by any appropriate means, a power series expansion for the function and the radius of convergence of the series.

3. $1/\left(1 - x^3\right)$

4. $\left(1 + x^2\right)/\left(4 - x^2\right)$

5. $\left(e^x + e^{-x}\right)/2$

6. $\ln\left(\frac{1+x}{1-x}\right)$ *Hint.* Think about algebraic properties of logarithms.

7. $\ln(5 - x)$

8. $\ln\left(1/\left(5 - x\right)\right)$

9. $x \arctan x$

10. $x \sin(x/2)$

11. $\cos x + \sin x$

12. $\int x \cos\left(x^2\right)\, dx$

13. $\int x^3 e^{-x^2}\, dx$

14. $\int \frac{\arctan x}{x}\, dx$

15. $\sin^2 x$ *Hint.* Use a trigonometric identity.

16. $x + \cos^2 x$

For problems 17 - 20, use power series methods to evaluate the limit.

17. $\lim_{x \to 0} \left(1 - \cos x\right)/x^2$

18. $\lim_{x \to 0} \left(1 - \cos x\right)/\left(1 + x - e^{-x}\right)$

19. $\lim_{x \to 0} \left(x - \arctan x\right)/x^3$

20. $\lim_{x \to 0} (\tan x - x)/x^3$

For problems 21 - 24, find, by any convenient means, the first 4 nonzero terms in the power series expansion of the given function. On what interval can you guarantee that the series converges absolutely? Why?

21. $(\arctan x)/e^x$

22. $e^{-x}/(1-x)$

23. $e^{2x}\arctan x$

24. $\ln x/\cos x$

For problems 25 - 27, find the sum of the series by relating it to a series whose sum you know.

25. $x - x^2 + x^3 - x^4 + - \cdots$

26. $\frac{1}{2!} + \frac{z}{3!} + \frac{z^2}{4!} + \frac{z^3}{5!} + \cdots$

27. $3t + \frac{9t^2}{2} + \frac{27t^3}{3} + \frac{81t^4}{4} + \cdots$

28. Use power series methods to approximate $\int_0^{1/4} \frac{1}{1+x^3}\, dx$ correct to within 4 decimal places; that is, the error must be less than 0.00005.

29. (a) Find a power series representation for $\arctan\left(x^2\right)$. (b) Use the representation to calculate $\int_0^{1/2} \arctan\left(x^2\right)\, dx$ correct to within 10^{-6}.

The *Fresnel integral*, named for the French physicist noted for his work in optics, is

$$S\left(x\right) = \int_0^x \sin\left(\frac{\pi}{2}t^2\right)\, dt$$

30. Find a power series representation for the Fresnel integral $S\left(x\right)$ and determine the values of x for which the expansion is valid.

31. Use power series methods to evaluate $S\left(1\right)$ correct to within 0.001.

The *Bessel function of order zero*, $J_0\left(x\right)$, is defined by

$$J_0\left(x\right) = \sum_{n=0}^{\infty} (-1)^n \frac{x^{2n}}{4^n\left(n!\right)^2}.$$

32. Show that the series converges for all x and satisfies the differential equation

$$x^2 y'' + xy' + x^2 y = 0,$$

which is *Bessel's differential equation of order 0*.

33. Use power series methods to evaluate $J_0(1)$ correct to within 0.001.

34. Find *exactly* the sum of the series $\sum_{n=1}^{\infty} \frac{n}{3^n}$. *Hint.* First find the sum of the series $\sum_{n=1}^{\infty} nx^n$.

35. Find *exactly* the sum of the series $\sum_{n=1}^{\infty} \frac{1}{n3^n}$. *Hint.* The hint from Problem 34 should give you a hint.

36. In Example 3 the power series expansion

$$\ln x = \sum_{n=1}^{\infty} (-1)^{n+1} \frac{(x-1)^n}{n} \quad \text{for } 0 < x < 2$$

was established.

(a) Show that the power series has interval of convergence $0 < x \le 2$.

(b) With the aid of continuity properties of power series, explain *carefully* why the power series expansion for $\ln x$ is valid for all x in the interval of convergence. What does the choice $x = 2$ establish about the alternating harmonic series?

37. Do the following:

(a) Make a change of variable in $\sum_{n=0}^{\infty} x^n = 1/(1-x)$ for $|x| < 1$ to obtain a power series expansion for the function $1/(1+x^2)$.

(b) Find the interval of convergence of the power series about 0 you found in (a).

(c) Use power series methods and the result of (a) to find a power series representation for $\arctan x$ and state, with justification, the values of x for which the series representation is valid.

(d) Use (c) to find an infinite series expansion for $\pi/4$.

38. Find a power series solution to the given initial value problem. Give the sum of the series if you know it:

$$y' - 2y = 4, \quad y(0) = 3.$$

39. Find a power series solution to the given initial value problem. Give the sum of the series if you know it:

$$y' + xy = 0, \quad y(0) = 3.$$

40. Do the following:

    (a) Use the power series method to solve the initial value problem $y'' - 6y' + 9y = 0$, $y(0) = 2$, $y'(0) = 4$.

    (b) Find the sum of the power series you found in part (a).

41. Let $a \neq 0$ be a constant.

    (a) Use the power series method to solve the initial value problem $y'' - a^2 y = 0$, $y(0) = 1$, $y'(0) = 0$.

    (b) Find the sum of the power series you found in part (a).

42. Bessel's differential equation of order zero, $x^2 y'' + xy' + x^2 y = 0$, has one solution that is given by a power series $y = \sum_{n=0}^{\infty} a_n x^n$.

    (a) Find the first four nonzero terms in the series solution.

    (b) Find the recursion relation for the coefficients a_n and use it to find a general formula for a_n.

43. The initial value problem $y'' + 3xy' - 9y = -9$, $y(0) = 1$, $y'(0) = 1$ has a power series solution. Find it. What is special about it?

44. The *Laguerre differential equation* has the form $xy'' + (1-x)y' + ay = 0$ where a is a parameter.

    (a) Show that the Laguerre differential equation has a power series solution $\sum a_n x^n$ by determining the recurrence relation satisfied by the coefficients and using it to determine the radius of convergence of the series solution.

    (b) For what special values of a does the Laguerre differential equation have a polynomial solution? Explain.

45. The power series solution to the Airy equation in Example 10 is an alternating series for $x > 0$. Let $y_N(x) = \sum_{n=0}^{N} a_{3n} x^{3n}$, a partial sum approximation of the solution $y(x)$. Find N so that $|y_N(x) - y(x)| < 0.001$ for all x in the interval $0 \leq x \leq 2$.

46. Let $|x| \leq 2$ and let $y_N(x)$ and $y(x)$ be as in the previous problem. Find N so that $|y_N(x) - y(x)| < 0.001$ for all x in the interval $|x| \leq 2$. *Comment.* For $|x| < 2$, the power series solution to the Airy equation in Example 10 is not an alternating series. So you will need a new approach. *Hint.* Use the error estimate related to the ratio test. It may help to first express the solution y as a power series in $t = x^3$: $y = \sum_{n=0}^{\infty} b_n t^n$ where $b_n = a_{3n}$. What recursion relates b_{n+1} and b_n? What t-interval corresponds to $|x| \leq 2$.

47. Fix $k > 0$. Show that $n^k x^n \to 0$ as $n \to \infty$ for any x with $|x| < 1$. *Hint.* Show that the series $\sum_{n=1}^{\infty} n^k x^n$ converges for $|x| < 1$.

48. Term-by-term differentiation of $f(x) = \sum_{n=0}^{\infty} a_n x^n$ gives
    $f'(x) = \sum_{n=0}^{\infty} n a_n x^{n-1}$.

    (a) In the second boxed result of this lesson, the result of term-by-term differentiation is expressed as $f'(x) = \sum_{n=1}^{\infty} n a_n x^{n-1}$. Why are both formulas for $f'(x)$ correct?

    (b) Find two formulas for $f''(x)$ that correspond to the two formulas in part (a) for $f'(x)$.

49. Show that the series $\sum_{n=1}^{\infty} \dfrac{\sin nx}{n^2}$ converges for all x. Show that the series obtained by term-by-term differentiation diverges when $x = 2\pi n$ for any integer n. Why doesn't this contradict a basic property of power series?

Lesson 18

Power Series and Complex Calculus

18.1   Goals

- Evaluate limits of simple expressions involving functions of a complex variable

- Define continuity and differentiability for functions of a complex variable

- Learn the definitions and basic properties of the complex functions e^z, $\sin z$, and $\cos z$

- Learn the Euler identities

18.2   Overview

In this lesson you will glimpse the beginnings of the differential calculus of complex-valued functions and its connection to power series expansions. You will learn the Euler identities that play a key role in various parts of pure and applied mathematics, especially in differential equations. In several instances the discussion closely parallels material familiar from real differential calculus. When that is the case, your instructor may just cover the highlights and leave the rest to you.

18.3   Differential Calculus and Power Series

We treat limits in the complex domain informally, much as real limits were treated when you first studied real differential calculus. Let $f(z)$ be a function of a complex variable z. Assume the domain of f includes all points of a small open disk centered at the complex number c. Then

$$\lim_{z \to c} f(z) = L \qquad (L \text{ a complex number})$$

means that $f(z)$ is as close to L as desired when $z \neq c$ is close enough to c. More precisely, for $z \neq c$, $|f(z) - L|$ is as close to zero as desired when $|z - c|$ is close enough to zero.

The same reasoning used in connection with real limits yields the same algebraic limit laws that you learned earlier in calculus. For example,

$$\lim_{z \to c} (f(z) + g(z)) = \lim_{z \to c} f(z) + \lim_{z \to c} g(z)$$

provided the limits on the right exist. Also, for any positive integer n,

$$\lim_{z \to c} z^n = c^n,$$
$$\lim_{z \to c} \frac{1}{z^n} = \frac{1}{c^n} \qquad c \neq 0.$$

As in real calculus, the algebraic limit laws and knowledge of a few basic limits make it easy to find many other limits virtually by inspection. For example,

$$\lim_{z \to 2} \left(z^2 - 4iz + 5\right) = 4 - 8i + 5 = 9 - 8i$$

and

$$\lim_{z \to 2-i} \frac{z^2}{z - 1} = \frac{(2 - i)^2}{1 - i} = \frac{3 - 4i}{1 - i} = \frac{7}{2} - \frac{1}{2}i.$$

Once complex limits have been defined, the definitions of continuity and differentiability in complex calculus are the same as for real calculus. A function $f(z)$ is **continuous at c** if

$$\lim_{z \to c} f(z) = f(c).$$

The special limit, $\lim_{z \to c} z^n = c^n$, show that the function $f(z) = z^n$ is continuous (meaning continuous at c for every c in its domain). The algebraic limit laws then imply that any polynomial in z with real or complex coefficients,

$$p(z) = a_0 + a_1 z + \cdots + a_n z^n$$

is continuous. Likewise, any rational function (a quotient of two such polynomials) is continuous.

A function $f(z)$ is **differentiable at z** if

$$f'(z) = \lim_{h \to 0} \frac{f(z + h) - f(z)}{h} \qquad \text{exists.}$$

Example 1 *If $f(z) = z^2$, show that $f'(z) = 2z$.*

Solution.

$$f'(z) = \lim_{h \to 0} \frac{(z+h)^2 - z^2}{h} = \lim_{h \to 0} \frac{2zh + h^2}{h} = \lim_{h \to 0} (2z + h) = 2z. \quad \square$$

The definition of differentiability and the calculation in the foregoing example should look familiar. On the surface, the calculus of complex functions looks very much like the calculus for real functions. For example, the derivative is still linear and the product, quotient, and chain rules still hold. Furthermore, virtually every derivative formula you learned in real calculus continues to hold in the complex domain. For example,

$$\frac{d}{dz} z^n = n z^{n-1}, \frac{d}{dz} \sin z = \cos z, \frac{d}{dz} e^z = e^z, \dots .$$

These formulas should look appealing to you, but only the first one really makes sense now. After all we don't know what $\sin z$, $\cos z$, and e^z mean when the variable z is complex! So what can we make of the derivative formulas now? Stay tuned.

Although the complex and real calculus look much the same on the surface there are profound differences. The differences all stem from the fact that the limits of real calculus are one-dimensional ($x \to a$ along the number line) whereas the limits of complex calculus are two-dimensional ($z \to c$ along any path in the complex plane). Here is one of the fundamental differences: A function that is differentiable in the complex sense at all points in a domain of the complex plane must have a power series expansion about each point in that domain. Since power series can be differentiated indefinitely, it follows that a function that is differentiable in the complex sense automatically has derivatives of all orders. The corresponding statement is false for real differentiability.

Real functions $f(x)$ that have power series expansions have analogues in the complex calculus obtained simply by replacing the real variable x by the complex variable z. For instance, replace x by z in the power series (Taylor series) expansions we found in Lesson 11 for e^x, $\sin x$, and $\cos x$ to obtain the complex functions

$$e^z = \sum_{n=0}^{\infty} \frac{z^n}{n!} = 1 + z + \frac{z^2}{2!} + \frac{z^3}{3!} + \frac{z^4}{4!} + \cdots ,$$

$$\sin z = \sum_{n=0}^{\infty} \frac{(-1)^n z^{2n+1}}{(2n+1)!} = z - \frac{z^3}{3!} + \frac{z^5}{5!} - \frac{z^7}{7!} + - \cdots ,$$

$$\cos z = \sum_{n=0}^{\infty} \frac{(-1)^n z^{2n}}{(2n)!} = 1 - \frac{z^2}{2!} + \frac{z^4}{4!} - \frac{z^6}{6!} + - \cdots .$$

The complex power series on the right converge for all z by the ratio text. If $z = x$ is real, the series sum respectively to e^x, $\sin x$, and $\cos x$. Thus, it is reasonable to use the complex power series to define e^z, $\sin z$, and $\cos z$ for z

any complex number. Moreover, these "extended" functions satisfy the same relations as when z is real. For example, term-by-term differentiation (check it) of the power series shows that

$$\frac{d}{dz}e^z = e^z, \quad \frac{d}{dz}\sin z = \cos z, \quad \frac{d}{dz}\cos z = -\sin z.$$

Also, algebraic manipulations with power series can be used to confirm that

$$e^{z+w} = e^z e^w \quad \text{and} \quad \sin^2 z + \cos^2 z = 1.$$

There is an elegant and fundamental reason for the persistence of these and other familiar formulas, but that is a story for a course in complex variables. An easy and useful consequence of the basic exponential law is

$$(e^z)^n = e^{nz}$$

for any integer n, positive, negative, or zero.

18.4   Euler Identities

One surprise, discovered by Euler, comes from the three power series for e^z, $\sin z$, and $\cos z$. Set $z = i\theta$ where θ is real into the power series for e^z and use $i^2 = -1$, $i^3 = -i$, $i^4 = 1$, etc. to obtain

$$
\begin{aligned}
e^{i\theta} &= 1 + i\theta + \frac{(i\theta)^2}{2!} + \frac{(i\theta)^3}{3!} + \frac{(i\theta)^4}{4!} + \frac{(i\theta)^5}{5!} + \cdots \\
&= 1 + i\theta - \frac{\theta^2}{2!} - i\frac{\theta^3}{3!} + \frac{\theta^4}{4!} + i\frac{\theta^5}{5!} - - + + \cdots \\
&= \left(1 - \frac{\theta^2}{2!} + \frac{\theta^4}{4!} - + \cdots\right) + i\left(\theta - \frac{\theta^3}{3!} + \frac{\theta^5}{5!} - + \cdots\right) \\
&= \cos\theta + i\sin\theta.
\end{aligned}
$$

Check the steps and include a few more terms to be sure of the pattern. This result is **Euler's formula (or identity)**

$$\boxed{e^{i\theta} = \cos\theta + i\sin\theta.}$$

Replace θ by $-\theta$ to obtain the companion formula

$$e^{-i\theta} = \cos\theta - i\sin\theta.$$

This pair of equations can be solved for $\cos\theta$ and $\sin\theta$:

$$\cos\theta = \frac{e^{i\theta} + e^{-i\theta}}{2} \quad \text{and} \quad \sin\theta = \frac{e^{i\theta} - e^{-i\theta}}{2i}.$$

You will find these Euler formulas very useful in differential equations.

Euler's formula and the rules of exponents enable us to express e^z in standard form: If $z = x + iy$, then $e^z = e^{x+iy} = e^x e^{iy}$ and, hence,

$$\boxed{e^z = e^x \left(\cos y + i \sin y \right) = e^x \cos y + i e^x \sin y.}$$

Calculators and computers use this formula to evaluate e^z. What are the exact values of e^{3+4i} and $e^{i\pi}$?

Recall that $e^x \neq 0$ for all x. Since $\cos y$ and $\sin y$ are never simultaneously equal to zero, the formula above reveals that

$$\boxed{e^z \neq 0 \quad \text{for all} \quad z.}$$

The same formula contains a surprise. Since the sine and cosine functions have fundamental period 2π, when the imaginary part y of $z = x + iy$ is increased by 2π the value of e^z is unchanged. That is, the complex exponential function is periodic with fundamental period $2\pi i$:

$$\boxed{e^{z+2\pi i} = e^z}$$

for all z. Repeated application of this result yields

$$e^{z+2\pi i n} = e^z$$

for any integer n. The choices $z = 0$ and $n = 1$ yield

$$\boxed{e^{2\pi i} = 1.}$$

Finally, the Euler identity enables us to express the polar form of a complex number in an especially convenient way:

$$\begin{aligned} z &= r \cos\theta + i r \sin\theta \\ &= r \left(\cos\theta + i \sin\theta \right) = r e^{i\theta}. \end{aligned}$$

Thus, the complex number $z = x + iy$ has polar representation

$$z = r e^{i\theta}$$

where $x = r\cos\theta$ and $y = r\sin\theta$. All polar representations of z are

$$z = r e^{i(\theta + 2\pi n)}.$$

(Why?)

18.5   Suggested Problems

For problems 1 - 4, evaluate the limit.

1. $\lim_{z \to i} \left(z^2 - 4iz + 5 \right)$

2. $\lim_{z \to 1-i} \dfrac{z - 4}{z^2}$

3. $\lim_{z \to 1-i} \dfrac{z - 1 + i}{z^2}$

4. $\lim_{z \to 1-i} \dfrac{z - 1 + i}{z^2 - 2z + 2}$

For problems 5 - 8, use the *definition* of the derivative $f'(z) = \lim_{h \to 0} \frac{f(z+h)-f(z)}{h}$ to find the derivative of the function.

5. $f(z) = 2 - 7i$

6. $f(z) = z$

7. $f(z) = 1/z$

8. $f(z) = 1/z^2$

For problems 9 - 11, use term-by-term differentiation to establish:

9. $\frac{d}{dz} e^z = e^z$

10. $\frac{d}{dz} \cos z = -\sin z$

11. $\frac{d}{dz} \sin z = \cos z$

For problems 12 - 15, use the product, quotient, and/or chain rules to find the derivative of the given functions.

12. $g(z) = z^3$

13. $h(z) = 1/z^4$

14. $k(z) = (\sin z) / \left(1 + z^2 \right)$

15. $l(z) = \cos \left(\left(4 + 3z - z^2 \right)^3 \right)$

For problems 16 - 20, find *exactly* the standard form for the given complex number.

16. e^{2+2i}

17. e^{-3+4i}

18. $e^{\pi i}$

19. $e^{\pi i/2}$

20. $e^{4\pi i}$

The Complex Trigonometric Functions: Now that $\sin z$ and $\cos z$ have been defined via power series for complex z, the definitions $\tan z = \sin z / \cos z$, $\cot z = \cos z / \sin z$, $\sec z = 1/\cos z$, and $\csc z = 1/\sin z$ define complex-valued trigonometric functions that reduce to the corresponding real functions when z is real.

21. Use the foregoing definitions, the known derivatives of the $\sin z$ and $\cos z$, and the familiar rules of differentiation and $\sin^2 z + \cos^2 z = 1$ to verify that

(a) $\frac{d}{dz} \tan z = \sec^2 z$

(b) $\frac{d}{dz} \sec z = \sec z \tan z$

22. *(The Complex Logarithm)*

(a) Use the power series expansion for $\ln x$ about $x = 1$ to define $\ln z$. For what complex z have you defined $\ln z$?

(b) Use power series methods to verify that $\frac{d}{dz} \ln z = 1/z$.

23. For *complex* z establish:

(a) $e^{iz} = \cos z + i \sin z$

(b) $e^{-iz} = \cos z - i \sin z$

(c) $\cos z = \frac{1}{2} \left(e^{iz} + e^{-iz} \right)$

(d) $\sin z = \frac{1}{2i} \left(e^{iz} - e^{-iz} \right)$

24. Use parts (c) and (d) of the foregoing problem to confirm that $\sin^2 z + \cos^2 z = 1$ for all complex z.

25. Let $z_0 = r_0 e^{i\theta_0}$ and $z = r e^{i\theta}$. Describe geometrically how to obtain $z_0 z$ from z. Illustrate with a figure.

26. Describe geometrically how to obtain iz from z. Illustrate with a figure.

27. Carefully sketch the vector that represents the complex number $z = e^{i\theta}$. Then carefully sketch the graph of the equation $z = e^{i\theta}$ for $0 \leq \theta \leq 2\pi$ in the complex plane. Describe the graph precisely in words. *Hint.* What is the length of $e^{i\theta}$?

28. Check directly that $e^{2\pi i} = 1$. Then use this result to establish that $e^{2\pi i n} = 1$ and that $e^{z + 2\pi i} = e^z$ for any integer n and any complex number z.

Lesson 19

Catch Up and Review

This is a self-study lesson. Now is the time to go back and clear up any points of confusion in Lessons 9–18. Get help if you need it. Ask your instructor, your GTA, and your fellow classmates. Don't forget the MLC! Review the goals given in Lessons 9–18. Have you achieved all of them? Have you solved *all* the assigned problems? If not, finish the unsolved problems from earlier lessons before you start on the additional problems below. Also, be sure that you really understand how you solved each problem. Could you clearly explain how to solve the problem to a confused classmate? Good luck with your review. A little extra effort here will really payoff.

Review Problems

1. Review all previously assigned problems on homeworks, quizzes, and tests!

2. Determine whether the given series converges. *Justify your answers!*

   (a) $\sum_{n=1}^{\infty} \dfrac{2}{3^n}$

   (b) $\dfrac{1}{3} - \dfrac{2}{4} + \dfrac{3}{5} - \cdots + (-1)^{n-1}\dfrac{n}{n+2} + \cdots$

   (c) $\sum_{n=2}^{\infty} \dfrac{1}{n\ln n}$ (*Hint:* use the integral test. Recall: $\int \dfrac{dx}{x\ln x} = \ln\ln x + C$.)

   (d) $\sum_{n=2}^{\infty} \dfrac{1-3n}{3+4n}$

3. Consider the alternating series $\sum_{n=1}^{\infty} \frac{(-1)^{n-1}}{\sqrt{n}}$.

   (a) The series converges. Why?

   (b) How many terms of the series do we need to add in order to find the sum of the series correct to three decimal places?

4. Do the following for $\sum_{n=1}^{\infty}(-1)^n \frac{(x-3)^n}{n^3}$.

   (a) Find the radius of convergence of the power series.

   (b) Find the interval of convergence of the power series.

5. Let $f(x) = \cos x$.

   (a) Find the third degree Taylor polynomial $T_3(x)$ of $f(x)$ centered at $a = 0$.

   (b) Write down an expression for the third degree remainder term $R_3(x)$ of $f(x)$ for $a = 0$, and show that if $|x| < 0.1$ then $|R_3(x)| < 5 \cdot 10^{-6}$.

6. Let $f(x) = \sin x$.

   (a) What is the maximum error possible in using the approximation $\sin x \approx x - x^3/3! + x^5/5!$ if $0 \le x \le 0.3$?

   (b) For what values of x is this approximation accurate to within 0.00005?

7. Let $f(x) = \sqrt{1 + x^3}$.

   (a) Find the Taylor series of $f(x)$ about 0.

   (b) Use your answer to part (a) to find $f^{(12)}(0)$.

8. Find the *interval of convergence* of the series $\sum_{n=1}^{\infty} \frac{(2x-1)^n}{n^3}$.

9. Find a power series representation with $a = 0$ for the function $f(x) = x^2/(1-2x)^2$.

10. Let $T_n(x) = \sum_{k=0}^{n} \frac{x^k}{k!}$ be the nth degree Taylor polynomial of the function $f(x) = e^x$ at $a = 0$. Show that $\lim_{n\to\infty} T_n(x) = e^x$ for all x.

11. Find the Taylor series expansion of the complex valued function $f(z) = (z-1)/(z-1-i)$ based at $a = i$. Use your answer to compute the derivative $f^{(9)}(i)$.

12. Find the nth degree Taylor polynomial of $f(x) = \sin x$ centered at $a = \pi/4$. Find an expression for the remainder $R_n(x)$ and show that $\lim_{n\to\infty} R_n(x) = 0$ for all x. What do you conclude?

13. Let $f(x) = \ln x$.

(a) Find the Taylor series of $f(x) = \ln x$ centered at $x = 1$. What is the interval of convergence of the series? Does the series converge to $f(x)$ there? Explain.

(b) Now replace x by the complex variable $z = x + iy$ in the Taylor series in part (a). Discuss the convergence of the resulting complex power series.

(c) In its domain of convergence, the power series in part (b) defines a complex analytic function $\ln z$ which agrees with the real natural log-function when z is real. Recall that we defined a complex analytic exponential function e^z using power series. Is the function $\ln z$ the inverse of e^z also for complex z? Explain!

14. Do the following.

(a) Find the power series expansion of the function $f(x) = 2x/(10 + 4x^4)$ at $a = 0$. Discuss the convergence of the resulting series. Compute the derivative $f^{(20)}(0)$.

(b) Find a power series expansion for $g(x) = \cos\sqrt{x}$ at $a = 0$.

15. Do the following.

(a) Use the integral test to show that the series $\sum_{n=2}^{\infty} 1/(n(\ln n)^3)$ converges.

(b) How many terms of the series would you have to add up to approximate its sum to within 10^{-4}?

(c) How can you get the same accuracy of approximation as in (b) with much less work? Carry out your plan!

16. Lesson 13, problems 20 and 22.

17. Evaluate the improper integrals.

(a) $\int_{-\infty}^{\infty} \dfrac{x}{x^2 + 2}\, dx$

(b) $\int_{-1}^{2} \dfrac{1}{(2x - 1)^{1/3}}\, dx$

18. Determine whether the given series converges. *Justify your answer!* If the series converges, also find its sum.

    (a) $\dfrac{1}{2} + \dfrac{2}{3} + \dfrac{3}{4} + \cdots + \dfrac{n}{n+1} + \cdots$

    (b) $\sum_{n=2}^{\infty} \dfrac{1}{\sqrt{n}\ln n}$

    (c) $\sum_{n=1}^{\infty} \dfrac{2}{n^2 + 2n}$

    (d) $\sum_{n=1}^{\infty} \dfrac{3^{n+1}}{\pi^n}$

19. Lesson 15, problems 29 and 30.

20. Do the following.

    (a) Use the integral test to show that the series $\sum_{n=2}^{\infty} 1/(n\ln n(\ln\ln n)^3)$ converges.

    (b) How many terms would you have to add up the series to approximate the sum of the series within 10^{-4}?

    (c) Next use the formula

$$U_N = S_N + \int_{N+1}^{\infty} f(x)\, dx$$

    given in the study guide to approximate the sum of the series. Find N so that the error is at most 10^{-4}.

21. Do the following.

    (a) Use the ratio test to show that the series $\sum_{n=0}^{\infty} (n^2 + n)/2^n$ converges.

    (b) Write $a_n = (n^2 + n)/2^n$. Find N_0 so that $a_{n+1}/a_n < 3/4$ for $n > N_0$.

    (c) Next use part (b) to find an estimate for the error $|S - S_N|$, where $N \geq N_0$.

    (d) Finally find N so that S_N approximates the sum of the series within 0.001.

22. Lesson 16, problems 15, 22, and 26.

23. Lesson 18, problems 8 and 27.

24. Find the limit

$$\lim_{x \to 0} \frac{\cos(x^2) - 1 + x^4/2 - x^8/24}{\exp(x^5) - 1 - x^5}.$$

25. Find exactly the sum of the series $\sum_{n=1}^{\infty} \dfrac{n^3}{2^n}$. *Hint.* See Example 4 in Lesson 17.)

26. Find a power series solution to the differential equation

$$y''(x) + x^2 y(x) = 0, \quad y(0) = 1, \quad y'(0) = 3.$$

Part IV

Supplemental Material

Appendix A

Lab/Recitation Projects

A.1 Group Projects

Your instructor may use some of the following group projects, probably as part of the work required in a recitation/lab class meeting.

Your instructor will give explicit directions concerning a group project such as whether it will be collected, the due date, the credit assigned to the project, and the format of an acceptable group report, if one is required. **Be sure to check with your instructor about what is required and any due dates.**

Typically you will work together in groups of three or four. You can share information among groups. These projects are collaborative learning activities.

The table on the next page lists all the group projects and the lessons they support. An * is appended to the name of a group project if the project covers material that is *essential* for MTH 306 and the topic of the project normally is covered in a recitation class meeting.

Group Project	Suitable for use with
Complex Numbers and the Complex Plane	Lesson 1
Solving Linear Systems I	Lesson 3
Solving Linear Systems II	Lesson 3
Finding the Inverse of a Matrix	Lesson 4
Linear Dependence and Independence	Lesson 5
Matrices and Linear Transformations	Lesson 6
Reflection Matrices	Lesson 6
Eigenvalue Problems I	Lesson 7
Eigenvalue Problems II	Lesson 7
Special Limits*	Lesson 9, 10
L'Hôpital's Rule and Taylor Polynomials*	Lessons 9
Taylor Polynomial Approximation	Lesson 9
Taylor Series Representations	Lesson 11
Series With Positive Terms and the Integral Test	Lesson 12
Comparison Tests	Lesson 13
Conditional and Absolute Convergence	Lesson 14
The Ratio and Root Tests	Lesson 15
Algebraic Manipulation of Power Series	Lesson 16
Enrichment Projects	
Population Dynamics	Lesson 7
Systems of Differential Equations	Lesson 7
Special Relativity 1	Lesson 9
Series in Action: Heat Conduction	Lesson 12 – 17
Effective Calculation of Logarithms	Lesson 17
The Binomial Series	Lesson 17
Special Relativity 2	Lesson 17

Enrichment projects indicate some areas in which the mathematical ideas of MTH 306 are applied and typically are a little more demanding.

The projects are printed on tear-out pages.

Group Project:
Complex Numbers and the Complex Plane

Names: _____

_____

Directions: Solve the following problems. **Be sure to check with your lab/recitation instructor about what is required.** Will you have to turn in a project report? If so, when will it be due? Is there a required format for the report? Be clear on what is expected before your group starts to work.

This project will give you some practice with complex numbers, review the quadratic formula, and helps you think geometrically about distances in the complex plane, and makes contact with a curve you know from precalculus or calculus.

One Route to the Quadratic Formula: A long time ago in an algebra class you learned the quadratic formula and probably saw how it can be established by completing the square. Here is another approach. Either one can be used to show that the quadratic formula gives the roots of any quadratic equation $az^2 + bz + c = 0$ whose coefficients may be real or complex numbers. Of course, assume throughout that $a \neq 0$.

1. Let g be a given complex number. Show by the following steps that the equation $w^2 = g$ has exactly two solutions $w = \pm\sqrt{g}$ where $\sqrt{g}$ stands for one of the solutions.

   (a) Let $g = re^{i\gamma}$ be a fixed polar form of g. Check that $\left(\sqrt{r}e^{i\gamma/2}\right)^2 = g$ where $\sqrt{r}$ is the usual real square root of r. So $\sqrt{g} = \sqrt{r}e^{i\gamma/2}$ is one square root of g.

   (b) Check that the identity $\alpha^2 - \beta^2 = (\alpha - \beta)(\alpha + \beta)$ holds for complex numbers.

   (c) Given the square root in (a) the equation $w^2 = g$ can be expressed as $w^2 - \left(\sqrt{g}\right)^2 = 0$. Show that the only solutions of this equation are $\pm\sqrt{g}$.

2. The quadratic equation $az^2 + bz + c = 0$ would be easy to solve if $b = 0$. Why? The following steps reduce the solution of a general quadratic to this case. You get to carry them out and rediscover the quadratic formula.

   (a) Let d be a complex number to be determined. Make the change of variables $z = w - d$ in the quadratic equation $az^2 + bz + c = 0$ to obtain a quadratic equation for w.

   (b) What choice of d enables you to reduce the equation for w to one you know how to solve?

    (c) Make that choice, find w, and then find z. You should wind up with the quadratic formula.

3. Let z and c be complex numbers.

    (a) What is the geometric interpretation of $|z-c|$ and $|z+c|$ in the complex plane. Make a sketch.

    (b) Sketch the graph of $|z-i| \le 1$ and $|z+i| < 1$ in the complex plane.

    (c) What is the graph of $|z-i| + |z+i| = 1$ in the complex plane? Explain.

    (d) Find four distinct points in the complex plane that lie on the graph of $|z-i| + |z+i| = 4$.

    (e) Sketch a careful graph of the equation in (d).

    (f) The curve in (e) occurs in precalculus and calculus. Name it. Explain how you know you are correct. *Hint.* There are two natural explanations. One involves no algebraic steps.

Group Project:
Solving Linear Systems I: Systematic Elimination of Unknowns

Names: _____

_____

Directions: Solve the following problems. **Be sure to check with your lab/recitation instructor about what is required.** Will you have to turn in a project report? If so, when will it be due? Is there a required format for the report? Be clear on what is expected before your group starts to work.

This project will help reinforce some key ideas related to solving linear systems.

Do the following for each of the linear systems given below:

- Find the determinant of the system. Based on the determinant what can you say about the number of solutions of the system? Explain briefly.

- Use systematic elimination of unknowns to solve the system.

- Interpret you solution in geometric terms.

1. $\begin{cases} 4x + y - 5z = 13 \\ x + 2y + z = 0 \\ 3x - 3y + z = -12 \end{cases}$

2. $\begin{cases} r - y + 2w = -1 \\ r + 2y - w = 2 \\ 5r + 7y - 2w = 7 \end{cases}$

3. $\begin{cases} 2a - b + c = 1 \\ a + 3b - 5c = 3 \\ -4a + 2b - 2c = 3 \end{cases}$

Group Project:
Solving Linear Systems II: How many solutions will there be?

Names: _____

_____

Directions: Solve the following problems. **Be sure to check with your lab/recitation instructor about what is required.** Will you have to turn in a project report? If so, when will it be due? Is there a required format for the report? Be clear on what is expected before your group starts to work.

This project will help reinforce some key ideas related to solving linear systems.

Answer the following questions about the linear system

$$\begin{cases} x \phantom{{}-2y} + cz = 6 \\ 3x - 2y + z = 2 \\ 2x - y + z = 4 \end{cases}$$

1. Set $c = -1$ and find the unique solution to this system of equations.

2. Find the value of c that corresponds to an infinite number of solutions to this system of equations.

3. Describe the family of solutions given by the value of c in Problem 2.

4. Is there a value of c for which this system has no solutions? Explain why or why not.

Group Project:
Matrix Inverses and Transposes

Names: _____

_____

Directions: Solve the following problems. **Be sure to check with your lab/recitation instructor about what is required.** Will you have to turn in a project report? If so, when will it be due? Is there a required format for the report? Be clear on what is expected before your group starts to work.

Do the following for the matrices given below:

- Use determinants to determine which of the matrices have an inverse.

- Use the systematic method in Lesson 4 to find the inverse of those matrices that have an inverse.

1.

$$\text{(a)} \quad \begin{bmatrix} 1 & 2 \\ 3 & 4 \end{bmatrix} \quad \text{and} \quad \text{(b)} \quad \begin{bmatrix} 1 & 2 \\ 2 & 4 \end{bmatrix}$$

2.

$$\text{(a)} \quad \begin{bmatrix} 0 & 1 & 0 \\ 1 & 0 & 2 \\ 0 & 0 & 1 \end{bmatrix} \quad \text{and} \quad \text{(b)} \quad \begin{bmatrix} 1 & 2 & 1 \\ -1 & 1 & 2 \\ 1 & 0 & 1 \end{bmatrix}$$

3. Let

$$A = \begin{bmatrix} 1 & 0 & 0 \\ 0 & 0 & 1 \\ 0 & 1 & 0 \end{bmatrix}$$

(a) Find A^T, AA^T, and $A^T A$.

(b) Find A^{-1}.

4. Let a 3×3 matrix A, whose entries are real numbers, be expressed in term of its rows by

$$A = \begin{bmatrix} \mathbf{r}_1 \\ \mathbf{r}_2 \\ \mathbf{r}_3 \end{bmatrix}$$

(a) Express A^T in terms of its columns using the transpose operation and the row vectors of A.

(b) Show that the entry in row i and column j of AA^T is given by the (matrix) product $\mathbf{r}_i \mathbf{r}_j^T$. Now express this entry as a dot product.

(c) Suppose $AA^T = I$. What special geometric properties do the rows of A have?

(d) If (c) holds, then $A^T A =$?

(e) What is the geometric interpretation of (d)?

Group Project:
Linear Dependence and Linear Independence

Names: _____

_____

Directions: Solve the following problems. **Be sure to check with your lab/recitation instructor about what is required.** Will you have to turn in a project report? If so, when will it be due? Is there a required format for the report? Be clear on what is expected before your group starts to work.

Do the following for each set of vectors:

- Determine whether the vectors in the set are linearly dependent or independent

- If dependent find a **nontrivial** linear combination of the vectors that has sum **0**.

- In each case give a geometric description of the span of the given set of vectors.

1.
$$\text{(a)} \quad \begin{bmatrix} -1 \\ -1 \end{bmatrix}, \begin{bmatrix} 1 \\ -3 \end{bmatrix} \quad \text{and} \quad \text{(b)} \quad \begin{bmatrix} 3 \\ -1 \end{bmatrix}, \begin{bmatrix} 1 \\ -3 \end{bmatrix}$$

2.
$$\text{(a)} \quad \begin{bmatrix} 2 \\ 1 \\ 0 \end{bmatrix}, \begin{bmatrix} 1 \\ 1 \\ 1 \end{bmatrix}, \begin{bmatrix} 0 \\ 1 \\ -1 \end{bmatrix} \quad \text{and} \quad \text{(b)} \quad \begin{bmatrix} -2 \\ 0 \\ 0 \end{bmatrix}, \begin{bmatrix} -2 \\ 2 \\ -2 \end{bmatrix}, \begin{bmatrix} 3 \\ -2 \\ 2 \end{bmatrix}$$

3.
$$\text{(a)} \quad \begin{bmatrix} 2 \\ 0 \\ 1 \\ 0 \end{bmatrix}, \begin{bmatrix} 1 \\ 1 \\ 1 \\ 1 \end{bmatrix}, \begin{bmatrix} 1 \\ -3 \\ -1 \\ -3 \end{bmatrix} \quad \text{and} \quad \text{(b)} \quad \begin{bmatrix} -2 \\ 0 \\ 1 \\ 0 \end{bmatrix}, \begin{bmatrix} -2 \\ 2 \\ 0 \\ -2 \end{bmatrix}, \begin{bmatrix} 3 \\ -2 \\ 1 \\ 2 \end{bmatrix}$$

Group Project:
Matrices and Linear Transformations

Names: _____

_____

Directions: Solve the following problems. **Be sure to check with your lab/recitation instructor about what is required.** Will you have to turn in a project report? If so, when will it be due? Is there a required format for the report? Be clear on what is expected before your group starts to work.

This project is designed to help you better visualize the action of a matrix in geometric terms. It also shows how to take advantage of the matrix representation of a linear transformation.

1. Give a geometric description in words and with sketches of the transformation $T : \mathbb{R}^3 \to \mathbb{R}^3$ that is multiplication by the matrix

$$A = \begin{bmatrix} 1 & 0 & 0 \\ 0 & -1 & 0 \\ 0 & 0 & 1 \end{bmatrix}$$

2. Give a geometric description in words and with sketches of the transformation $T : \mathbb{R}^3 \to \mathbb{R}^2$ that is multiplication by the matrix

$$A = \begin{bmatrix} 1 & 0 & 0 \\ 0 & -1 & 0 \end{bmatrix}$$

3. Do the following:

   (a) Find the matrix of the linear transformation $T : \mathbb{R}^2 \to \mathbb{R}^2$ where $T(\mathbf{v})$ is the reflection of $\mathbf{v}$ across the line $y = (1/2)\, x$.

   (b) Find the reflection of the vector $[2\ 3]^T$ across the line $y = (1/2)\, x$.

4. Let $\mathbf{a} = [1\ 2\ 3]^T$ and define a linear transformation $T : \mathbb{R}^3 \to \mathbb{R}^3$ as follows: For each position vector $\mathbf{v}$ in $\mathbb{R}^3$ let $T(\mathbf{v})$ be the position vector with the property that the line segment from the tip of $\mathbf{v}$ to the tip of $T(\mathbf{v})$ is parallel to $\mathbf{a}$ and such that the tip of $T(\mathbf{v})$ is in the xy-plane. Do the following:

   (a) Find the matrix A of T.

   (b) Determine whether or not A is a projection matrix. If it is, is it an orthogonal projection? Explain.

Group Project:
Reflection Matrices

Names:

_____

_____

Directions: Solve the following problems. **Be sure to check with your lab/recitation instructor about what is required.** Will you have to turn in a project report? If so, when will it be due? Is there a required format for the report? Be clear on what is expected before your group starts to work.

1. Goal: Find the 3×3 matrix A that reflects vectors across the plane Π with equation

$$z = 2x - y$$

by the following steps:

   (a) Let $\mathbf{n}$ be a unit vector that is normal to Π. Find $\mathbf{n}$. (There are 2 possible $\mathbf{n}$'s.)

   (b) Find $\text{comp}_\mathbf{n} \, \mathbf{e}_i$ for $i = 1, 2, 3$.

   (c) For $i = 1, 2, 3$, find $\mathbf{b}_i = \text{proj}_\mathbf{n} \, \mathbf{e}_i$.

   (d) Find the vector $A\mathbf{b}_i$ for $i = 1, 2, 3$. (What do you want A to do to $\mathbf{b}_i$?)

   (e) For $i = 1, 2, 3$, find $\mathbf{c}_i = \mathbf{e}_i - \mathbf{b}_i$.

   (f) Find the vector $A\mathbf{c}_i$ for $i = 1, 2, 3$. (What do you want A to do to $\mathbf{c}_i$?)

   (g) For $i = 1, 2, 3$, $\mathbf{e}_i = \mathbf{b}_i + \mathbf{c}_i$. Use this together with (d) and (f) to give $A\mathbf{e}_i$ for $i = 1, 2, 3$.

   (h) Find the matrix A.

   (i) Without any computation, give a candidate for A^{-1}.

   (j) Check (i).

   (k) Find the 3×3 matrix B that reflects vectors across the plane Π with equation $z = 2x - y$ and triples their magnitude.

   (l) Give B^{-1}.

Group Project:
Eigenvalue Problems I

Names: _____

_____

Directions: Solve the following problems. **Be sure to check with your lab/recitation instructor about what is required.** Will you have to turn in a project report? If so, when will it be due? Is there a required format for the report? Be clear on what is expected before your group starts to work.

1. Solve the eigenvalue problem for the given matrix as follows:

- Find the characteristic equation of the matrix and use it to determine all the eigenvalues of the matrix.

- For each eigenvalue find **all** the corresponding eigenvectors.

- For each eigenvalue list a full set of linearly independent eigenvectors and describe in geometric terms the span of the linearly independent eigenvectors corresponding to each eigenvalue.

$$\text{(a)} \begin{bmatrix} 8 & 5 \\ -10 & -7 \end{bmatrix} \qquad \text{(b)} \begin{bmatrix} -2 & 0 \\ 0 & -2 \end{bmatrix}$$

$$\text{(c)} \begin{bmatrix} 2 & 1 & 1 \\ -2 & -1 & -2 \\ -2 & -2 & -1 \end{bmatrix} \qquad \text{(d)} \begin{bmatrix} 5 & 5 & -1 \\ -1 & -4 & 5 \\ -1 & 2 & -1 \end{bmatrix}$$

Sometimes it is easier to find eigenvectors and eigenvalues by a geometric analysis. Review the geometric meaning of the equation $T(\mathbf{v}) = \lambda \mathbf{v}$ for a nonzero vector $\mathbf{v}$. Now solve the following problem:

2. The transformation $T : \mathbb{R}^3 \to \mathbb{R}^3$ that reflects each vector in the plane $x + y + z = 0$ and then reverses the direction of the reflected vector and doubles its length is a linear transformation. Use geometric reasoning to find all the eigenvectors and corresponding eigenvalues of T.

Group Project:
Eigenvalue Problems II

Names: _____

_____

Directions: Solve the following problems. **Be sure to check with your lab/recitation instructor about what is required.** Will you have to turn in a project report? If so, when will it be due? Is there a required format for the report? Be clear on what is expected before your group starts to work.

1. The goal of this problem is to find the eigenvalues and eigenvectors for the following matrix:
$$A = \begin{bmatrix} 1 & -8 \\ 1 & -3 \end{bmatrix}.$$

   (a) Find the eigenvalues of A.

   (b) Find an eigenvector $\mathbf{v_1}$ corresponding to one of the eigenvalues.

   (c) Use $\mathbf{v_1}$ to find an eigenvector $\mathbf{v_2}$ corresponding to the remaining eigenvalue.

2. The goal of this problem is to find the eigenvalues and eigenvectors for the following matrix:
$$B = \begin{bmatrix} 3 & 4 \\ 4 & -3 \end{bmatrix}.$$

   (a) Find the eigenvalues of B.

   (b) Find an eigenvector $\mathbf{v_1}$ corresponding to one of the eigenvalues.

   (c) Find an eigenvector $\mathbf{v_2}$ corresponding to the remaining eigenvalue.

   (d) Calculate $\mathbf{v_1} \cdot \mathbf{v_2}$. Are $\mathbf{v_1}$ and $\mathbf{v_2}$ linearly independent, orthogonal, both, or neither?

3. The goal of this problem is to find the eigenvalues and choose orthogonal eigenvectors for the following matrix:
$$C = \begin{bmatrix} 3 & 0 & -4 \\ 0 & 5 & 0 \\ -4 & 0 & -3 \end{bmatrix}.$$

   (a) Find the eigenvalues of C. (There are two distinct eigenvalues; one negative and one positive. The positive eigenvalue appears as a double root of the characteristic equation.)

   (b) Find an eigenvector $\mathbf{v_1}$ corresponding to the negative eigenvalue.

   (c) Find an eigenvector $\mathbf{v_2}$ corresponding to the positive eigenvalue. It should be orthogonal to $\mathbf{v_1}$. Why?

   (d) Find another eigenvector $\mathbf{v_3}$ corresponding to the positive eigenvalue. Choose it to be orthogonal to both $\mathbf{v_1}$ and $\mathbf{v_2}$.

Group Project:
Special Limits

Names: _____

_____

Directions: Solve the following problems. **Be sure to check with your lab/recitation instructor about what is required.** Will you have to turn in a project report? If so, when will it be due? Is there a required format for the report? Be clear on what is expected before your group starts to work.

In each problem do the following:

- Perform numerical experiments and/or use graphs to determine the behavior as $n \to \infty$ of the given expressions. Experiment with small, medium, and large values for n.

- If you believe an expression has a limit, state what you believe the limit is. If you believe there is no limit state that. In either case, provide tables and/or graphs that support your assertions.

This project is designed to acquaint you with some important limits that come up in calculus, especially in the study of infinite series. You will use these results frequently during the rest of the term.

1. Fix a real number a. This problem concerns the behavior of a^n as $n \to \infty$. Determine the behavior in the following cases. Comment on any qualitative differences you notice:

    (a) $(1/2)^n$, 2^n

    (b) $(-1/2)^n$, $(-2)^n$

    (c) $(.9)^n$, $(.99)^n$

    (d) $(1.1)^n$, $(1.01)^n$

2. Based on the results in Problem 1 what do you believe about $\lim_{n\to\infty} a^n$? Be specific.

3. Fix a positive real number a. This problem concerns the behavior of $a^{1/n} = \sqrt[n]{a}$ as $n \to \infty$. Determine the behavior in the following cases. Comment on any qualitative differences you notice:

    (a) $1^{1/n}$, $(.9)^{1/n}$, $(1.1)^{1/n}$

    (b) $(0.1)^{1/n}$, $(0.5)^{1/n}$

   (c) $(0.01)^{1/n}$, $(100)^{1/n}$, $(1000)^{1/n}$

4. Based on the results in Problem 3 what do you believe about $\lim_{n\to\infty} a^{1/n}$? Be specific.

5. This problem concerns the behavior as $n \to \infty$ of $n^{1/n}$. Make a table of n versus $n^{1/n} = \sqrt[n]{n}$ for $n = 1, 5, 10, 20, 30, 40, 50, 75, 100, 1000$. Plot the graph of $y = x^{1/x}$ for $0 < x \leq 1000$. Based on the results state what you believe about $\lim_{n\to\infty} n^{1/n}$?

6. Let x be a real number. Determine the behavior as $n \to \infty$ of $|x|^n / n!$. *Hint.* On the same screen, graph $|x|^n / n!$ for $n = 1, 2, 3, 5, 10, 20, 100$. Start with $n = 1$ and plot the graph. Then append the graphs for the other values of n, one at a time.

7. Let x be a real number. Determine the behavior as $n \to \infty$ of $(1 + x/n)^n$. *Hint.* On the same screen, graph $(1 + x/n)^n$ for $n = 1, 2, 3, 5, 10, 20, 100$. Do the graphs remind you of a familiar function?

Group Project:
L'Hôpital's Rule and Taylor Polynomials

Names:

_____

_____

Directions: Solve the following problems. **Be sure to check with your lab/recitation instructor about what is required.** Will you have to turn in a project report? If so, when will it be due? Is there a required format for the report? Be clear on what is expected before your group starts to work.

This project is designed to help you discover a very useful way to find subtle limits that come up in calculus.

$$\lim_{x \to 1} \frac{\ln x}{\sin \pi x} = ?$$

1. Why isn't this an easy limit to evaluate? Discuss briefly but be specific.

2. Use a graphing calculator to graph $y = \ln x$ and $y = \sin \pi x$ on the same plot. Use a graphing window of $0 \le x \le 3$, $-1.5 \le y \le 1.5$.

3. Find the first order Taylor polynomial approximation at 1 to $y = \ln x$. Call this approximation $T_1(x)$. Find the first order Taylor polynomial approximation at 1 to $y = \sin \pi x$. Call this approximation $S_1(x)$. Record your results:

$$T_1(x) =$$
$$S_1(x) =$$

4. Append the graphs of $y = T_1(x)$ and $y = S_1(x)$ to the plot in Problem 2. Zoom in on the point $(1, 0)$ and think about what you are seeing.

5. Why is it reasonable to suspect that

$$\lim_{x \to 1} \frac{\ln x}{\sin \pi x} = \lim_{x \to 1} \frac{T_1(x)}{S_1(x)}?$$

6. Finally, use the result in Problem 5 to find $\lim_{x \to 1} \ln x / \sin \pi x$.

7. Let $f(x) = \ln x$ and $g(x) = \sin \pi x$. Now express the result of Problem 5 in the form

$$\lim_{x \to 1} \frac{f(x)}{g(x)} = \lim_{x \to 1} \frac{?}{?}$$

where this time the question marks are expressed *directly* in terms of the functions f and g with no reference to $T_1(x)$ and $S_1(x)$. Congratulations, you have discovered the essence of l'Hôpital's rule.

Toward the end of your recitation class your instructor may put your work on Problems 1-7 in a broader context. If so you will learn what an indeterminate form is and a precise statement of l'Hôpital's Rule for the indeterminate forms $0/0$ and ∞/∞ and perhaps an indication of how to handle the indeterminate forms 0^0 and 1^∞.

Group Project:
Taylor Polynomial Approximation

Names:

_____

_____

Directions: Solve the following problems. **Be sure to check with your lab/recitation instructor about what is required.** Will you have to turn in a project report? If so, when will it be due? Is there a required format for the report? Be clear on what is expected before your group starts to work.

In this project $f(x) = 1/\sqrt{1-x}$ and you investigate the behavior of some Taylor polynomial approximations to $1/\sqrt{1-x}$ about 0.

1. Find the zeroth, first, second, and third Taylor polynomials, $T_0(x)$, $T_1(x)$, $T_2(x)$, and $T_3(x)$, about 0 for $f(x) = 1/\sqrt{1-x}$. Can you predict what all terms in $T_4(x)$ will be, except for the term involving x^4?

2. *(What do you see?)* Use a graphing calculator to make graphs for $-0.7 \le x \le 0.7$ and $0 \le y \le 2$ as follows: On the same coordinate axes first graph $1/\sqrt{1-x}$, then add the graph of $T_0(x)$, then add the graph of $T_1(x)$, then add the graph of $T_2(x)$, and then add the graph of $T_3(x)$. Look carefully at what happens. Discuss any trends you see related to how well the successive Taylor polynomials approximate $1/\sqrt{1-x}$. Be as specific as you can. (Sometimes graphs are too close together to distinguish. Zoom in with an appropriate graphing window to see how they differ in terms of how well they approximate $1/\sqrt{1-x}$.)

3. *(From eyeball to measurement)* For $0 \le x \le 1/2$ show that

$$\frac{1}{\sqrt{1-x}} = T_0(x) + R_0(x), \quad \frac{1}{\sqrt{1-x}} = T_1(x) + R_1(x), \quad \frac{1}{\sqrt{1-x}} = T_2(x) + R_2(x)$$

where the error in approximation satisfies

$$|R_0(x)| \le \sqrt{2}x, \quad |R_1(x)| \le \frac{3\sqrt{2}}{2}x^2, \quad |R_2(x)| \le \frac{5\sqrt{2}}{2}x^3$$

4. Sketch a graph of $1/\sqrt{1-x}$ and of $T_2(x)$ on the same coordinate axes. Indicate on the graph the meaning of the remainder (error) $R_2(x)$ at $x = 0$, $1/4$, and $1/2$.

5. Each error estimate in Problem 3 is most pessimistic at $x = 1/2$ and gets better (smaller) the nearer x is to zero. Does this make sense? Explain.

Group Project:
Taylor Series Representations

Names:
_____

_____

Directions: Solve the following problems. **Be sure to check with your lab/recitation instructor about what is required.** Will you have to turn in a project report? If so, when will it be due? Is there a required format for the report? Be clear on what is expected before your group starts to work.

1. Find the Taylor series about 0 for $f(x) = \ln(4 + x)$.

2. Use a graphing calculator to make graphs for $-2 \leq x \leq 2$ and $0 \leq y \leq 2$ as follows: On the same coordinate axes first graph $\ln(4 + x)$, then add the graph of $T_0(x)$, then add the graph of $T_1(x)$, then add the graph of $T_2(x)$, and then add the graph of $T_3(x)$. Look carefully at what happens. Discuss any trends you see related to how well the successive Taylor polynomials approximate $\ln(4 + x)$. Be as specific as you can. (Sometimes graphs are too close together to distinguish. Zoom in with an appropriate graphing window to see how they differ in terms of how well they approximate $\ln(4 + x)$.)

3. Show that $\ln(4 + x)$ is the sum of its Taylor series for $-2 \leq x \leq 2$.

4. Find the first three *nonzero* terms in the Taylor series expansion of $f(x) = \sec(x^2)$ by evaluating enough derivatives of f at 0. Do you think that you can find all the terms in the Taylor series of f by continuing in this fashion? Explain briefly.

5. Use Taylor series expansions already established in these lessons and changes of variables to find an infinite series expansion for the function

$$f(x) = \cos\sqrt{x} + \frac{\sin\sqrt{x}}{\sqrt{x}}$$

valid when $x > 0$.

Group Project:
Series With Positive Terms and the Integral Test

Names: _____

_____

Directions: Solve the following problems. **Be sure to check with your lab/recitation instructor about what is required.** Will you have to turn in a project report? If so, when will it be due? Is there a required format for the report? Be clear on what is expected before your group starts to work.

1. Explain briefly why the integral test cannot be applied *directly* to the series

$$\frac{1}{3} + \frac{1}{2} + \frac{1}{3^2} + \frac{1}{2^2} + \frac{1}{3^3} + \frac{1}{2^3} + \frac{1}{3^4} + \frac{1}{2^4} + \cdots$$

to determine whether it converges or diverges.

2. Show by any convenient means that the series in Problem 1 does converge and find its (exact) sum.

3. Let S_N be the Nth partial sum of the series $\sum_{n=1}^{\infty} 1/\sqrt{n}$. Do the following:

   (a) Show that $S_1 \geq 1$, $S_2 \geq \sqrt{2}$, $S_3 \geq \sqrt{3}$, $S_4 \geq \sqrt{4}$, and in general that $S_n \geq \sqrt{n}$.

   (b) Use (a) to determine whether the series $\sum_{n=1}^{\infty} 1/\sqrt{n}$ converges or diverges.

   (c) Deduce the convergence or divergence of $\sum_{n=1}^{\infty} 1/\sqrt{n}$ by any other method.

4. Let S_N be the Nth partial sum of the series $\sum_{n=1}^{\infty} n2^{-n}$ and S its sum. Show that the series converges. Then find an approximation to S that is accurate to within 0.005.

Group Project:
Comparison Tests

Names:

_____

_____

Directions: Solve the following problems. **Be sure to check with your lab/recitation instructor about what is required.** Will you have to turn in a project report? If so, when will it be due? Is there a required format for the report? Be clear on what is expected before your group starts to work.

This group project will help you gain experience in using the basic comparison test and the limit comparison test. It will also help you gain insight into which of these tests is easier to apply, if both are applicable.

For each of the following series do the following:

- Determine if it converges or diverges by the basic comparison test.

- Determine if it converges or diverges by the limit comparison test.

- If you were able to apply both tests which was easier? Why?

- If you were able to apply one test but not the other explain as clearly as you can either why the other test does not apply or why you could not figure out how to apply it.

1. (a) $\sum_{n=0}^{\infty} \frac{3^n}{4^n+2^n}$ (b) $\sum_{n=0}^{\infty} \frac{3^n}{4^n-2^n}$

2. $\sum_{n=0}^{\infty} \frac{1-\cos(n\pi/2)}{n^2+1}$

3. $\sum_{n=1}^{\infty} \frac{\sin(1/n)}{n}$

4. $\sum_{n=1}^{\infty} \frac{\cos(1/n)}{n}$

5. $\sum_{n=0}^{\infty} \frac{(n!)^2}{(2n)!}$

Group Project:
Conditional and Absolute Convergence

Names: _____

_____

Directions: Solve the following problems. **Be sure to check with your lab/recitation instructor about what is required.** Will you have to turn in a project report? If so, when will it be due? Is there a required format for the report? Be clear on what is expected before your group starts to work.

This group project will help you to better appreciate the distinction between conditional convergence and absolute convergence. It also indicates one way to treat an alternating series that converges but whose convergence cannot be deduced from the alternating series test.

1. Explain briefly why the alternating harmonic series

$$1 - \frac{1}{2} + \frac{1}{3} - \frac{1}{4} + \frac{1}{5} - \frac{1}{6} + \frac{1}{7} - \frac{1}{8} + - \cdots$$

   is conditionally convergent but not absolutely convergent.

   You know the alternating harmonic series converges by Problem 1. Its sum is $\ln 2$. You may use this fact in the following problems. Rearrange the terms in the alternating harmonic series to obtain the series

$$1 + \frac{1}{3} - \frac{1}{2} + \frac{1}{5} + \frac{1}{7} - \frac{1}{4} + \frac{1}{9} + \frac{1}{11} - \frac{1}{6} + + - \cdots \qquad (*)$$

2. Explain why

$$\frac{1}{2} - \frac{1}{4} + \frac{1}{6} - \frac{1}{8} + - \cdots = \frac{1}{2} \ln 2$$

3. Now insert 0 terms into the series in Problem 2 (including before the first term) in such a way that the sum of the modified series and the alternating harmonic series is the rearranged series in (*). Conclude that

$$1 + \frac{1}{3} - \frac{1}{2} + \frac{1}{5} + \frac{1}{7} - \frac{1}{4} + \frac{1}{9} + \frac{1}{11} - \frac{1}{6} + + - \cdots = \frac{3}{2} \ln 2$$

   Thus rearranging the order of appearance of the terms in the alternating harmonic series leads to a new series with a different sum! Seeing is believing!

4. Explain briefly why the alternating series test does not apply to the series

$$\sum a_n = \frac{1}{2^3} - \frac{1}{2^2} + \frac{1}{3^3} - \frac{1}{3^2} + \frac{1}{4^3} - \frac{1}{4^2} + \frac{1}{5^3} - \frac{1}{5^2} + - \cdots$$

5. Show that the series in Problem 4 does converge. *Hint.* $|a_n| \leq b_n$ for

$$\sum b_n = \frac{1}{2^2} + \frac{1}{2^2} + \frac{1}{3^2} + \frac{1}{3^2} + \frac{1}{4^2} + \frac{1}{4^2} + \frac{1}{5^2} + \frac{1}{5^2} + \cdots$$

6. Find N so that the Nth partial sum S_N of $\sum a_n$ in Problem 4 approximates the sum S to within 0.001. *Hint.* $|S_N - S| \leq b_{N+1} + b_{N+2} + \cdots$

Group Project:
The Ratio and Root Tests

Names: _____

_____

Directions: Solve the following problems. **Be sure to check with your lab/recitation instructor about what is required.** Will you have to turn in a project report? If so, when will it be due? Is there a required format for the report? Be clear on what is expected before your group starts to work.

1. Show that the series $\sum_{n=1}^{\infty} \frac{n^2}{3^n}$ converges by (a) the ratio test and (b) the root test.

   In Problems 2 and 3 you will need to make choices for M and r in the error estimates associated with the ratio and root tests. Experiment with different permissible choices of M and r. For different choices you normally determine a different partial sum S_N that provides the required approximation to the sum S of the series. Try to determine M and r that give the smallest N such the partial sum S_N provides the required approximation to S.

2. Use the error estimate associated with the ratio test to find the sum S of the series in Problem 1 correct to within 0.005.

3. Use the error estimate associated with the root test to find the sum S of the series in Problem 1 correct to within 0.005.

4. Consider the power series $\sum_{n=1}^{\infty} \frac{x^n}{n^n}$.

   (a) Is it a geometric series? Explain.

   (b) Find the radius of convergence of the power series.

   (c) Let $S(x)$ be the sum of the series and $S_N(x)$ be its Nth partial sum. Find N so that $|S(x) - S_N(x)| < 0.0005$ for all x with $-5 \leq x \leq 5$.

Group Project:
Algebraic Manipulation of Power Series

Names: _____

_____

Directions: Solve the following problems. **Be sure to check with your lab/recitation instructor about what is required.** Will you have to turn in a project report? If so, when will it be due? Is there a required format for the report? Be clear on what is expected before your group starts to work.

In each of the following problems, you are asked to use algebraic manipulations to calculate the first few nonzero terms in the power series expansion of a given function. Do this as follows:

- First, before performing any calculations, determine with justification the largest open interval you can such that the power series expansion will converge absolutely there.

- Second, use known power series expansions and algebraic manipulations to find the first three nonzero terms in the power series expansion of each function.

- Third, if you have a computer and computer algebra system software available find several more terms of the series expansion.

1. For (a) follow the directions above. Then solve (b).

   (a) $\cos^2 x - \sin^2 x$

   (b) $\cos^2 x - \sin^2 x$ can be expressed as the cosine of something. What and why? Now find the full power series expansion of $\cos^2 x - \sin^2 x$ determine its radius of convergence directly using some test.

2. *(Turn Division into Multiplication)*

   (a) For the function $\cos x / (\cos x - \sin x)$ follow the general directions above and use long division.

   (b) Here is another approach. Explain why you know that

   $$\frac{\cos x}{\cos x - \sin x} = b_0 + b_1 x + b_2 x^2 + \cdots$$

   on some interval about the base point 0. Equivalently,

   $$\cos x = (\cos x - \sin x)\left(b_0 + b_1 x + b_2 x^2 + \cdots\right).$$

   How can you use this equation to determine the first three nonzero terms in the power series expansion of $\cos x / (\cos x - \sin x)$? Carry out the calculations.

3. For the function $1/\sqrt{1-x}$ follow the general directions above. *Hint.* Square the equation

$$\frac{1}{\sqrt{1-x}} = b_0 + b_1 x + b_2 x^2 + \cdots$$

and use what you know.

A.2 Enrichment Projects

Enrichment projects indicate some areas in which the mathematical ideas of MTH 306 are applied and typically are a little more demanding. These projects are suitable for independent study and/or, at the discretion of your instructor, extra credit.

Group Project:
Eigenvalues and Eigenvectors in Action
Population Dynamics

Names:

_____

_____

Directions: Solve the following problems. Check with your recitation/lab instructor about the format required for the written report on this group project and the date the report is due.

This group project illustrates a typical situation where eigenvalues and eigenvectors come up in practice. Suppose students attend only OSU or LBCC sometimes transferring to the other school at the end of a term. The matrix

$$A = \begin{bmatrix} .8 & .3 \\ .2 & .7 \end{bmatrix}$$

describes the transition of students from term to term. The first column gives the probabilities that a student currently at OSU will either stay at OSU next term or transfer to LBCC. The probability is .8 that a student currently at OSU will remain at OSU next term and the probability is .2 that a student current at OSU will switch to LBCC next term. The second column gives the corresponding information about a student currently at LBCC. Such a student transfers to OSU next term with probability .3 and remains at LBCC next term with probability .7. In what follows superscripts refer to terms. Let

$$\mathbf{v}^{(1)} = \begin{bmatrix} p \\ q \end{bmatrix}$$

be the initial proportion of students attending OSU and LBCC, respectively, during the first term (of this study). So $p, q \geq 0$ and $p + q = 1$. By the rules of probability, the proportions attending each school during the second term will be $\mathbf{v}^{(2)} = A\mathbf{v}^{(1)}$. The proportions will be $\mathbf{v}^{(3)} = A\mathbf{v}^{(2)}$ during the third term, and so forth. The problems that follow deal with the "long term" behavior of a cohort of students who started at OSU and LBCC in the proportions p and q respectively.

1. Show that $\mathbf{v}^{(N+1)} = A\mathbf{v}^{(N)}$ and that $\mathbf{v}^{(N+1)} = A^N\mathbf{v}^{(1)}$ for $N = 1, 2, 3, \ldots$. Notice that $\mathbf{v}^{(1)}$ has nonnegative components that sum to 1. Show that $\mathbf{v}^{(2)}$ has the same property. Now, what about $\mathbf{v}^{(N)}$ for $N \geq 3$? Explain briefly.

2. For $\mathbf{v}^{(1)} = \begin{bmatrix} .3 \\ .7 \end{bmatrix}$ find what happens for the next two years. That is, find $\mathbf{v}^{(1)}, \mathbf{v}^{(2)}, \ldots, \mathbf{v}^{(6)}$.

3. Do the results in Problem 2 suggest any long-term trend? Discuss briefly.

4. Suppose $\mathbf{v}^{(N)} \to \mathbf{v}$, a limiting distribution of students between OSU and LBCC. Show that $A\mathbf{v} = \mathbf{v}$ and explain why each component of $\mathbf{v}$ is nonnegative and why the sum of the components of $\mathbf{v}$ is 1.

   Problem 4 reveals that the limiting distribution of students is an eigenvector $\mathbf{v}$ of A corresponding to the eigenvalue $\lambda = 1$. The limiting distribution $\mathbf{v}$ is *the* eigenvector (corresponding to eigenvalue $\lambda = 1$) with nonnegative components that sum to 1.

5. Use the results of Problem 4 to find the limiting population distribution $\mathbf{v}$.

Group Project:
Eigenvalues and Eigenvectors in Action
Systems of Differential Equations

Names:

Directions: Solve the following problems. Check with your recitation/lab instructor about the format required for the written report on this group project and the date the report is due.

This group project illustrates a typical situation where eigenvalues and eigenvectors come up in differential equations. The project deals with systems of first order *linear* differential equations but the methods extend readily to higher order linear systems. These methods also are essential for the study of the stability of both linear and nonlinear systems of equations in the neighborhood of an equilibrium point. (Such points can be stable or unstable. Think about a pendulum. In principle the pendulum can be in equilibrium as it hangs a rest in either the straight up or straight down position relative to its pivot. One position is stable and the other is not.) In typical physical situations eigenvalues and eigenvectors reveal the stability properties of the system and its qualitative behavior near an equilibrium point.

Let $y' = dy/dt$. Recall that all solutions to the exponential growth/decay equation $y' = ky$ are given by

$$y = ce^{kt} = e^{kt}c$$

where c is an arbitrary constant.

1. An analogous system of two differential equations in two unknowns is

$$\begin{aligned} u' &= au + bv \\ v' &= cu + dv \end{aligned}$$

where u and v are unknown functions of time t and a, b, c, and d are constants.

(a) Show that the system can be expressed as $\mathbf{w}' = A\mathbf{w}$ where

$$A = \begin{bmatrix} a & b \\ c & d \end{bmatrix} \quad \text{and} \quad \mathbf{w} = \begin{bmatrix} u \\ v \end{bmatrix}$$

(b) Check that $\mathbf{w}' = A\mathbf{w}$ has the trivial solution $\mathbf{w} = \mathbf{0}$.

(c) Check that linear combinations of solutions of $\mathbf{w}' = A\mathbf{w}$ are solution of the system. That is, if α and β are scalars and $\mathbf{w}_1$ and $\mathbf{w}_2$ are solutions of $\mathbf{w}' = A\mathbf{w}$ then $\mathbf{w} = \alpha\mathbf{w}_1 + \beta\mathbf{w}_2$ also is a solution.

2. By analogy to the growth/decay equation $y' = ky$, it is reasonable to guess that $\mathbf{w}' = A\mathbf{w}$ may have solutions of the form

$$\mathbf{w} = e^{\lambda t}\mathbf{v}$$

Substitute this guess into $\mathbf{w}' = A\mathbf{w}$ and determine conditions on λ and $\mathbf{v}$ so that $\mathbf{w} = e^{\lambda t}\mathbf{v}$ is a *nontrivial* solution of the given system of differential equations.

3. Use the results of Problem 2 to find two different (linearly independent) solutions to the system

$$\begin{aligned} u' &= u + v \\ v' &= 4u + v \end{aligned}$$

4. Use the result of Problems 1 and 3 to solve the initial value problem

$$\begin{aligned} u' &= u + v \qquad u(0) = -2 \\ v' &= 4u + v \qquad v(0) = 3 \end{aligned}$$

Group Project:
Special Relativity 1

Names:

_____

_____

Directions: Solve the following problems. Check with your recitation/lab instructor about the format required for the written report on this group project and the date the report is due.

Einstein developed the theory of special relativity to help explain experimental results that were no longer consistent with classical physics. Here is a brief table comparing some quantities from particle mechanics under the two theories:

Particle Property	Relativistic	Classical
Mass	$m = \dfrac{m_0}{\sqrt{1-v^2/c^2}}$	m_0
Momentum	$mv = \dfrac{m_0 v}{\sqrt{1-v^2/c^2}}$	$m_0 v$
Kinetic Energy	$\left(\dfrac{1}{\sqrt{1-v^2/c^2}} - 1 \right) m_0 c^2$	$\frac{1}{2}m_0 v^2$

In the table m_0 is the rest mass of the particle which is also it mass in classical physics, c is the speed of light in a vacuum, and v is the speed of the particle. The formula for the relativistic kinetic energy comes from Einstein's famous formula $E = mc^2$ for the total energy of a particle with relativistic mass m. When a particle is at rest, its has rest energy $E_0 = m_0 c^2$. When the same particle has speed v, the added energy of motion (kinetic energy) is

$$\mathrm{KE} = E - E_0 = mc^2 - m_0 c^2 = \left(\frac{1}{\sqrt{1 - v^2/c^2}} - 1 \right) m_0 c^2.$$

Since classical mechanics is in extremely good accord with experimental results when speeds are small compared with the speed of light and the formulas of special relativity give extremely good agreement with experimental results for all speeds v, we must expect that the relativistic quantities in the table and their corresponding classical counterparts are indistinguishable when v/c is small. In mathematical terms, the difference between any pair of relativistic and classical formulas in the table should tend to zero as $v/c \to 0$, equivalently, as $v \to 0$. Furthermore, in practice, the simpler classical formulas can be used if the experimental uncertainty in the measurements is greater than the difference between the corresponding relativistic and classical quantities in the table. So two key questions emerge:

- How can you see that the difference between each relativistic quantity and its classical counterpart tends to zero as $v \to 0$?

- How well do the classical quantities approximate the relativistic ones for v small compared to c?

In this project you will use Taylor polynomials to answers to these questions. You may use any of the results in a previous group project on Taylor approximation of $1/\sqrt{1-x}$ even if that group project was not assigned.

1. Let R be any one of the relativistic mass, relativistic momentum, or relativistic kinetic energy. Let C be the corresponding classical quantity in the table. For an object whose rest mass m_0 is at most 1 kg, determine for each of the three cases a range of speeds v over which you can be certain that
$$|R - C| < 10^{-6}$$
Express your velocity ranges in terms of m/s and mi/hr.

   Remark: In practical terms this means that if experimental errors prevent measurement of the mass, momentum, or kinetic energy to an accuracy of better than one part in a million you can safely use classical mechanics to predict experimental behavior of the corresponding quantity over the given velocity ranges.

2. Show that $m \approx m_0$, $mv \approx m_0 v$, and $\mathrm{KE}_{relativistic} \approx \mathrm{KE}_{classical}$ for v small compared to c and that the approximate equality becomes more nearly an equality as v becomes increasingly small compared to c (approaches 0 if you prefer).

Group Project:
Series in Action – Heat Conduction in a Rod

Names:

_____

_____

Directions: Solve the following problems. Check with your recitation/lab instructor about the format required for the written report on this group project and the date the report is due.

This group project illustrates a typical situation where infinite series come up in practice. The temperature $u(x, t)$ at time t and position x in a certain laterally insulated circular rod of unit length, modeled as a cylinder along the x-axis from $0 \leq x \leq 1$, is gotten by solving the heat equation with appropriate boundary and initial conditions. If the ends of the rod are held against ice blocks starting at time $t = 0$ and if initially (at time zero) the temperature of the rod is $f(x) = 100x(1 - x)$ in degrees centigrade, then

$$u(x, t) = \frac{400}{\pi^3} \sum_{n=1}^{\infty} \frac{1 - (-1)^n}{n^3} e^{-n^2 \pi^2 t / 10} \sin n\pi x$$

for $t \geq 0$ and $0 \leq x \leq 1$.

1. Just to be sure everything seems to be on the up and up, show that the series converges for all $t \geq 0$ and $0 \leq x \leq 1$.

   Since $u(x, 0) = 100x(1 - x)$,

   $$100x(1 - x) = \frac{400}{\pi^3} \sum_{n=1}^{\infty} \frac{1 - (-1)^n}{n^3} \sin n\pi x$$

   Let $S_N(x)$ be the Nth partial sum of this series.

2. Plot $100x(1 - x)$ and the partial sums $S_N(x)$ for $N = 1$, 3, and 5 one-by-one on the same graph to get a feeling for how well the partial sums of the series approximate the initial temperature profile.

3. Now, find N so that $S_N(x)$ approximates $100x(1 - x)$ to within 10^{-6}. (Remember $0 \leq x \leq 1$.) *Hint.* Express the error $|u(x, 0) - S_N(x)|$ as an infinite series and make an area comparison to estimate the size of the error series.

4. Use

   $$u(x, t) \approx \frac{400}{\pi^3} \sum_{n=1}^{5} \frac{1 - (-1)^n}{n^3} e^{-n^2 \pi^2 t / 10} \sin n\pi x$$

   to graph the temperature profiles in the rod at the times $t = 1$, 2, 3, and 5 seconds. Put all four plots on the same graph.

5. What do the plots in Problem 4 suggest about $\lim_{t \to \infty} u(x,t)$? Is this physically reasonable? Explain.

6. Derive and use the estimate

$$|u(x,t)| \le \frac{800}{\pi^3} e^{-\pi^2 t/10} \sum_{k=0}^{\infty} \frac{1}{(2k+1)^3}$$

to verify the limit in Problem 5.

Group Project:

Effective Calculation of Logarithms

Names:

_____

_____

Directions: Solve the following problems. Check with your recitation/lab instructor about the format required for the written report on this group project and the date the report is due.

This group project is designed to help you better understand how power series can be used in practical calculations, here of logarithms. The problems give first steps toward the effective calculation of logarithms. The results are quite reasonable for the effort involved. Numerical methods of this type and their progeny have led to the code programmed in the calculators and the computers you use.

1. Replace x by $-x$ in the power series representation of $\ln(1-x)$ to find that

$$\ln(1+x) = x - \frac{x^2}{2} + \frac{x^3}{3} - \frac{x^4}{4} + - \cdots \quad \text{for} \quad -1 < x < 1$$

2. The series for $\ln(1-x)$ and for $\ln(1+x)$ coverage too slowly to be useful for practical calculation of logarithms. However, they can be use to find such a series. Show that

$$\ln\left(\frac{1+x}{1-x}\right) = 2\left(x + \frac{x^3}{3} + \frac{x^5}{5} + \frac{x^7}{7} + \cdots\right) \quad \text{for} \quad -1 < x < 1$$

This series is much better for calculating logarithms.

3. Let $y = (1+x)/(1-x)$ for $-1 < x < 1$. Show that $y \to 0$ as $x \to -1^+$ and that $y \to \infty$ as $x \to 1^-$. Conclude that the series in Problem 2 for $\ln y$ with $y = (1+x)/(1-x)$ gives the logarithm of every positive real number. Equally important the series converges rather rapidly "near" $x = 0$. Techniques beyond those covered here take advantage of that fact. But for now, let $x = 1/3$ and show that

$$\ln(2) = 2\left(\frac{1}{3} + \frac{1}{3}\cdot\frac{1}{3^3} + \frac{1}{5}\cdot\frac{1}{3^5} + \frac{1}{7}\cdot\frac{1}{3^7} + \cdots\right)$$

Use five terms of the series to find $\ln(2) \approx 0.69315$. Use your calculator to check that this approximation is correct to five decimal places (assuming your calculator knows what it is doing).

4. This problem indicates how you can use a partial sum of the series for $\ln\left((1+x)/(1-x)\right)$ to approximate a logarithm to any desired accuracy. To be specific use $x = 1/3$ as in the previous problem.

(a) Explain why

$$0 \quad < \quad \ln 2 - 2\left(\frac{1}{3} + \frac{1}{3} \cdot \frac{1}{3^3} + \frac{1}{5} \cdot \frac{1}{3^5}\right)$$

$$< \quad \frac{2}{7}\left(\frac{1}{3^7} + \frac{1}{3^9} + \frac{1}{3^{11}} + \cdots\right) = \frac{1}{28 \cdot 3^5} \approx 1.47 \times 10^{-4}$$

rounded up. Calculate the 3-term sum that approximates $\ln 2$ and compare it with your calculator's value. The difference between the 3-term sum and your calculator's version of $\ln 2$ should be less than 1.47×10^{-4}. Check this. Did you calculator get it right?

(b) Determine N (as small as you can) and the corresponding partial sum S_N of the series for $\ln 2$ in Problem 3 so that S_N approximates $\ln 2$ to within 10^{-6}. (Compare your S_N against your calculator's approximation of $\ln 2$.)

Group Project:
The Binomial Series

Names: _____

_____

Directions: Solve the following problems. Check with your recitation/lab instructor about the format required for the written report on this group project and the date the report is due.

This group project introduces you to an important series expansion, called the binomial series, that was discovered by Newton. The binomial series is the Taylor series for $(1+x)^\alpha$, where α is a real number. Assume $\alpha \neq 0$ because the case $\alpha = 0$ is of no interest. The binomial series is most useful for fractional powers such as $(1+x)^{1/2}$, $(1+x)^{-1/2}$, and $(1+x)^{1/3}$.

1. Fix $\alpha \neq 0$. Show that the Taylor series of $(1+x)^\alpha$ is

$$1 + \sum_{k=1}^{\infty} \binom{\alpha}{k} x^k = 1 + \alpha x + \frac{\alpha(\alpha-1)}{1\cdot 2}x^2 + \frac{\alpha(\alpha-1)(\alpha-2)}{1\cdot 2\cdot 3}x^3 +$$

$$\frac{\alpha(\alpha-1)(\alpha-2)(\alpha-3)}{1\cdot 2\cdot 3\cdot 4}x^4 + \cdots$$

where the coefficient of x^k, called a **binomial coefficient**, is

$$\binom{\alpha}{k} = \frac{\alpha(\alpha-1)(\alpha-2)\cdots(\alpha-k+1)}{1\cdot 2\cdot 3\cdots\cdot k}$$

2. If $\alpha = n$ is a positive integer, show that the series reduces to a polynomial of degree n.

3. If α is not a positive integer, show that the Taylor series in Problem 1 has radius of convergence $r = 1$.

From now on assume that α is not a positive integer. It is natural to expect that the Taylor series of $(1+x)^\alpha$ has sum $(1+x)^\alpha$ for $-1 < x < 1$. This is indeed the case as you will show in the following problems. The bottom line is

$$(1+x)^\alpha = 1 + \alpha x + \frac{\alpha(\alpha-1)}{1\cdot 2}x^2 + \frac{\alpha(\alpha-1)(\alpha-2)}{1\cdot 2\cdot 3}x^3 + \cdots$$

for $-1 < x < 1$, which is the **binomial series** expansion.

4. Let $S(x)$ be the sum of the binomial series for $-1 < x < 1$. Use term-by-term differentiation to show that

$$(1 + x) S'(x) = \alpha S(x)$$

Verify that

$$\frac{d}{dx} (1 + x)^{-\alpha} S(x) = 0$$

conclude that

$$(1 + x)^{-\alpha} S(x) = C$$

for some constant C and finally show that $C = 1$ to deduce that $(1 + x)^{\alpha} = S(x)$, which establishes the binomial series expansion.

5. Let $a > 0$. In several physics and engineering applications it is informative to expand

$$\frac{1}{\sqrt{a^2 + x^2}}$$

in an infinite series. There is one series when $|x| < a$ and another when $|x| > a$. Find both series.

Group Project:

Special Relativity 2

Names:

_____

_____

Directions: Solve the following problems. Check with your recitation/lab instructor about the format required for the written report on this group project and the date the report is due.

Einstein developed the theory of special relativity to help explain experimental results that were no longer consistent with classical physics. Refer to the group project, Special Relativity 1, for more background for this project.

Particle Property	Relativistic	Classical
Mass	$m = \dfrac{m_0}{\sqrt{1-v^2/c^2}}$	m_0
Momentum	$mv = \dfrac{m_0 v}{\sqrt{1-v^2/c^2}}$	$m_0 v$

According to Einstein's fundamental discovery the total energy of a particle moving with speed v is

$$E = mc^2 = \frac{m_0 c^2}{\sqrt{1 - v^2/c^2}}$$

- How can you see that the relativistic quantities tend to their classical counterparts as $v \to 0$?

- How well do the classical quantities approximate the relativistic ones for v small compared to c?

If you did the earlier relativity lab you answered these questions using Taylor polynomial approximations to $1/\sqrt{1-x}$. Now you will answer them using the Taylor (power) series for $1/\sqrt{1-x}$ which enables you to find power series expansions for the relativistic mass, momentum, and energy. You may use the binomial series

$$(1+x)^\alpha = 1 + \alpha x + \frac{\alpha(\alpha-1)}{1\cdot 2}x^2 + \frac{\alpha(\alpha-1)(\alpha-2)}{1\cdot 2\cdot 3}x^3 + \frac{\alpha(\alpha-1)(\alpha-2)(\alpha-3)}{1\cdot 2\cdot 3\cdot 4}x^4 + \cdots$$

for all $|x| < 1$. Here the exponent α can be any real number.

1. If $0 < v < c$, show that

$$\frac{1}{\sqrt{1-v^2/c^2}} = 1 + \frac{1}{2}\left(\frac{v^2}{c^2}\right) + \frac{3}{8}\left(\frac{v^2}{c^2}\right)^2 + \frac{5}{16}\left(\frac{v^2}{c^2}\right)^3 + \cdots$$

2. Express the relativistic mass, momentum, and kinetic energy of a particle as a power series in powers of v^2/c^2.

3. Show that $m \approx m_0$, $mv \approx m_0 v$, and $E \approx m_0 c^2 + \frac{1}{2} m_0 v^2$ for v small compared to c and that the approximate equality becomes more nearly an equality as v becomes increasingly small compared to c (approaches 0 if you prefer). In particular, for speeds v small compared to c the energy of motion of an object is nearly $\frac{1}{2} m_0 v^2$, its classical kinetic energy.

4. Assume (it is true) that the coefficient of $\left(v^2/c^2\right)^n$ for $n \geq 1$ of the power series in Problem 1 is less than 1/2. Write

$$\frac{1}{\sqrt{1 - v^2/c^2}} = S_n + R_n$$

where S_n is the partial sum of the series in Problem 1 with last term involving $\left(v^2/c^2\right)^n$ and R_n is the corresponding remainder. Compare the remainder series with a geometric series to show that

$$0 < R_n < \frac{1}{2\left(1 - v^2/c^2\right)} \left(\frac{v^2}{c^2}\right)^{n+1} \approx \frac{1}{2} \left(\frac{v^2}{c^2}\right)^{n+1}$$

if $v^2/c^2 \ll 1$.

5. Scientists often use the series in Problem 1 to approximate the corresponding relativistic quantities by cutting off the series with the last term that is above the level of error associated with a particular experiment. The implicit assumption in doing this is that the total error involved in this cut off is roughly the size of the first term not used in the full series. Is this a reasonable assumption? Explain.

6. Just to dot all the i's and cross all the t's show that the coefficient of $\left(v^2/c^2\right)^n$ in the series expansion of $1/\sqrt{1 - v^2/c^2}$ is

$$\frac{(1/2)\,(3/2)\,(5/2) \cdots ((2n-1)/2)}{1 \cdot 2 \cdot 3 \cdots n}$$

and deduce that this coefficient has absolute value $\leq 1/2$ for all $n \geq 1$.

Appendix B

Sample Exams

Some instructors give one midterm others give two midterms. Check with your instructor about what will happen in your class. The material covered on the midterm(s) varies depending on when the exam(s) are scheduled. Your instructor will tell you the coverage for your midterm(s) and the final exam.

Sample Midterms and Finals

A few midterms and finals, given by different instructors, follow. These sample tests illustrate the types of problems that might be asked on a midterm or final this term and give you some idea of the approximate level of difficulty of past test questions.

No answers are provided for these sample exams. Part of checking your understanding and preparing for an exam is for you to know when you have solved a problem correctly and when you have not.

Disclaimer: The appearance of a type of question on past exams is neither a necessary nor a sufficient condition that you will get such a question on the exams you take.

Construct Your Own Sample Midterms and Finals

Really! You can do this by yourself but it may be better to work with a group. Here are suggestions about how to proceed:

- Your source of problems – all the problems in this text and any other sources you may have.

- Think about what are the most important topics covered in the course and try to pick problems that will test them – this is what you instructor does.

- Write down selected problems on separate sheets of paper and mix them up so you don't know what section of the text they came from.

- Now make up tests using your problems. Each test question you choose should test a different topic or idea.

- You must decide how many questions to put on the exam. You must judge what a reasonable 50 minute midterm is and what a reasonable 1 hour and 50 minute final is.

- If you are working alone, wait a day or two before taking a test that you made up so that you will not remember the exact section of text from which your problems came.

- If you are working with a group, exchange the test you made up for the test made up by another member of your group.

- This can even be fun!

B.1 Sample Midterms

MTH 306   **Exam 1**   **Spring 2007**

Instructions

1. There are 7 problems on 7 pages including the cover page.

2. No books or notes are allowed.

3. You must show sufficient work to justify all answers. Correct answers with inconsistent work will not be given any credit.

4. Write your final answers in the boxes provided, where appropriate.

5. The exam is self-explanatory. Please do not ask the instructor to interpret any of the exam questions.

(13 pts) 1. Find the cube roots of $-1 + i$. (Hint: Use DeMoivre's formula)

(12 pts) 2. For what values of a does the homogeneous system

$$\begin{aligned} (1-a)x + 2y \quad &= 0 \\ 3x + (2-a)y &= 0 \end{aligned}$$

have a nontrivial solution?

(12 pts) 3. Let A be the 3×3 matrix

$$A = \begin{bmatrix} 1 & 2 & 1 \\ 0 & 2 & 4 \\ 3 & h & 1 \end{bmatrix}$$

where h is a real number. For what values of h is the matrix invertible?

(15 pts) 4. Consider the linear system

$$\begin{aligned} 3x + 3y \quad &= -1 \\ 2x + y + z &= 0 \\ x - y + 2z &= 1. \end{aligned}$$

Find all solutions, if any exist, by systematic elimination using an augmented matrix.

(16 pts) 5. Given the vectors

$$\mathbf{v_1} = \begin{bmatrix} 4 \\ 2 \\ 6 \end{bmatrix}, \quad \mathbf{v_2} = \begin{bmatrix} 0 \\ -3 \\ 5 \end{bmatrix}, \quad \mathbf{v_3} = \begin{bmatrix} -1 \\ -2 \\ 1 \end{bmatrix},$$

(a) determine whether they are linearly dependent or linearly independent.
(b) If they are linearly dependent, find a nontrivial linear relation that they satisfy.

(16 pts) 6. Let

$$A = \begin{bmatrix} 2 & 3 \\ 5 & 4 \end{bmatrix}.$$

(a) Find the eigenvalues of A and eigenvectors corresponding to those eigenvalues.

(b) Does A have a simple structure (diagonalizable)? Explain.

(16 pts) 7. Let T_1 be the linear transformation that is multiplication by the matrix $\begin{bmatrix} 0 & -1 \\ 1 & 0 \end{bmatrix}$ and let $T_2 : \mathbb{R}^2 \to \mathbb{R}^2$ be the transformation where $T_2(\mathbf{v})$ is the reflection of $\mathbf{v}$ across the line $y = -x$.

(a) Give a geometric description of T_1.

(b) Find the standard matrix of T_2.

(c) Find the standard matrix of $T_1 \circ T_2$ (in which T_2 acts first and T_1 acts second on any input vector).

MTH 306   **Exam 2**   **Spring 2007**

Instructions

1. There are 6 problems on 7 pages including the cover page and the formula page.

2. No books, notes are allowed.

3. You may use a scientific calculator, but **no** graphing, programmable calculators are allowed.

4. The last page contains some useful formulas.

5. You must show sufficient work to justify all answers. Correct answers with inconsistent work will not be given any credit.

6. Write your final answers in the boxes provided, where appropriate.

7. The exam is self-explanatory. Please do not ask the instructor to interpret any of the exam questions.

(14 pts) 1.   (a) Find the sum of $\sum_{n=0}^{\infty} \frac{(-1)^n}{4^n}$, if it exists.

        (b) A ball is dropped from a height of 9 m. After hitting the ground, it rebounds to a height of 3 m and then continues to rebound at one-third of its former height thereafter. Find the total distance traveled by the ball.

(16 pts) 2. Let $f(x) = \ln x$.

        (a) Find $T_3(x)$, the 3rd Taylor polynomial of $f(x)$ about 1.

        (b) Use $T_3(x)$ to approximate $\ln 0.9$.

        (c) If the approximation is used for x in the interval $0.6 \le x \le 1.4$, estimate the maximum error possible in the approximation. Give your answer correct to **five decimal places**.

(14 pts) 3. We know that $\frac{1}{1-x} = \sum_{n=0}^{\infty} x^n$ for $-1 < x < 1$. Use an appropriate change of variable to find the Taylor series of $\frac{x}{1-3x^2}$ and find the values of x for which the series converges.

(14 pts) 4. Consider the infinite series $\sum_{n=1}^{\infty} ne^{-n^2}$. Use the integral test to check for convergence or divergence of the series.

(18 pts) 5. Consider the series $\sum_{n=1}^{\infty} \frac{(-1)^{n+1}}{3n-1}$.

        (a) Prove that the series converges. Specify the test you use.

           (i) Name of test:_____

           (ii) Details of test:

(b) What is the smallest N such that $|S - S_N| < 0.004$? Here, S is the sum of the series and S_N is the Nth partial sum.

(c) Determine whether the series is absolutely convergent or conditionally convergent. Explain in detail.

(24 pts) 6. Determine if the following infinite series converges or diverges.

(a) $\sum_{n=1}^{\infty} \frac{\cos^2 n}{n\sqrt{n}}$.

   (i) Name of test:_____

   (ii) Details of test:

   (iii) Conclusion:_____

(b) $\sum_{n=1}^{\infty} \frac{2n^2}{3n^2 - 7n + 1}$.

   (i) Name of test:_____

   (ii) Details of test:

   (iii) Conclusion:_____

(c) $\sum_{n=1}^{\infty} \frac{3n^2}{n!}$.

   (i) Name of test:_____

   (ii) Details of test:

   (iii) Conclusion:_____

FORMULAS

Taylor Series

- The Taylor Series of f about a is

$$\sum_{n=0}^{\infty} \frac{f^{(n)}(a)}{n!}(x-a)^n = f(a) + f'(a)(x-a) + \frac{f''(a)}{2!}(x-a)^2 + \cdots .$$

- Let $R_n(x) = f(x) - T_n(x)$. If $\left|f^{(n+1)}(x)\right| \le B$ for all x between a and b, then

$$|R_n(x)| \le B\frac{|x-a|^{n+1}}{(n+1)!}, \quad \text{for all } x \text{ between } a \text{ and } b.$$

- Examples:

$$e^x = \sum_{n=0}^{\infty} \frac{x^n}{n!} \text{ for all } x, \qquad \frac{1}{1-x} = \sum_{n=0}^{\infty} x^n \text{ for all } -1 < x < 1.$$

Approximation of Series That Converges By The Integral Test

Assume that the series $\sum_{n=0}^{\infty} a_n$ converges by the integral test applied to the positive, decreasing, continuous function $f(x)$ with $f(n) = a_n$. Let $U_N = S_N + \int_{N+1}^{\infty} f(x)\,dx$. Then

$$0 < S - U_N < a_{N+1}.$$

Error of Approximation in an Alternating Series

If the series $\sum_{n=1}^{\infty}(-1)^{n+1}b_n$, $b_n \geq 0$, converges, then

$$|S - S_N| < b_{N+1}.$$

Special Limits

- $\frac{\ln n}{n^p} \to 0$ if $p > 0$.

- $n^{\frac{1}{n}} \to 1$.

- $\left(1 + \frac{x}{n}\right)^n \to e^x$ for all x.

- $\frac{x^n}{n!} \to 0$ for all x.

- $(n!)^{\frac{1}{n}} \to \infty$.

MTH 306   **Exam 1**   **Fall 2006**

Directions: No books or notes are allowed. Calculators may be used to verify numerical computations, but work must be shown to receive credit. There are 6 problems on the exam. Problems 1 - 5 are worth 15 points each. Problem 6 is worth 25 points. Total = 100 points.

1. (15 points) Let $z = 1 + i$ and $w = 1 + 2i$.

   (a) Compute zw and $\frac{1}{z}$. Give your answers in standard form.

   (b) Write z in polar form $z = re^{i\theta} = r(\cos(\theta) + i\sin(\theta))$ and then compute z^8.

2. (15 points) Let A, B, C be the matrices given below.
$$A = \begin{pmatrix} 1 & 1 & 1 \\ 1 & 1 & 1 \end{pmatrix} \quad B = \begin{pmatrix} 1 & 1 & 1 \\ 1 & 1 & 1 \\ 1 & 1 & 1 \end{pmatrix}, \quad C = \begin{pmatrix} 1 & 1 \\ 1 & 1 \\ 1 & 1 \end{pmatrix}.$$
   Determine which of the four products AB, BA, AC, CA are defined. If the product is not defined, state so. If the product is defined, compute it.

3. (15 points)

   (a) Find a vector parametric equation of the line passing through the points $(1, 1, 3)$ and $(3, 2, 4)$.

   (b) Find the equation of the plane, in standard form, that is normal to the line in part (a) and passes through the point $(1, 1, 1)$.

4. (15 points) Show that the matrix $A = \begin{pmatrix} 1 & 4 \\ 3 & 5 \end{pmatrix}$ is invertible. Then find A^{-1}. (You may use either the algorithm for finding the inverse of a square matrix or the formula for the inverse of a 2×2 matrix.) Check your answer by an appropriate matrix multiplication.

5. (15 points) Let $A = \begin{pmatrix} 2 & 3 \\ 5 & 4 \end{pmatrix}$.

   (a) Find the eigenvalues of A and eigenvectors corresponding to those eigenvalues.

   (b) Find an invertible matrix P and a diagonal matrix D such that $P^{-1}AP = D$. (You need not find P^{-1}).

6. (25 points) Consider the system of equations
$$\begin{aligned} x - 2y + 2z &= 1 \\ -2x + 3y - 2z &= -6 \\ x - 3y + 4z &= -3. \end{aligned}$$

(Be careful with your computations in (a) and (b). These are crucial and the remaining parts of the problem can be done easily from the results of these computations.)

(a) Write out the coefficient matrix, A, of the system and compute its determinant.

(b) Write out the augmented matrix of the system and using elementary row operations on this matrix find all solutions to the given system. Write the solution set in vector form.

(c) Find all solutions to the corresponding homogeneous equation $A\mathbf{x} = \mathbf{0}$.

(d) Are the columns of the coefficient matrix linearly dependent or linearly independent? Explain! If linearly dependent find scalars c_1, c_2, c_3 such that $c_1\mathbf{v}_1 + c_2\mathbf{v}_2 + c_3\mathbf{v}_3 = \mathbf{0}$, where $\mathbf{v}_1$, $\mathbf{v}_2$, $\mathbf{v}_3$ are the columns of A (in order).

MTH 306   **Exam 2**   **Fall 2006**

Directions: No books or notes are allowed. Calculators may be used to verify numerical computations, but work must be shown to receive credit. Many problems involve convergence or divergence of a series. All such questions must be answered by applying an appropriate test. An answer of "converges" or "diverges" will receive little, if any, credit. There are 6 problems on the exam. Problems 2 and 4 are worth 18 points each. The remaining problems are worth 16 points each.

1. (16 points) A certain function f has continuous derivatives of order ≤ 3 at all points. Suppose that $f(0) = 1$, $f'(0) = 1/2$, $f''(0) = -1/4$, and $|f'''(x)| \leq 3/8$ when $0 \leq x \leq 1$.

   (a) Find $T_2(x)$, the Taylor polynomial of f centered at 0.

   (b) Use T_2 to approximate $f(0.1)$ and find an upper bound for the error in your approximation.

2. (18 points) Consider the infinite series $\sum_{n=1}^{\infty} ne^{-n^2}$.

   (a) Show that the function $f(x) = xe^{-x^2}$ is decreasing on the interval $[1, \infty)$ (and hence the integral test may be used to check for convergence or divergence of the series.)

   (b) Show that the series converges and then use the integral test error estimate to find the smallest number N such that $U_N = \sum_{n=1}^{N} ne^{-n^2} + \int_{N+1}^{\infty} xe^{-x^2} dx$ approximates the sum of the series with an error < 0.0005.

3. Consider the series $\sum_{n=1}^{\infty} (-1)^{n+1} e^{-\sqrt{n}}$.

   (a) (12 points) Show that the series converges and find the smallest number N such that $S_N = \sum_{n=1}^{N} (-1)^{n+1} e^{-\sqrt{n}}$ approximates the sum of the series with an error < 0.0005.

   (b) (4 points) Determine whether the series $\sum_{n=1}^{\infty} (-1)^{n+1} e^{-\sqrt{n}}$ is absolutely convergent or conditionally convergent. Explain.

4. (18 points) Determine whether each of the following series is absolutely convergent, conditionally convergent, or divergent. Justify your answer by applying appropriate tests for convergence or divergence.

   (a) $\sum_{n=1}^{\infty} \frac{\cos(n)}{2n^5}$.

   (b) $\sum_{n=1}^{\infty} \frac{(-1)^{n-1}}{\sqrt{n+2}}$.

   (c) $\sum_{n=1}^{\infty} \frac{n^5 - 5n}{100n^5 + n^4 + 72}$.

5. (16 points) Find the sum of each convergent series below.

   (a) $\sum_{n=0}^{\infty} \frac{3(2^n)}{7^n}$.

   (b) $\sum_{n=0}^{\infty} \frac{3(2^n)+2^{2n}}{7^n}$.

6. (16 points) Find the radius of convergence and interval of convergence of the power series $\sum_{n=0}^{\infty} \frac{(-1)^n x^n}{(n+1)4^n}$. At which points is the series absolutely convergent? At which points, if any, is the series, conditionally convergent?

B.2 Sample Finals

MTH 306 FINAL SPRING 2008

Instructions:

- There are 10 problems worth 5 points each. Some problems have parts.

- Four problems are multiple choice. This means there is one correct answer and you must circle the correct answer to receive any credit.

- Three problems list five statements. You must mark the letter T next to each true statement and the letter F next to each false statement in the space _____ provided next to each statement. You will earn 1 point for each correctly marked response.

- Three problems are long-answer problems where you may earn partial credit depending on your work. Each problem has a space in which to write your answer. **Expect to lose credit if you do not put your answer in the space provided.** Space also is provided for you to show your supporting work. **Expect to receive no credit for a correct answer that your work does not support.** This means that you **must present the mathematical reasoning needed to justify your answers.**

- You may use any correct method to solve a particular problem, *unless that problem directs otherwise.*

- You may use a calculator for standard numerical calculations but not for symbolic differentiation, integration, or other calculus operations. You may use the calculator to check your work, but on the long-answer questions you **must include the mathematical methods needed to obtain any answer you give just as if you didn't have a calculator available during the exam.** I want to know what you know, not what your calculator knows.

- **Give exact answers** whenever possible. Decimal approximations to answers that can be given exactly will not receive full credit.

- Solve the problems in the order that is easiest for you. Skip problems that you find harder and come back to them later.

- The exam is closed book and no notes are allowed.

You may use the following reminders related to error estimates. However, for each error estimate you need to know the circumstances under which it can be applied.

- (Taylor Polynomial Error Estimate) For Taylor polynomials with base point a

$$R_n\left(x\right) = f^{(n+1)}\left(c\right)\frac{\left(x-a\right)^{n+1}}{\left(n+1\right)!}$$

for some c between a and x.

- (Integral Test Error Estimate) If a series $\sum_{n=1}^{\infty} a_n$ converges by the integral test and $a_n = f(n)$, then

$$\int_{N+1}^{\infty} f(x)\, dx \leq S - S_N \leq a_{N+1} + \int_{N+1}^{\infty} f(x)\, dx$$

and

$$0 \leq S - U_N \leq a_{N+1}$$

where

$$U_N = S_N + \int_{N+1}^{\infty} f(x)\, dx.$$

- (Alternating Series Error Estimate) You should be able to remember the error estimate associated with the alternating series test. It will not be provided on the exam.

- (Root Test Error Estimate) If a series $\sum_{n=1}^{\infty} a_n$ converges by the root test and if $|a_n|^{1/n} \leq r < 1$ for all $n \geq M$, then

$$|S - S_N| < \frac{r^{N+1}}{1 - r} \text{ for all } N \geq M.$$

- (Ratio Test Error Estimate) If a series $\sum_{n=1}^{\infty} a_n$ converges by the ratio test and if $|a_{n+1}/a_n| \leq r < 1$ for all $n \geq M$, then

$$|S - S_N| < \frac{|a_{N+1}|}{1 - r} \text{ for all } N \geq M.$$

1. (5 points) **Circle the letter corresponding to the statement that is true.** The interval of convergence of the power series

$$\sum_{n=1}^{\infty} \frac{(x+2)^n}{(-3)^n\, n}$$

is

    (a) $-5 < x \leq 1$

    (b) $-5 \leq x < 1$

    (c) $-3 \leq x \leq 3$

    (d) $-1 < x \leq 5$

    (e) $-1 \leq x \leq 5$

    (f) $-3 < x \leq 3$

2. (5 points) **Circle the letter corresponding to the statement that is true.** The third Taylor polynomial $T_3(x)$ about 1 (with base point 1) for $f(x) = x \ln x$ is

(a) $(x-1) + \frac{1}{2}(x-1)^2 - \frac{1}{6}(x-1)^3$

(b) $x + \frac{1}{2}x^2 - \frac{1}{6}x^3$

(c) $(x-1) + (x-1)^2 - (x-1)^3$

(d) $(x-1) - \frac{1}{2}(x-1)^2 + \frac{1}{3}(x-1)^3$

(e) $x + x^2 - x^3$

(f) $(x-1) + \frac{1}{2}(x-1)^2 + \frac{1}{6}(x-1)^3$

3. (5 points) **Circle the letter corresponding to the statement that is true.** You use the third Taylor polynomial $T_3(x)$ about 1 (with base point 1) of $f(x) = x \ln x$ to approximate the exact value of $1.5 \ln(1.5)$. Based on the error estimates for Taylor polynomials given in this course, the **best** estimate that can be given of the error $|1.5 \ln(1.5) - T_3(1.5)|$ is

(a) $27/64$

(b) $1/192$

(c) $1/8$

(d) $3/128$

(e) $1/32$

(f) $1/72$

4. (5 points) Let c and b be constants for which the following system of equations has a unique solution. **Circle the letter corresponding to the statement that is true** about the solution to the system

$$\begin{aligned} x - 2y + 2z &= 0 \\ -x + 3y + cz &= b \\ 2x + z &= 0 \end{aligned}$$

(a) $z = 4b/c$

(b) $z = b/(4c - 9)$

(c) $z = 4b/(11 - 4c)$

(d) $z = 4b/(4c + 11)$

(e) $z = 4b/(4c - 9)$

(f) $z = b/4c$

5. (5 points) **In the space provided next to each statement below write the letter T if the statement is true and write the letter F if the statement is false.** Let $A\mathbf{x} = \mathbf{b}$ be a linear system of 3 equations in 3 unknowns. Given that

$$\mathbf{x}_1 = \begin{bmatrix} 1 \\ 2 \\ 3 \end{bmatrix} \text{ and } \mathbf{x}_2 = \begin{bmatrix} -1 \\ 2 \\ 3 \end{bmatrix}$$

are solutions of the system,

(a) The matrix A is invertible. _____

(b) The system $A\mathbf{x} = \mathbf{b}$ has exactly two solutions. _____

(c) The system $A\mathbf{x} = \mathbf{0}$ has nontrivial solutions. _____

(d) The columns of the matrix A are linearly independent. _____

(e) $2\mathbf{x}_1 - \mathbf{x}_2$ is a solution of $A\mathbf{x} = \mathbf{b}$. _____

6. (5 points) **In the space provided next to each statement below write the letter T if the statement is true and write the letter F if the statement is false.** Let

$$M = \begin{bmatrix} 5 & 0 & 0 \\ 0 & -3 & 1 \\ 0 & 1 & -3 \end{bmatrix}.$$

(a) All the eigenvalues of M are real. _____

(b) The eigenvectors of M corresponding to distinct eigenvalues are orthogonal. _____

(c) $\lambda = -3$ is an eigenvalue of M with multiplicity 2. _____

(d) The columns of M are linearly dependent. _____

(e) The characteristic equation of M is $(\lambda - 5)\left(\lambda^2 + 6\lambda + 8\right) = 0$. _____

7. (5 points) **In the space provided next to each statement below write the letter T if the statement is true and write the letter F if the statement is false.**

(a) The series $\sum \cos(1/n)$ diverges by the Basic Divergence Test. _____

(b) The series $\sum (-1)^n \sin(1/n)$ converges by the Alternating Series Test.

_____

(c) The series $\sum_{n=1}^{\infty} (-1)^{n+1} \frac{e^{-nx}}{n^2}$ is absolutely convergent for all x by comparison with the series $\sum 1/n^2$. _____

(d) The series $\sum_{n=1}^{\infty} (-1)^{n+1}/\sqrt{n}$ is convergent by the Alternating Series Test but is not absolutely convergent. _____

(e) The series $\sum_{n=0}^{\infty} \frac{(-1)^n x^n}{n!}$ clearly converges when $x = 0$. It is absolutely convergent for all other x by the ratio test. _____

8. (5 points) A power series is given by

$$1 + 2x + \frac{4!}{(2!)^2}x^2 + \frac{6!}{(3!)^2}x^3 + \frac{8!}{(4!)^2}x^4 + \frac{10!}{(5!)^2}x^5 + \cdots$$

(a) Express this series in sigma notation; that is write the series as $\sum_{n=0}^{\infty} a_n x^n$ for appropriate coefficients a_n.

Your answer: _____

Your work: (no justification is required for part (a) but if you answer incorrectly your work might result in some partial credit)

(b) Find the radius of convergence of the given series.

Your answer: The radius of convergence is _____

Your work:

9. (5 points) You need to approximate the value of the nasty integral

$$\int_0^1 \frac{\sin x}{x}\,dx$$

so the error is less than 10^{-6}. Use power series methods covered in this course to do the following.

(a) Express the value of the integral as an infinite series.
    Your answer: The integral is equal to
    _____
    Your work:

(b) Let S_N be the Nth partial sum of the series you found in (a). Use any applicable error estimate developed in this course to determine N so that S_N approximates the integral to within the required accuracy of 10^{-6}.

Your answer: $N = $ _____
Your work:

10. (5 points) Do the following for the series $\sum_{n=1}^{\infty} n e^{-n^2}$

(a) Show the series converges.
    Your work:

(b) Let S be the sum of the series. You want to approximate S so that the error in your approximation is less than 10^{-4}. To accomplish this you decide to use (**Circle your choice A or B**):

   A. a partial sum S_N of the series

   B. an area adjusted approximation U_N

   For your choice (A or B), based on error estimates developed in this course, find the **smallest** N such that your choice of approximation will have the required accuracy.
   Your answer: $N =$

   Important: Put your supporting work on the next page. That work must include a correct explanation of why the error estimate you use can be used in this situation, to receive any credit on this problem.)

MTH 306   **FINAL EXAM**   **Winter 2008**

Instructions

1. There are 13 problems on 9 pages including the cover and formula pages.

2. No books or notes are allowed.

3. A scientific calculator with no advanced functions (differentiation and/or integration) will be allowed.

4. You must show sufficient work to justify all answers. Correct answers with inconsistent work will not be given any credit.

5. The exam is self-explanatory. Please do not ask the instructor to interpret any of the exam questions.

Section I: Multiple Choice Problems
Circle the correct (only one) answer for each problem. **No** partial credit.

1. Find $\left[\cos\left(\frac{1}{5}\right) + i\sin\left(\frac{1}{5}\right)\right]^{10}$.

   (a) $\cos^{10}\left(\frac{1}{5}\right) + i\sin^{10}\left(\frac{1}{5}\right)$.
   (b) $\cos 2 + i\sin 2$.
   (c) $10\left(\cos\left(\frac{1}{5}\right) + i\sin\left(\frac{1}{5}\right)\right)$.
   (d) $\cos\left(\frac{1}{5^{10}}\right) + i\sin\left(\frac{1}{5^{10}}\right)$.
   (e) $10\left(\cos 2 + i\sin 2\right)$.

2. Let $A = \begin{bmatrix} -7 & 0 & 2 \\ 2 & -5 & 1 \\ 3 & 10 & h \end{bmatrix}$. For what values of h will the matrix A have **no** inverse?

   (a) $h = -4$.
   (b) $h \neq -4$.
   (c) $h = 4$.
   (d) $h \neq 4$.
   (e) $h = 4, -4$.

3. Suppose that the system of equations

$$x + 2y - 3z = a$$
$$2x + 3y + z = b$$
$$5x + 9y - 8z = c$$

has a solution. Which equation must a, b and c satisfy?

(a) $3a - b + c = 0.$

(b) $a - 3b + c = 0.$

(c) $3a + b - c = 0.$

(d) $7a - b - c = 0.$

(e) $a + b + c = 0.$

4. Find the power series expansion of $f(x) = \frac{1}{2+3x}$.

(a) $\sum_{n=0}^{\infty} (-1)^n 3^n x^{2n}$ for $|x| < 1.$

(b) $\sum_{n=0}^{\infty} \frac{3^n x^{2n}}{2}$ for $|x| < 3.$

(c) $\sum_{n=0}^{\infty} \frac{3^n x^{2n}}{2^{n+1}}$ for $|x| < \frac{3}{2}.$

(d) $\sum_{n=0}^{\infty} (-1)^n \frac{3^n x^{2n}}{2^{n+1}}$ for $|x| < \sqrt{\frac{2}{3}}.$

(e) $\sum_{n=0}^{\infty} (-1)^n \frac{2^n x^{2n}}{3^{n+1}}$ for $|x| < \sqrt{\frac{3}{2}}.$

5. $e^{\frac{5\pi i}{4}}$ equals

(a) $e^{\frac{5\pi}{4}} i.$

(b) $e^{\frac{1}{4}(\cos 5\pi + i \sin 5\pi)}.$

(c) $\cos \frac{5\pi}{4} + i \sin \frac{5\pi}{4}.$

(d) $e^5 (\cos \frac{\pi}{4} + i \sin \frac{\pi}{4}).$

(e) $\sin \frac{5\pi}{4} + i \cos \frac{5\pi}{4}.$

6. Estimate $\int_0^{\frac{1}{2}} \ln(1+x)\, dx$ to within an error of 0.001. (Hint: Use the fact that $\ln(1+x) = \sum_{n=1}^{\infty} \frac{(-1)^{n+1} x^n}{n}$ for $|x| < 1$ and use your knowledge of alternating series.)

(a) 0.1042

(b) 0.1078

(c) 0.1094

(d) 0.125

(e) 0.4055

Section II: You must show all your work to receive credit.

(12 pts) 7. Find the eigenvalues and associated eigenvectors for $\begin{bmatrix} 3 & 2 \\ -3 & -2 \end{bmatrix}$.

(12 pts) 8. For what values of x are the vectors $\left\{ \begin{bmatrix} 1 \\ 1 \\ 1 \end{bmatrix}, \begin{bmatrix} -2 \\ 0 \\ 1 \end{bmatrix}, \begin{bmatrix} x \\ 1 \\ 3 \end{bmatrix} \right\}$ linearly dependent?

(14 pts) 9. Find the sum of the following series.

  (a) $\sum_{n=0}^{\infty} \frac{(-1)^n 2^n}{5^n}$.

  (b) $\sum_{n=0}^{\infty} (-1)^n \frac{\left(\frac{\pi}{4}\right)^{2n}}{(2n)!}$. (Hint: Use a Taylor series)

(14 pts) 10. Consider the infinite series $\sum_{n=1}^{\infty} \frac{x^n}{3^n \sqrt{n}}$.

  (a) Find the radius of convergence for the series.

  (b) Find the interval of convergence.

(12 pts) 11. Two transformations T and S are linear. For each $\mathbf{v} \in \mathbb{R}^2$, $T(\mathbf{v})$ is the reflection of $\mathbf{v}$ across the line $y = x$ and S is governed by $S(x,y) = (x+y, 2x-y)$. Find the standard matrix of $T \circ S$.

(12 pts) 12. Find the 2nd Taylor polynomial $T_2(x)$ of the function $f(x) = \sqrt[3]{1+x}$ about $x = 0$.

(14 pts) 13. Determine if the following infinite series converge or diverge.

  (a) $\sum_{n=1}^{\infty} \frac{n\sqrt{n}}{n^2+n-1}$.
      (i)   Name of test:_____
      (ii) Details of test:
      (iii) Conclusion:_____

  (b) $\sum_{n=0}^{\infty} \frac{n^3}{2^n}$.
      (i)   Name of test:_____
      (ii) Details of test:
      (iii) Conclusion:_____

FORMULAS

Taylor Series

- The Taylor Series of f about a is

$$\sum_{n=0}^{\infty} \frac{f^{(n)}(a)}{n!} (x-a)^n = f(a) + f'(a)(x-a) + \frac{f''(a)}{2!} (x-a)^2 + \cdots .$$

- Let $R_n(x) = f(x) - T_n(x)$. Then

$$|R_n(x)| \le B\frac{|x-a|^{n+1}}{(n+1)!}, \ \forall x \in [a-b, a+b], \ \text{where} \ B = \max_{a-b \le x \le a+b}\left|f^{(n+1)}(x)\right|.$$

- Examples:

$$e^x = \sum_{n=0}^{\infty}\frac{x^n}{n!} \ \text{for all } x, \qquad\qquad \frac{1}{1-x} = \sum_{n=0}^{\infty}x^n \ \text{for all } -1 < x < 1.$$

$$\sin x = \sum_{n=0}^{\infty}\frac{(-1)^n x^{2n+1}}{(2n+1)!} \ \text{for all } x, \qquad \cos x = \sum_{n=0}^{\infty}\frac{(-1)^n x^{2n}}{(2n)!} \ \text{for all } x.$$

Error of Approximation in an Alternating Series
If the series $\sum_{n=1}^{\infty}(-1)^{n+1}b_n$, $b_n \ge 0$, converges, then

$$|S - S_N| < b_{N+1}.$$

Special Limits

- $\frac{\ln n}{n^p} \to 0$ if $p > 0$.

- $n^{\frac{1}{n}} \to 1$.

- $\left(1 + \frac{x}{n}\right)^n \to e^x$ for all x.

- $\frac{x^n}{n!} \to 0$ for all x.

$(n!)^{\frac{1}{n}} \to \infty$.

MTH 306   **FINAL EXAM**   **Winter 2006**

Directions: No books or notes are allowed. Calculators may be used, but sufficient work or explanation must be provided to receive credit. Many problems ask if a given series converges or diverges. Answers to such without sufficient justification will receive no credit. Read each problem carefully.

1. (10 points) Let $\mathbf{v} = \langle 1, 2, -3 \rangle$ and $\mathbf{w} = \langle 2, 1, 3 \rangle$.

   (a) Compute the cosine of the angle between $\mathbf{v}$ and $\mathbf{w}$.

   (b) Compute $\text{proj}_{\mathbf{w}} \mathbf{v}$ and $\text{comp}_{\mathbf{w}} \mathbf{v}$, the vector projection of $\mathbf{v}$ onto $\mathbf{w}$ and the component of the vector projection of $\mathbf{v}$ onto $\mathbf{w}$.

2. (12 points) Consider the following two systems of linear equations

$$\begin{cases} x + 2y + z = 4 \\ 3x + 4y + 3z = 8 \\ 2x + 5y + 2z = 10 \end{cases} \qquad \begin{cases} x + y + z = 4 \\ 2x + y + z = 5 \\ x - y + z = -2 \end{cases}$$

   (a) Which system, if either, has a unique solution? Explain.

   (b) Form the augmented matrix for one of the systems (your choice) and use elementary row operations to find all solutions to the system.

3. (14 points) Let $A = \begin{pmatrix} 1 & 0 & 0 \\ 0 & 2 & 4 \\ 2 & 3 & 1 \end{pmatrix}$.

   (a) Find all the eigenvalues of the matrix A.

   (b) Find an eigenvector corresponding to the largest eigenvalue of A. (If $\lambda_1 \leq \lambda_2 \leq \lambda_3$ are the eigenvalues of A, then λ_3 is the largest eigenvalue.)

4. (14 points) Let $T : \mathbb{R}^2 \to \mathbb{R}^2$ be the linear transformation defined by $T \begin{pmatrix} x \\ y \end{pmatrix} = \begin{pmatrix} y - x \\ -y \end{pmatrix}$.

   (a) Find the standard matrix A associated to T, that is find the matrix A such that $T \begin{pmatrix} x \\ y \end{pmatrix} = A \begin{pmatrix} x \\ y \end{pmatrix}$.

   (b) Find the eigenvalues of A and determine whether A is diagonalizable; that is does there exist an invertible matrix P such that $P^{-1}AP = D$, where D is a diagonal matrix. If P exists, find P and D. If no such P exists, explain why.

5. (10 points) Determine whether the series below converge or diverge. If the series converges, find the sum. When the series involves a complex quantity, put your answer in standard form.

(a) $\sum_{k=2}^{\infty} 5\frac{3^k}{2^k+3^k}$.

(b) $\sum_{k=1}^{\infty} \left(\frac{2}{1+2i}\right)^k$.

6. (12 points) Let $f(x) = \frac{x^2}{2+x^5}$.

(a) Using the formula for the geometric series and an appropriate change of variable or substitution, find the Taylor series of f centered at 0.

(b) Using your series in part (a) compute an infinite series that converges to $\int_0^1 \frac{x^2}{2+x^5}dx$, then use the resulting series to approximate the integral with an error < 0.005.

7. (14 points) The function f is defined by the power series $\sum_{n=0}^{\infty} \frac{x^n}{2^n(n^2+1)}$.

(a) Find the radius of convergence and interval of convergence of the power series. At which points, if any, is the series absolutely convergent? Conditionally convergent?

(b) Compute a power series representation for the derivative $f'(x)$. Find the radius of convergence and interval of convergence of the power series for f'. At which points, if any, is the power series for f' absolutely convergent? Conditionally convergent?

8. (14 points) Let $f(x) = \sqrt{1+x}$.

(a) Compute the Taylor polynomial $T_2(x)$ of f centered at 0.

(b) Use $T_2(x)$ to approximate $f(0.1) = \sqrt{1.1}$ and use the Taylor theorem error, or remainder, formula to bound (estimate) the error in your approximation.

(c) Compute $\sqrt{1.1}$ on your calculator and compare your bound on the error with the actual error. (Of course, the actual error should be smaller than your bound (estimate).)

Appendix C

Selected Answers

Lesson 1: Complex Numbers

1. $-4 + 3i$
3. $-11 + 29i$
5. $-\frac{31}{74} - \frac{1}{74}i$
7. 13
9. 1
11. $x = \pm\frac{3}{2}i$
17. $2\left(\cos\frac{\pi}{3} + i\sin\frac{\pi}{3}\right)$ or $2e^{i\pi/3}$
21. (a) $z = x + iy$, $iz = -y + ix$, iz is obtained from z by rotating z counterclockwise by $\pi/2$ radians. (b) $z = re^{i\theta}$, $iz = re^{i(\theta+\pi/2)}$, iz is obtained from z by rotating z counterclockwise by $\pi/2$ radians.
23. -2^{50}
25. $1, -\frac{1}{2} + \frac{1}{2}i\sqrt{3}, -\frac{1}{2} - \frac{1}{2}i\sqrt{3}$
27. Circle in the complex plane with center at 1 and radius 3
29. The exterior of the circle in the complex plane with center at 0 and radius 4
31. The circle and the exterior of the circle in the complex plane with center at $-i$ and radius 1
33. Circle in the complex plane with center at 2 and radius 3
35. $f(i) = 0$, $f(2-i) = \frac{12}{5} - \frac{4}{5}i$
37. $h(i) = 0$, $h\left(\frac{5-2i}{2-i}\right) = 12$
39. All $z \neq 0$
41. $f(z) = x + \frac{x}{x^2+y^2} + i\left(y - \frac{y}{x^2+y^2}\right)$

Lesson 2: Vectors, Lines, Planes

1. The sum of the squares of diagonals of a parallelogram are equal to the sum of the squares of its four sides
3. (c) $\mathbf{a}$ is perpendicular to the plane spanned by $\mathbf{b}$ and $\mathbf{c}$.
9. $x = -2 + 7t$, $y = 4t$, $z = 3 - 4t$. (Other parametric equations may give the same line.)

11. $4(x+2) + 81y + 88(z-3) = 0$, equivalently, $4x + 81y + 88z = 256$

Lesson 3: Linear Equations
1. $x = 1 \quad y = 2$
3. $x = -3 \quad y = 0$
5. $x = -1/3 \quad y = 7/3 \quad z = -1/3$
7. no solution
9. There are infinitely many solutions u, v, w where $u = -w$, $v = w+1$, and w can be given any value. Another way to express the solutions is: $u = -t \quad v = t+1 \quad w = t$ for any value of t. These equations are parametric equations for a line in space through the point $(0,1,0)$ that is parallel to the vector $\langle -1, 1, 1 \rangle$. The planes whose equations are given intersect in that line.
11. 5
13. 0
15. 0
17. The system has a unique solution because its determinant is not zero.
19. The system has a unique solution because its determinant is not zero.
21. $\lambda = -1, 3$
23. $\lambda = 8, -1, -1$
25. (a) determinant nonzero   (b) $x = y = z = 0$

Lesson 4: Matrices and Linear Systems
1. (b) $A - 3B = \begin{bmatrix} -11 & -23 \\ 15 & 6 \end{bmatrix}$ (d) $BA = \begin{bmatrix} 4 & 13 \\ -5 & 7 \end{bmatrix}$

   (e) $A\mathbf{x} = \begin{bmatrix} 3 \\ -3 \end{bmatrix}$

3. (c) $AB = \begin{bmatrix} 5 & -1 & 11 \\ 4 & 1 & 1 \\ 10 & 1 & 15 \end{bmatrix}$

9. $x = 1, y = 1, z = 3, w = 4$

11. $A = \begin{bmatrix} 4 & -2 & 1 \\ -5 & 7 & 4 \\ 3 & -1 & 0 \end{bmatrix}$, $\mathbf{b} = \begin{bmatrix} 6 \\ 0 \\ 5 \end{bmatrix}$, $\mathbf{x} = \begin{bmatrix} x \\ y \\ z \end{bmatrix}$

13. $A = \begin{bmatrix} 4 & -2 & 1 \\ -5 & 7 & 4 \\ 3 & -1 & 0 \\ 1 & -2 & 1 \end{bmatrix}$, $\mathbf{b} = \begin{bmatrix} 6 \\ 0 \\ 5 \\ 3 \end{bmatrix}$, $\mathbf{x} = \begin{bmatrix} x \\ y \\ z \end{bmatrix}$

15. $A^{-1} = \begin{bmatrix} \frac{1}{2} & \frac{1}{2} & -\frac{1}{2} \\ -\frac{1}{2} & \frac{1}{2} & \frac{1}{2} \\ \frac{1}{2} & -\frac{1}{2} & \frac{1}{2} \end{bmatrix}$

17. $A^{-1} = \begin{bmatrix} \frac{1}{6} & \frac{1}{3} & \frac{1}{6} \\ -\frac{1}{6} & \frac{1}{6} & \frac{1}{3} \\ \frac{1}{6} & 0 & \frac{1}{6} \end{bmatrix}$

Lesson 5: Linear Dependence and Independence
1. linearly independent
3. linearly independent
5. linearly dependent

$$\begin{bmatrix} -1 \\ 3 \\ -2 \end{bmatrix} - \begin{bmatrix} 3 \\ 1 \\ 0 \end{bmatrix} + 2 \begin{bmatrix} 2 \\ -1 \\ 1 \end{bmatrix} = \begin{bmatrix} 0 \\ 0 \\ 0 \end{bmatrix}$$

7. linearly independent

Lesson 6: Matrices and Linear Transformations
1. (a) Reflection across the y-axis
   (c) Reflection across the xz-plane
   (f) Counterclockwise rotation by $90°$ about the origin

2. (b) $A = \begin{bmatrix} 0 & -1 \\ -1 & 0 \end{bmatrix}$

   (d) $A = \begin{bmatrix} -3/5 & 4/5 \\ 4/5 & 3/5 \end{bmatrix}$

   (f) $A = \begin{bmatrix} 0 & 1 & 0 \\ 1 & 0 & 0 \\ 0 & 0 & 0 \end{bmatrix}$

   (i) $A = \begin{bmatrix} \cos\theta & \sin\theta \\ -\sin\theta & \cos\theta \end{bmatrix}$

   (l) $A = \begin{bmatrix} 1 & 0 & 0 \\ 0 & 1 & 0 \end{bmatrix}$

7. There is no such vector; that is, $T(\mathbf{v}) = \begin{bmatrix} 1 & 4 & 2 \end{bmatrix}^T$ has no solution.

9. $\mathbf{v} = \begin{bmatrix} 4 & -3 \end{bmatrix}^T$

11. There is no such vector; that is, $T(\mathbf{v}) = \begin{bmatrix} -6 & -11 & 7 \end{bmatrix}^T$ has no solution.

12. 6×5

17. $A = \begin{bmatrix} 1/5 & -2/5 \\ -2/5 & 4/5 \end{bmatrix} \begin{bmatrix} 1/\sqrt{2} & -1/\sqrt{2} \\ 1/\sqrt{2} & 1/\sqrt{2} \end{bmatrix} \begin{bmatrix} 0 & 1 \\ 1 & 0 \end{bmatrix}$

and $T\left([3 \; -3]^T\right) = \begin{bmatrix} \frac{-3}{10}\sqrt{2} & \frac{-1}{10}\sqrt{2} \\ \frac{3}{5}\sqrt{2} & \frac{1}{5}\sqrt{2} \end{bmatrix} \begin{bmatrix} 3 \\ -3 \end{bmatrix} = -\frac{3}{5}\sqrt{2} \begin{bmatrix} 1 \\ -2 \end{bmatrix}$

19. $A = \frac{1}{29} \begin{bmatrix} 21 & 12 & -16 \\ 12 & 11 & 24 \\ -16 & 24 & -3 \end{bmatrix}$ and $T\left(\begin{bmatrix} x \\ y \\ z \end{bmatrix}\right) = \frac{1}{29} \begin{bmatrix} 21x + 12y - 16z \\ 12x + 11y + 24z \\ -16x + 24y - 3z \end{bmatrix}$

21. (a) $P = \begin{bmatrix} 1/3 & 1/3 \\ 2/3 & 2/3 \end{bmatrix}$ (c) P projects onto the line L but is not an orthogonal projection

Lesson 7: Eigenvalue Problems

1. $\left\{\begin{bmatrix}1\\1\end{bmatrix}\right\}\leftrightarrow 4,\quad\left\{\begin{bmatrix}1\\3\end{bmatrix}\right\}\leftrightarrow 2$

3. $\left\{\begin{bmatrix}1\\1\end{bmatrix}\right\}\leftrightarrow -3$

5. $\left\{\begin{bmatrix}1\\1-i\end{bmatrix}\right\}\leftrightarrow 1+2i,\left\{\begin{bmatrix}1\\1+i\end{bmatrix}\right\}\leftrightarrow 1-2i$

7. $\left\{\begin{bmatrix}-1\\4\\1\end{bmatrix}\right\}\leftrightarrow 1,\left\{\begin{bmatrix}1\\2\\1\end{bmatrix}\right\}\leftrightarrow 3,\left\{\begin{bmatrix}-1\\1\\1\end{bmatrix}\right\}\leftrightarrow -2$

9. $\left\{\begin{bmatrix}1\\-\frac{3}{2}\\1\end{bmatrix}\right\}\leftrightarrow 1,\left\{\begin{bmatrix}0\\1\\-i\end{bmatrix}\right\}\leftrightarrow 1+2i,\left\{\begin{bmatrix}0\\1\\i\end{bmatrix}\right\}\leftrightarrow 1-2i$

11. $\left\{\begin{bmatrix}1\\-2\\0\end{bmatrix},\begin{bmatrix}4\\2\\-5\end{bmatrix}\right\}\leftrightarrow 0,\left\{\begin{bmatrix}2\\1\\2\end{bmatrix}\right\}\leftrightarrow 9$ (The first pair of orthogo-

nal eigenvectors may be replaced by any other pair of orthogonal vectors in the plane spanned by the given pair.)

13. $\left\{\begin{bmatrix}-3\\2\\1\end{bmatrix}\right\}\leftrightarrow -1,\left\{\begin{bmatrix}1\\1\\1\end{bmatrix}\right\}\leftrightarrow 1,\left\{\begin{bmatrix}-\frac{1}{5}\\-\frac{4}{5}\\1\end{bmatrix}\right\}\leftrightarrow 13$

19. $\lambda^4\mathbf{v}$

29. $P_1=\frac{1}{9}\begin{bmatrix}5&-2&-4\\-2&8&-2\\-4&-2&5\end{bmatrix},\quad P_3=\frac{1}{9}\begin{bmatrix}4&2&4\\2&1&2\\4&2&4\end{bmatrix}$

Lesson 8: Catch up and Review

3. (a) $\left\{\begin{bmatrix}1\\-\frac{3}{4}+\frac{1}{4}\sqrt{33}\end{bmatrix}\right\}\leftrightarrow -\frac{1}{2}+\frac{1}{2}\sqrt{33},$

$\left\{\begin{bmatrix}1\\-\frac{3}{4}-\frac{1}{4}\sqrt{33}\end{bmatrix}\right\}\leftrightarrow -\frac{1}{2}-\frac{1}{2}\sqrt{33}$

(b) $\left\{\begin{bmatrix}\frac{1}{2}+\frac{1}{6}i\sqrt{15}\\1\end{bmatrix}\right\}\leftrightarrow -\frac{1}{2}+\frac{1}{2}i\sqrt{15},$

$\left\{\begin{bmatrix}\frac{1}{2}-\frac{1}{6}i\sqrt{15}\\1\end{bmatrix}\right\}\leftrightarrow -\frac{1}{2}-\frac{1}{2}i\sqrt{15}$

5. $x=-\frac{15}{7},\ y=-\frac{4}{7}$

7. (a, b) $\left\{\begin{bmatrix}2\\1\end{bmatrix}\right\}\leftrightarrow 10,\left\{\begin{bmatrix}1\\-2\end{bmatrix}\right\}\leftrightarrow -5$

(c) Yes, the eigenvectors are linearly independent in $\mathbb{R}^2$.

9. (a) $C=\begin{bmatrix}\frac{1}{25}&\frac{3}{25}\\\frac{3}{25}&-\frac{7}{50}\end{bmatrix}$ (b) $\begin{bmatrix}5&30\\-10&40\end{bmatrix}$ (c) $\begin{bmatrix}29&-18\\2&16\end{bmatrix}$

13. $\begin{bmatrix}2\\-4\\9\end{bmatrix}$

15. $\begin{bmatrix} 11 & 4 \\ 9 & 9 \end{bmatrix}$

19. linearly independent

Lesson 9: Taylor Polynomial Approximation

1. $(x-1) - \frac{1}{2}(x-1)^2 + \frac{1}{3}(x-1)^3 - \frac{1}{4}(x-1)^4 + +\frac{1}{5}(x-1)^5$

3. $1 + 2\left(x - \frac{1}{4}\pi\right) + 2\left(x - \frac{1}{4}\pi\right)^2 + \frac{8}{3}\left(x - \frac{1}{4}\pi\right)^3 + \frac{10}{3}\left(x - \frac{1}{4}\pi\right)^4$

5. $T_5(x) = 2x - \frac{4}{3}x^3 + \frac{4}{15}x^5$ and $\sin(0.5) \approx 0.479427$

7. $s(t) \approx 50 - 30t + 8t^2$

9. $t < \left(\frac{30}{.35}\right)^{1/3} \approx 4.4091$

11. $\theta(t) \approx 1 - 3t - (\sin 1)t^2 + (\cos 1)t^3$

13. $|R_3(x)| \le \frac{3}{8}\frac{(0.6)^3}{3!} = 0.0135$

15. (a) $T_1(x) = x = T_2(x)$, $T_3(x) = x - x^3/3! = T_4(x)$,
        $T_5(x) = x - x^3/3! + x^5/5! = T_6(x)$,
        $T_7(x) = x - x^3/3! + x^5/5! - x^7/7! = T_8(x)$

    (b) For n odd, Taylor polynomials for $\sin x$ satisfy $T_n(x) = T_{n+1}(x)$

Lesson 10: Infinite Series

1. convergent, sum 12

3. divergent

5. convergent, sum 3/2

7. $\sum_{n=3}^{\infty} x^n = \frac{x^3}{1-x}$ for $|x| < 1$

11. $\sum_{n=0}^{\infty} \frac{x^n}{1+x^2} = \frac{1}{(1+x^2)(1-x)}$ for $|x| < 1$

13. $\sum_{n=0}^{\infty} \frac{x^{2n}}{(1+x^2)^n} = 1 + x^2$ for all x

15. $\sum_{n=0}^{\infty} 2^n x^{n+1}$ for $|x| < 1/2$

17. $\sum_{n=0}^{\infty} 4^n x^{2n+2}$ for $|x| < 1/2$

19. (a) and (b) $\sum_{n=0}^{\infty} t^{n/2} = \frac{1}{1-\sqrt{t}}$ for $0 \le t < 1$

21. $\sum_{n=0}^{\infty} 2^n \sin^n t$ for $|\sin t| < 1/2$ which means $-\pi/6 + k\pi < t < \pi/6 + k\pi$
    for any $k = 0, \pm 1, \pm 2, \ldots$

23. (a) Since $\cos(1/n) \to \cos 0 = 1$, the series diverges by the basic divergence test

    (b) Since $\sin(1/n) \to \sin 0 = 0$, the basic divergence test gives no information

27. 1

29. 1/4

31. $H(1+r)/(1-r)$

Lesson 11: Taylor Series Representations

1. (c) $\sum_{n=0}^{\infty} x^{n+1}/n!$

    (e) $1 + \frac{1}{2}x + \sum_{n=2}^{\infty} (-1)^{n-1} \frac{1 \cdot 3 \cdot 5 \cdots (2n-3)}{2^n n!} x^n =$
        $1 + \frac{1}{2}x - \frac{1}{2^2 2!}x^2 + \frac{3}{2^3 3!}x^3 - \frac{3 \cdot 5}{2^4 4!}x^4 + \frac{3 \cdot 5 \cdot 7}{2^5 5!}x^5 - + \cdots$

5. (a) $\frac{1}{2} + \frac{\sqrt{3}}{2}\left(x - \frac{\pi}{6}\right) - \frac{1}{2!}\frac{1}{2}\left(x - \frac{\pi}{6}\right)^2 - \frac{1}{3!}\frac{\sqrt{3}}{2}\left(x - \frac{\pi}{6}\right)^3 + + - - \cdots$

    (d) $2 + \frac{1}{4}(x-4) + \sum_{n=2}^{\infty} (-1)^{n-1} \frac{1 \cdot 3 \cdots (2n-3)}{2^{3n-1} n!}(x-4)^n$

9. $e - 2$

11. $e^{-3} - 1$

13. 0

15. e^{-x}

17. $1 - x^2 + \frac{1}{2}x^4$

19. $1 + \frac{1}{2}x^2 + \frac{5}{24}x^4$

21. $\sin x^2 = \sum_{n=0}^{\infty} (-1)^n \frac{x^{4n+2}}{(2n+1)!}$

23. $\sum_{n=0}^{\infty} (-1)^n \frac{x^{n+1}}{n!} + \sum_{n=0}^{\infty} (-1)^n \frac{x^{2n}}{(2n)!} = \sum_{n=0}^{\infty} a_n x^n$ where

$$a_n = \begin{cases} 1/(n-1)! & \text{for} \quad n \text{ odd} \\ \left((-1)^{n/2} - n\right)/n! & \text{for} \quad n \text{ even} \end{cases}$$

25. $\frac{x}{1-x^4} = x \sum_{n=0}^{\infty} \left(x^4\right)^n = \sum_{n=0}^{\infty} x^{4n+1}$

Lesson 12: Series With Nonnegative Terms

1. $A = \sum_{n=2}^{7} a_n$, $B = \int_1^7 f(x)\,dx$, $C = \sum_{n=1}^{6} a_n$
3. converges
5. diverges
7. converges
9. $p > 1$
11. $\sum_{n=1}^{31} \frac{1}{n^2} + \frac{1}{32} \approx 1.6444$
13. $\sum_{n=1}^{2} ne^{-n^2} + \frac{1}{2}e^{-9} \approx 0.40457$
15. (b) $N \approx e^{10}$, e^{20}, e^{100} respectively.
    That is, $N \approx 22,026$, 4.85×10^8, 2.69×10^{43} respectively.
17. (b) $N = 14$ does the job and $U_{14} = S_{14} + \int_{15}^{\infty} \frac{1}{x\,(\ln x)^2}\,dx \approx 2.1051$

    (c). $N > e^{100} - 1 \approx 2.7 \times 10^{43}$

Lesson 13: Comparison Tests

1. converges
3. diverges
5. converges
7. diverges
9. converges
11. diverges
13. converges
15. diverges
17. converges for all $0 \le x \le 1$ and diverges for $x > 1$
19. converges for all $x > 0$ and diverges for $x = 0$
21. converges for all $x \ge 0$
23. the exponent is not constant;   the series diverges

Lesson 14: Alternating Series, Absolute Convergence

3. $|S - S_{10}| < 11/122$
5. $|S - S_{10}| < 11/2048$
7. absolutely convergent
9. diverges
11. conditionally convergent

13. conditionally convergent
15. (a) converges for $|x| \le 1$ (b) converges absolutely for $|x| \le 1$
17. (a) converges for all x (b) converges absolutely for all x
19. (b) $N = 10$
     (c) $S_{10} = \sum_{n=1}^{10} \frac{(-1)^{n+1}}{n^3} \approx 0.90112$
     (d) S_{10} ends with a negative term so it is less than S
21. (b) $N = 9$
     (c) $S_9 = \sum_{n=1}^{9} (-1)^{n+1} \frac{\sin(1/n)}{n^2} \approx 0.74817$
     (d) S_9 ends with a positive term so it is greater than S
23. $\sum_{n=1}^{\infty} \left| \frac{z^n}{n} \right|$ converges absolutely for $|z| < 1$ which is the open unit disk in the complex plane.
25. $\sum_{n=1}^{\infty} \left| (-1)^n \frac{z^n}{n\sqrt{n}} \right|$ converges absolutely for $|z| \le 1$ which is the closed unit disk in the complex plane.
27. underestimate

Lesson 15: Ratio and Root Tests
1. series diverges
3. the limit gives no information about converge or divergence
5. series converges absolutely
7. series converges absolutely
9. series converges absolutely
11. series diverges
13. either test is inconclusive
15. either test is inconclusive
17. series diverges
19. absolutely convergent
21. (b) $S_6 = \sum_{n=0}^{6} \frac{1}{n!} \approx 2.7181$
23. (b) $S_{11} = \sum_{n=0}^{11} \frac{n^2+n}{3^n} \approx 2.2495$
25. (b) $S_{10} = \sum_{n=0}^{10} \frac{1}{n!} \approx 2.7183$
27. (b) $S_4 = \sum_{n=0}^{4} (-1)^n \left(\frac{1}{1+n} \right)^n \approx 0.59709$
29. (b) $N = 13$
31. (a, b, c) Each series converges if $|x| < 1$ and diverges otherwise.
     (d) For p any positive integer, the series $\sum n^p x^n$ converges if $|x| < 1$ and diverges otherwise.
35. (a) $|z| < 1$ (b) the open unit disk
37. (a) $z = 0$ (b) the origin of the complex plane
39. series converges
41. (a) $N \ge 20$ (b) $N \ge 11$ (c) $N \ge 10$

Lesson 16: Power Series
5. $r = 2/3$; interval of convergence is $-2/3 \le x < 2/3$
7. $r = 2$; interval of convergence is $-3/2 \le x < 5/2$
9. $r = 2$; interval of convergence is $-7/2 < x \le 1/2$
11. $r = 1$; interval of convergence is $3 \le x \le 5$

13. $r = \infty$ (in this case there is no circle of convergence)
15. $r = 2/3$ and the circle of convergence is the circle with center at $2/3$ and radius $2/3$ in the complex plane.
17. domain is $|x| < \infty$
19. $\left(1 - x^2\right) / \left(1 - x^3\right)$ for $|x| < 1$
21. (a) $4 + x - x^2 + \cdots$ (b) $|x| < \infty$
23. (a) $x - \frac{2}{3}x^3 + \frac{2}{15}x^5 + \cdots$ (b) $|x| < \infty$
25. (a) $x + \frac{1}{3}x^3 + \frac{2}{15}x^5 + \cdots$ (b) $|x| < \pi/2$
27. (a) $x + x^2 + \frac{5}{6}x^3 + \cdots$ (b) $|x| < 1$

Lesson 17: Analytic Properties of Power Series

1. $r = 4$
3. $\sum_{n=0}^{\infty} x^{3n}$ and $r = 1$
5. $\sum_{n=0}^{\infty} \frac{x^{2n}}{(2n)!}$ and $r = \infty$
7. $\ln 5 - \sum_{n=0}^{\infty} \frac{x^{n+1}}{5^{n+1}(n+1)}$ and $r = 5$
9. $\sum_{n=0}^{\infty} (-1)^n \frac{x^{2n+2}}{2n+1}$ and $r = 1$
11. $1 + x - \frac{x^2}{2!} - \frac{x^3}{3!} + \frac{x^4}{4!} + \frac{x^5}{5!} - \frac{x^6}{6!} - \frac{x^7}{7!} + + - - \cdots$ and $r = \infty$
13. $\sum_{n=0}^{\infty} (-1)^n \frac{x^{2n+4}}{(2n+4)n!} + C$ and $r = \infty$
15. $\sum_{n=1}^{\infty} (-1)^{n+1} \frac{2^{2n-1}x^{2n}}{(2n)!}$ and $r = \infty$
17. $\frac{1}{2}$
19. $\frac{1}{3}$
21. $x - x^2 + \frac{1}{6}x^3 + \frac{1}{6}x^4$ and $|x| < 1$
23. $x + 2x^2 + \frac{5}{3}x^3 + \frac{2}{3}x^4$ and $|x| < 1$
25. $x/(1 + x)$
27. $-\ln(1 - 3t)$ for $|t| < 1/3$
29. (a) $\arctan x^2 = \sum_{n=0}^{\infty} (-1)^n \frac{x^{4n+2}}{2n+1}$
    (b) $\int_0^{1/2} \arctan x^2\, dx \approx \sum_{n=0}^{2} (-1)^n \frac{(1/2)^{4n+3}}{(4n+3)(2n+1)} \approx 4.1304 \times 10^{-2}$ correctly rounded
31. $S(1) \approx S_2 \approx 0.438563$ correctly rounded
33. $J_0(1) \approx S_2 = 0.765625$
35. $\ln \frac{3}{2}$
37. (a) $1/\left(1 + x^2\right) = \sum_{n=0}^{\infty} (-1)^n x^{2n}$ (b) $|x| < 1$
    (c) $\arctan x = \sum_{n=0}^{\infty} (-1)^n \frac{x^{2n+1}}{2n+1}$; $|x| \le 1$
    (d) $\frac{\pi}{4} = \sum_{n=0}^{\infty} (-1)^n \frac{1}{2n+1} = 1 - \frac{1}{3} + \frac{1}{5} - \frac{1}{7} + - \cdots$
39. $y = 3 \sum_{n=0}^{\infty} \frac{(-1)^n}{2^n n!} x^{2n} = 3e^{-x^2/2}$
41. (a) $y = \sum_{n=0}^{\infty} \frac{a^{2n}}{(2n)!} x^{2n}$
    (b) *Hint.* Subtract the power series for e^{-ax} from the power series for e^{ax}
43. $y = 1 + x + x^3$; the series reduces to a polynomial
45. $N \ge 4$

Lesson 18: Power Series and Complex Calculus

1.   8
3.   0
5. $f'(z) = 0$
7. $f'(z) = -1/z^2$
13. $h'(z) = -4/z^5$
15. $l'(z) = -3(4 + 3z - z^2)^2 (3 - 2z) \sin\left((4 + 3z - z^2)^3\right)$
17. $e^{-3} \cos 4 + i e^{-3} \sin 4$
19. i
25. Rotate the vector that represents z by the angle θ_0, counterclockwise (if $\theta_0 \geq 0$) and clockwise (if $\theta_0 < 0$) and then multiply the length of the rotated vector by r_0.
27. The unit circle in the complex plane swept out once in the counterclockwise sense

Lesson 19: Catch up and Review

3.   (a) By the alternating series test.
     (b) $4,000,000$
5.   (a) $T_3(x) = 1 - \frac{1}{2}x^2$
     (b) $R_3(x) = (\cos c) \frac{x^4}{4!}$ for some c between 0 and x
7.   (a) $\sum_{n=0}^{\infty} \binom{1/2}{n} x^{3n}$
     (b) $4! \binom{1/2}{4} = -\frac{15}{16}$
9. $\sum_{n=0}^{\infty} 2^{n-1} n x^{n+1}$ for $|x| < 1/2$
11. $(1-i) + \sum_{n=1}^{\infty} (-i)(z-i)^n \qquad f^{(9)}(i) = -(9!)i$
13. (a) see lesson 17, example 3 in your text
     (b) $\sum_{n=1}^{\infty} (-1)^{n+1} \frac{1}{n} (z-1)^n$ converges absolutely in $|z-1| < 1$.
     (c) Yes. *Hints.* $\ln z = \sum_{n=1}^{\infty} (-1)^{n+1} \frac{1}{n} (z-1)^n$ for $|z-1| < 1$.
          Deduce that $\frac{d}{dz} \ln z = \frac{1}{z}$. What is $\frac{d}{dz} \frac{e^{\ln z}}{z}$?
15. (b) In excess of 2.5×10^{30} terms!
     (c) The area corrected approximation $U_{101} = S_{101} + \frac{1}{2(\ln(102))^2}$ is accurate to with 10^{-4}.
17. (a) Does not exist
     (b) 0
21. (b) $N_0 = 4$
     (d) 23 or greater
25. 26

Index